Images of Japanese Women

Images of Japanese Women:
A Westerner's View

by
Bettina L. Knapp

The Whitston Publishing Company
Troy, New York
1992

Copyright 1992
Bettina L. Knapp

Library of Congress Catalog Card Number 91-67976

ISBN 0-87875-427-X

Printed in the United States of America

Contents

Preface vii

Time Line x

Introduction 1

Chapter 1:
    Murasaki Shikibu's *The Tale of Genji*:
    Search for the Mother 29

Chapter 2:
    The Heian Art Diary: Hidden Behind the Screens 72

Chapter 3:
    Women's Mysteries: Poetry and Noh in Feudal Japan ... 102

Chapter 4:
    The Arts and the "The Floating World"
    in the Edo Period: 1603-1867 122

Chapter 5:
    Ladies Make Waves in the Meiji Period: 1868-1912 154

Chapter 6:
    Modernism: The Circle Completed 179

Conclusion 244

Bibliography 248

Index 256

She pitied all women. How impossibly difficult was their position! If they shut themselves away, ignored the existence of beauty, tenderness—of all emotion—what was left, save to sit thinking of darkness and the grave?
(Murasaki Shikibu, *The Tale of Genji*)

Preface

I feel flattered to see images of our women emerge from Professor Knapp's pen, so beautiful, esoteric, positive and even powerful. Women from different times of Japanese history are given flesh and blood by the author's passionate interest and tender yet meticulous observation, and come alive to converse not only with the reader but also among themselves. It is truly a rare opportunity that the reader can meet so many representative Japanese women in one volume. None of these women belongs to the stereotype that most Western minds have been fed—that quiet figure, submissive and yielding, who always walks three steps behind her man.

Women writers and artists depicted truthfully by the author, are independent and intelligent with enough will power to stand their ground. They persist and they accomplish. Images of women created by men artists may appear more gentle and at times plaintive. But there is one thing these women share in common. They seem to be closely connected with nature from which the Japanese mind has long absorbed its nourishment and strength.

It is a delightful experience to meet these women. And while enjoying the experience, the reader is unawaringly introduced to a critical discussion of the material from which they are selected—the Japanese ancient chronicles, literature spanning more than ten centuries, theater, poetry and arts.

Professor Knapp states that she has to rely on English sources in writing this book since she does not read Japanese. But seeing the bibliography she lists, I am amazed both by the scope of the research that she has undertaken and by the quality of scholarship accomplished in this field. Although it is only during the last several decades that the number of Western scholars and translators interested in Japanese arts and literature has increased, the advance of the scholarship is rather breathtaking.

We Japanese are great translators. For more than one hundred years since we opened the country to the world, we have been translating foreign writing of all subjects into Japanese. It has been one of our efforts to catch up with the level of Western civilization. We have also understood the parallel necessity of introducing our culture to the world, but this necessity has not been successfully fulfilled, mainly because of the language difficulty. Even today, while a number of skilled translators display an excellent performance from English into Japanese, those who undertake the reverse are few. For this reason, I am very grateful that Western scholars are reaching out to us. And the present addition with our women in the limelight will certainly meet our heartfelt welcome.

During the first week of 1992, our newspapers report about various activities Japanese women are engaged in. A woman from Osaka, after her husband's sudden death in an accident, entered Columbia University, and now is working as a psychotherapist in a Brooklyn hospital. A woman of sixty-nine from Hiroshima is the president of the Association of Atomic Bomb Victims in Hokkaido where at least 700 victims reside. The association, after nine years of fund raising, is just about to open the No More Atomic Bomb Victims Museum, where mementoes from the Hiroshima and Nagasaki bombing will be displayed. A young woman in her early twenties earns close to a million dollars a year with her comic books.

A famous young Kabuki actor talks about how essential his wife is both to his family and to his profession. His lovely wife who had been a star performer of an all-girl dancing team, now plays many roles at the heart of his household. She is a wife, mother of three children, housekeeper, hostess to important patrons of the theater, her actor husband's manager, as well as their son's who has just begun his Kabuki acting career at the age of two. An article reports that for the last three years, the number of women entering the workforce after graduating from universities and colleges exceeded that of men. And more than sixty percent of these working women over thirty prefer single life to marriage.

The images of the modern Japanese women these newspaper articles present may be different from those of the past. Yet, I wonder what kind of portraits posterity will draw from them, or which women they will choose to delineate. I hope the images of our modern women that future generations will cherish can be as beautiful and enticing as these described in this book.

Kazuko Sugisaki
Professor of English,
Gifu College of Education, Japan,
and translator

Time Line: Japan

660 B.C.E.   Jimmu-Tenno becomes first Emperor according to mythical accounts.
260 C.E.   Approximate date of founding of the great shrine to the Sun Goddess Amaterasu at Ise. Shinto Shamanesses and Priests are in attendance. Thought to have been matriarchal society at outset.
297:   First Chinese account of Japan: *History of the Kingdom of Wei*. Equality of men and women. Women rulers: Pimiko, Iyo.

YAMATO PERIOD (645-709)

552:   Introduction of Buddhism to Japan. Shakyamuni Gautama (566-483 B.C.E.). Early Buddhist art.
592-628:   Reign of Empress Suiko. Empress Toyo-mike.
594:   Buddhism proclaimed the state religion.
660-690:   Princess Nukada.
645-702:   Empress Jito.

NARA PERIOD (710-794)

710:   Permanent capital established at Nara.
712:   *Records of Ancient Matters (Kojiki)*.
720:   *Chronicles of Japan (Nihongi)*.
   T'ang influence on Buddhist Art.
752:   Dedication of the Great Buddha (Daibutsu) of Todai-ji in Nara.
770:   Empress Shotoku.
8th cent.   Yosami, Lady Kii, Kasa no Iratsume.

HEIAN PERIOD (794-1185)

- 794: Heian-kyo (Kyoto) becomes the capital.
- 850: Ono no Komachi. Lady Ise.
- 858: Hereditary civil dictatorship of the *Fujiwara* family established. Court life.
- 990: Beginning of classic age of Japanese prose (*monogatari*). *The Tale of Genji* by Lady Murasaki Shikibu and *The Pillow Book* by Sei Shonagon.
  Heian art diary (*nikki*): *The Diary of Lady Murasaki; The Diary of Sarashina; The Diary of Izumi Shikibu; The Gossamer Years.*
  Esoteric Buddhism and art. Landscape painting.
- 1185: Defeat of Taira clan. Minamoto Yoritomo supreme in Japan.

KAMAKURA SHOGUNATE (1185-1333)

- 1192: Yoritomo becomes first Shogun.
- 1274: First Mongol invasion.
- 1281: Second Mongol invasion.
  Poets: Lady Eifuku Mon'in (c. 1310); Lady Junii Tamekko (c. 1290); Empress Eifuku (1271-1342); Lady Jusammi Chikako (c. 1300).
- 1258 b.*The Confessions of Lady Nijo.*
- 1333: Direct imperial rule under Go-Daigo.
- 1336: Go-Daigo flees to Yoshino. Rival emperor reigns in Kyoto under the protection of Ashikaga Takauji.
  Scroll painting. Zen Buddhism, the monk Eisai.

Warring States Period.

NANBOKUCHO —SOUTHERN AND NORTHERN COURTS (1333-1392)

ASHIKAGA SHOGUNATE or MUROMACHI PERIOD (1393-1572)

- 1338: Ashikaga Takauji becomes shogun.
- 1384: Kan'ami (1333-1384), master of Noh drama. *Matzukase* by Kan'ami. *Onnagata* (men portray women).
- 1443: Seami (1363-1443) master of Noh drama. *Matzukaze* reinterpreted by Seami.
  Zen inspiration in art: monochrome landscape painting.

Flower arrangements; landscape gardening. Tea ceremony.

AZUCHI-MOMOYAMA PERIOD (1573-1602)

1568: Occupation of Kyoto by Oda Nobunaga.
Capital controlled by Nobunaga.
1582: Nobunaga murdered.
1590: Hideyoshi supreme in Japan.
1593: Confucianism adopted as official cult of Tokugawa Japan.
1600: Tokugawa Ieyasu victorious at the Battle of Sekigahara.

TOKUGAWA SHOGUNATE or EDO PERIOD (1603-1867)

1603: Establishment of Tokugawa shogunate.
1685: Yamaga Soko (1622-1685), early proponent of the "Way of the Warrior" (Bushido).
"Floating World"; geisha; prostitution.
Courtesan poet: Ohashi.
Ukiyo-e prints; *shunga* prints. Utamaro, Kunisada, etc.
1688-1704: Genroku period: novels of Saikaku, plays by Chikamatsu, poems by Basho.
Haiku poets: Chine-jo; Seifu-jo.
Tea-house poets: Kaji, Yuri, Ike Gyokuran, etc.
Poet/painters: Ono Ozu. Ryonen Genso, Sasaki Shogen. Kaga no Chiyo. Tagami Kikusha, etc.
Painters: Tani Kankan; Kiyohara Yukinobu (Kano School founded by Masanobu); Kamazaki Ryu-jo.
1853: Perry expedition.
1856: Townsend Harris, first American minister to Japan.
1863: British bombardment of Kagoshima in retaliation for antiforeign outbursts.

MEIJI PERIOD (1868-1912)

1868: Meiji Restoration.
1871: Feudal domains abolished.
1872: Conscription.
1874: Tokyo Normal School for Women.
1877: Satsuma Rebellion.
1894-5: Sino-Japanese War.
Fiction/poetry/painting: Higuchi Ichiyo, Yosano Akiko, Yamakawa Tomiko, Okuhara Seiko, Noguchi Shonin, etc.

Time Line

1900: First Medical School for Women.
First College for Women.
1902: Anglo-Japanese alliance.
1904-5: Russo-Japanese War.
1910: Annexation of Korea.
1912: Death of Emperor Meiji.

TAISHO PERIOD (1912-1926)
SHOWA PERIOD (1926-)

1911: Founding of *Bluestocking* literary magazine and society to teach women about themselves: focuses on issues such as marriage, abortion, prostitution, etc.
Attempts at women's liberation.
1931: "Manchurian Incident."
1937: Outbreak of war with China.
Tanka poets: Saito Fumi, Baba Akiko, Nakagawa Mikiko, Sugita Hisajo, Hoshino Tatsuko, Yagi Mikajo, etc.
Free verse poets: Tada Chimako, Shiraishi Kazuko, etc.
Women activists: political, social, literary; imprisonments, etc.
Art/Life in short story and novel: Tamura Toshiko, Nogami Yaeko, Okamoto Kanoko, Uno Chiyo, Hayashi Fumiko, Setouchi Harumi, Tsushima Yuko, Hirabayashi Taio, etc.
1940: Rome-Berlin-Tokyo Axis.
1941-45: Dec. 7, Japan attacks Pearl Harbor. Pacific War.
1946: Women given vote. Emperor disclaims divinity; separation of religion and state.
1947: New Japanese Constitution: marriage based "on mutual consent of both sexes" etc. Primogeniture abolished (on paper—not always in actuality). Women still exploited in marketplace.
1952: End of military occupation by Allied Forces.
1905-1989: Enchi Fumiko: *Masks*, a woman's mystery.

Introduction

How could a society have veered so drastically away from what is thought to have been Japan's matriarchal beginnings to the extremes of a patriarchal system? What was the genesis of events that led to the virtual incarceration of women—at least those of higher classes whose lives were spent hidden behind screens and sliding doors? How did the incredibly complex laws governing the institution of marriage—and divorce—work to the detriment of women? If a double standard prevailed, how is it that some married and unmarried women not only had secret affairs, but that these relationships frequently came to be acceptable to the families? How did the forcibly reclusive women occupy themselves? How did their rigid control over their emotions affect their inner world, thoughts, feelings, rapport with other women living in seclusion, and with their parents, particularly the powerful Mother figure? What kind of relationship, if any, did wives have with their husbands? Were they merely sexual objects born and reared for man's pleasure? Or simply procreating devices? What were the roles played by second and third wives? Concubines? Prostitutes? Geishas? What were the psychological factors involved in a society so closed for women and open for men? How and why did this ultra-firm and restrictive grip on women finally begin to be released, ever so slowly, in the twentieth century? What lasting effects did the shackling of women leave on today's Japanese male? Answers, if there are any, are, at best, only temporary.

Although the main focus of our inquiry revolves around the probing of literary works—poems, novels, essays—written by Japanese women throughout the centuries, for a better understanding of the society and culture of which these women are a product, history, art, architecture, theatre, music, dance, and costume designs will also be considered in *Images of Japanese Women: A Westerner's View.*

To dwell at length on the verbal art, however, seemed to me an imperative, despite the fact that so many ancient texts by women are no longer extant. The act of writing—the only artistic expression, with few exceptions, left to us from early centuries—best reveals, although in coded language, elements of the manacled feminine inner world. Women's literary expression of their thoughts and feelings offer special insights and serve to enrich our knowledge of their situations. Our emphasis on the verbal art in no way precludes the fact that for later centuries we will undertake a brief exploration of the extant pictorial domain—its images, brush strokes, color tones, and rhythms—from an aesthetic, philosophical, and psychological point of view, with the hope of ferreting out those elusive mysteries of women.

In exploring poems, novels, and essays written by Japanese women one must proceed slowly, with circumspection, and via suggestion. To penetrate an inner dimension requires the removal, never complete, to be sure, of the mask—that social face worn to protect and conceal a frequently turbulent and painful personal existence. What is not said in the literary work, therefore, is frequently more significant than what is written. Silences and blank spaces are more telling that verbal prowess. Concision expresses more than prolixity. The legacy left us by talented and creative Japanese women, although relatively sparse until the twentieth century, opens up an immense storehouse of esthetic, philosophical, and psychological riches.

Is it not surprising to learn that, despite the restrictive climate in which women lived, *The Tale of Genji*—the greatest Japanese novel and one of the greatest in all world literature—was written by Murasaki Shikibu who lived in the tenth century? So extraordinary is this work that even today one is not only impressed by its author's incredible knowledge concerning her times and those past, but is also gripped by its beauty and depth as well as by its artistry and universality. Mention must also be made of the messages embedded in the many poems written by such women as Kasa no Iratsume (8th cent.) and Ono no Komachi (9th cent.). Their works are a feast for the senses. Useful contrast may be drawn between such ancient writings and the output of contemporary women novelists, such as Enchi Fumiko, and poets, such as Shiraishi Kazuko.

Could knowledge gleaned from a culture so vastly different from ours not serve to expand our consciousness? Could it not, perhaps, yield new insights to help us deal in a more positive manner with the pain, doubt, and the insecurities facing us and our contemporaries?

There is another aspect to our story which sheds light on our theme: the unusual nature of the religious scene in Japan. Shinto and Buddhism not only live in harmony with one another, but supplement each other's teachings. Certainly, head-on collisions occurred between the two in past centuries, since Buddhism was introduced to Japan in 552 C.E., while Shinto was native to the land. But neither Shinto nor Buddhism displaced or eradicated the other. They came to cohabit, and remain in harmony to this day.

Shinto beliefs cast a crucial and extraordinary light on our story. Indeed, in exploring its Creation myth psychologically, we see an unconscious attempt on the part of patriarchal forces to control and even to overrule the autochtonous matriarchal system. What justification is there for such a statement?

Unlike most world religions in which the Sun, and everything associated with it, is masculine, and the Moon is identified with feminine forces, Shinto presents an opposite picture. The glowing daylight celestial body, even in today's Japan, is a Goddess: Amaterasu. Some other ancient religions similarly embodied opposite identifications: the tribal Arabian Shamshu was a sun-Goddess; in the Sumerian, Babylonia, and Assyrian pantheon, both the Moon (Sin, Nanna) and the Sun (Utu, Shamash) were male; the right eye of the Egyptian, Hathor, Goddess of the Sky, became the Sun, and her left, the Moon. Hathor was also considered both mother and daughter to the Sun God, Ra. The definite article preceding the German noun Sun was feminine, although the Nordic deity, Baldur, was male.

Not only did Amaterasu-worship become the supreme cult of Japan, but Amaterasu also became the progenitrix of Japan's Imperial Line—and, by extension, of the entire race! Amaterasu's grandson descended from heaven, and his grandson, in turn, became the first Emperor of Japan, ascending the throne in 660 B.C.E. Thus does her cult embrace not only Nature-worship but ancestor-worship as well.

All the more astounding is the fact that despite the intensity of Amaterasu-worship the lot of women worsened progressively from the eighth century to the twentieth century. Not only were women deprecated and virtually enslaved, but they were associated with Evil: the Devil, Monsters, and Ghosts—angry spirits returning to extract their due vengeance on the male. Were these beliefs an expression of the male's subliminal fear of women?

Although some women struggled valiantly and at the cost of deep sacrifice to earn their independence as early as the seventeenth century, few reached the sought-for goal. Only after World War II, with the promulgation of the 1947 constitution, did the condition of women alter.

> There shall be no discrimination in political, economic or social relations, because of . . . sex. . . . Marriage shall be based only on the mutual consent of both sexes and it shall be maintained through mutual cooperation with the equal right of husband and wife as a basis. With regard to choice of spouse, property rights, inheritance, choice of domicile, divorce and other matters pertaining to marriage and the family, laws shall be enacted from the standpoint of individual dignity and the essential equality of the sexes (Edwin O. Reischauer, *The Japanese*, 211).

Although the law of the land may be imprinted on paper, it does not follow that the woman's lot has improved in actuality. Long strides must still be taken if women are to become the equals of men in Japan.

* * *

Let us look back in time to examine the historical, religious, and literary conditions which fomented the extreme imbalance between masculine and feminine rights.

Japan's beginnings are bathed in mystery. The first recorded date for the founding of the Japanese Empire—660 B.C.E.—appears in the *Chronicles of Japan* (*Nihongi*, 720). Fanciful, perhaps, since according to the punctilious records kept by the Chinese, Japan was referred to for the first time in 57 C.E. This later date refers to Japan not in terms of a unified land but one made up of some hundred tribal communities (*Sources of Japanese Tradition*, I, 1).

Although the inhabitants of Japan in Neolithic times were the ancestors of the partly proto-caucasoid Ainu, later groups, originating perhaps in the steppes of northeastern Asia, were possessed of distinctly Mongoloid features. Some invaders came from Korea to northern Kyushu and western Honshu.

Partly nomadic, they were horse-riding, warfaring people. Workers in iron, stone, and bronze, it was they who brought to Japan the long straight iron sword, the curved stone in the shape of a large comma, and the round bronze mirror. One of the invading clans gained dominance over the other groups; settling in the Yamato Plain, it won power over central and western Japan, and some sections of southern Korea (Edwin O. Reischauer, *Japan Past and Present*, 11-12).

What arrests our attention at this juncture of Japan's history is the political and religious substructure of its tribal units. Each was ruled by a chieftain—either a female priestess or a male priest. Documents refer to the "queen's country," indicating her leadership over the other clans. Such references not only are in keeping with Shinto cosmogony, but also shed light on the subject of female/male relationship.

We are told in the *Records of Ancient Matters* (*Kojiki*, 712) and the *Chronicles of Japan* (*Nihongi*, 720) that in the beginning "Heaven and Earth were not yet separated, and the *In* and *Yo* not yet divided." The *In* and *Yo* may be compared to the *Yang* and *Yin* of the Chinese Taoist cosmogony. In time, the *In* (male) and *Yo* (female) principles "formed a chaotic mass like an egg which was of obscurely defined limits and contained germs." When the egg took on life, its purer and clearer part was drawn to and formed Heaven; its heavier element became Earth, which was "compared to the floating of a fish sporting on the surface of the water." A form which looked like a reed-shoot suddenly manifested itself between Heaven and Earth, becoming a God: Kuni-toko-tachi ("Land-eternal-strand-of-august-thing"). Seven generations of Gods were then born, the last couple being Izanagi ("Male-who-invites") and Izanami ("Female-who-invites") (F. Hadland Davis, *Myths and Legends of Japan*, 21).

What is of particular interest to us is the marital relationship of the primal pair: Izanagi and Izanami. Although varying tales have been recounted, depending upon the text consulted, each indicates an ongoing conflict between male and female, the one vying for dominance over the other.

When Izanagi and Izanami were ordered by the Gods to stabilize and fertilize the mobile earth, analogized to "floating oil, moving like a jelly-fish," they did so. While standing on the "Floating Bridge of Heaven" they used the lance given them by the Gods to stir the mighty waters beneath them. Once coagulation began, they withdrew the lance and the drop that fell from its tip formed the island of Onokoro ("Naturally Coagulated").

Izanagi and Izanami descended onto the island that had just come into being, created a pillar in its center, and were now prepared to beget countries. In keeping with proscribed ritual, Izanagi, turning to the left, began walking around the pillar; while Izanami, doing likewise, went to the right. When the two met, Izanami spoke first:

> How delightful! I have met with a lovely youth.

Izanagi was angered.

> I am a man and by that right should have spoken first. How is it that on the contrary thou, a woman, shouldst have been the first to speak? This was unlucky. Let us go round again.

They did just that. When they again met, the male deity spoke first:

> How delightful I have met a lovely maiden.

He then asked:

> In thy body is there aught formed?

Izanami replied:

> In my body there is a place which is the source of femininity.

Izanagi said:

> In my body again there is a place which is the source of masculinity. I wish to unite this source-place of my body to the source-place of thy body (*Nihongi*, I, 12-3).

No sooner had the two become husband and wife than land, islands and other deities were born.

Another interpretation of the conversation between Izanagi and Izanami offers a different but equally illuminating account. After the couple had walked around the pillar, evidently a phallic symbol, and Izanami was the first to speak, thereby angering her future husband, she had already been impregnated. When she gave birth to a "leech-child," both she and her husband disowned him, setting him adrift on a raft. Thus did the island of Awa come into being.

So distressed was the primal pair after the birth of the "leech-child" that they returned to heaven to seek advice from the Gods. Informed that their abnormal offspring resulted from Izanami's crucial error—the female having spoken before the man—the onus was placed on the woman. The two were then ordered to carry out the ritual correctly after which were born the many islands of Japan, and the Gods: Wind, Trees, Mountains, Fire, etc. Following the birth of the last named, Izanami was badly burned, causing her intense suffering. She died after giving birth to the Goddess, Moaning River (*Nihongi*, I, 23).

So disconsolate was Izanagi that he cut off the child's head, and then went down to the Land of Yomi (Hell) to retrieve his wife. Upon meeting, Izanami said:

> My Lord and husband, why is thy coming so late? I have already eaten of the cooking-furnace of Yomi. Nevertheless, I am about to lie down to rest [in a house]. I pray thee do not look at me (*Nihongi*, I, 24).

Intense curiosity encouraged Izanagi to go against his wife's wishes. What did he see? Once beautiful, Izanami's body was now rotted and filled with maggots. Aghast, he fled, but not before Izanami had screamed out, "You have humiliated me!" She then ordered the "Eight Ugly Females of Yomi" to pursue and attack her husband. Thanks to his knowledge of magic, however, Izanagi was able to defend himself not only against the Ugly Females, but the pursuing Eight Thunder Gods, and the Soldiers of Hell as well. Gaining his freedom by reaching the upper slope of Yomi, he blocked its entrance with a huge boulder. When Izanami reached the spot, "he pronounced the formula of divorce." Her reply: "My dear Lord and husband, if thou sayest so, I will strangle to death the people of the country which thou dost govern, a thousand in one day" (*Nihongi*, I, 25).

Impervious to Izanami's threats, Izanagi is next to be found on the island of Tsukiji. Feelings of contamination and pollution carried over from his sojourn in Yomi prompted him to perform purification rituals. After washing his left eye, the great Sun Goddess, Amaterasu, came into being; upon washing his right eye, the God of the Moon, Tsuki-yumi emerged; through the washing of his nose, the God Susa-no-o took form.

Amaterasu no O kami (Heaven-Shining-Great-August-Deity) is described in the *Nihongi* as follows:

> The resplendent luster of this child shone throughout all the six quarters. Therefore the two Deities rejoiced, saying: "We have had many children, but none of them have been equal to this wondrous infant (*Nihongi*, I, 18).

The moon God, Tsuki-yumi (the "Counter-of-the-Months, therefore identified with time), was also radiant, but not so splendid as the Sun. As Amaterasu's consort, he would, however, share in her government. (Other versions state that these deities were born to both Izanagi and Izanami prior to her descent into the Land of Yomi.) Izanagi gave Amaterasu his jeweled necklace, and ordered her to rule the Plain of Heaven; Tsuki-yumi was told to rule the kingdom of night. Her brother, Susa-no-o ("His-Swift-Impetuous-Male Augustness") became the Storm God, who was not only endowed with a bitter temper, but a streak of cruelty (*Sources of Japanese Tradition*, I, 14).

> After this, Izanagi, his divine task having been accomplished, and his spirit-career about to suffer a change, built himself an abode of gloom in the island of Ahaji, where he dwelt for ever in silence and concealment" (Davis, 25).

Susa-no-o, who was frequently unruly, was banished from Heaven, went to Korea, and finally settled close by, in Izumo, on the Pana Sea coast, where he married the local princess. Although it was here that he fought and killed the horrendous eight-headed and eight-tailed serpent in whose mouth he found the great Sword, he did not stop playing pranks aimed, for the most part, at his sister. For example, after Amaterasu had planted her rice fields in the spring, carefully separating the narrow and long rice, Susa-no-o tore down the barriers, thereby confusing the two. When autumn arrived, he had piebald colts lie down on the fields, thus crushing the harvest. He then voided excrement in the New Temples constructed for the Festival of First Fruits in honor of Amaterasu.

Sibling rivalry found other expression: Amaterasu frequently dressed up as a shamanistic chieftain, wearing warrior's vestments. Conflict between brother and sister took on a highly dramatic form when Susa-no-o noticed his sister and her helpers weaving garments for the Gods in the great Weaving Hall. Intent upon tormenting them, he first made a hole in the roof, then threw down a piebald colt. Amaterasu was so alarmed that she pricked herself with her shuttle. One of her helpers, however, fell dead from fright. So enraged was Amaterasu by this incident that she went into the Rock-Cave of Heaven, fastened the door, and refused to come out. Thus the world was deprived of light. Eighty (some sources say countless) Gods met to try to remedy the catastrophe. Nothing seemed to work until the Goddess Amano-Uzume-no-Mikoto ("Her Augustness-Heavenly-Alarming-Female"), bedecked in a variety of plants and leaves, mounted an upside down tub at the cave's entrance, and began dancing. Her gestures took on the cast of obscenity.

> Then she became divinely possessed, exposed her breasts and pushed her skirt-band down to her genitals.
> Then [heaven and earth] shook as the eight hundred myriad deities laughed at once (Hayao Kawai, *The Japanese Psyche*, 50).

The noise aroused Amaterasu's curiosity: was another deity usurping her popularity? Looking out at the mirror that had been placed on the tree outside the cave, and fascinated by her own reflection, Amaterasu walked a little beyond the opening of the Rock-Cave of Heaven. No sooner had she done so than the God of Force blocked her return into the cave. As for Susa-no-o, he was severely punished by the Gods. (Japanese theatre was said to have originated from this event. See Chapter 3).

That the Japanese Imperial line traces its genealogy from Amaterasu and her brother, Susa-no-o, is not unusual, since brother and sister in most religions are the begetters of future generations. What is fascinating for our purposes is the manner in which their progeny came into being. Because Susa-no-o chewed some of Amaterasu's ornaments, giving birth to offspring from his mouth, he claimed them as his own, whereas Amaterasu sustained that the children were hers because the seed (or elements from which they were made) came from her (*Sources*, 17).

What is arresting in this myth is the fact that the normal route of sexual procreation was reversed: the male produced the progeny from his mouth; the women provided the semen. The separation of the sexes was decreed by Amaterasu who declared the following to Susa-no-o:

> As for the seed of the five male Deities born last, their birth was from things of mine; so undoubtedly they are my children. As for the seed of the three female Deities born first, their birth was from a thing of thine; so doubtless they are thy children (*Sources*, 17).

In time, Amaterasu sent to earth her divine Grandson, Ama-tsu-hiko-no-ninigi no Mikoto, bearing the sword, Kusanagi, which her brother, Susa-no-o, had found in the mouth of the eight-headed snake he had killed; the precious stones from the mountain-steps of Heaven; and the mirror into which Amaterasu had gazed from her cave. These three objects became the Three Imperial Regalia which are emblems of power even to this day. Amaterasu then commanded her August Grandchild:

> This Reed-plain-1500-autumns-fair-rice-ear Land is the region which my descendants shall be lords of. Do thou, my August grandchild, proceed thither and govern it. Go! and may prosperity attend thy dynasty, and may it, like Heaven and Earth, endure forever (*Nihongi*, 77).

Amaterasu added: "Adore this mirror as our souls, adore it as you adore us."

Ninigi's great grandson, Emperor Kami Yamato Iharebiko, known in history as Jimmu Tenno, founded the Imperial line of Japan in 660 B.C.E., the point at which Japan's "official" history begins, bringing with it the struggle between the Yamato and Izumo clans, and the establishment of the cult of Amaterasu as the progenitrix of the Imperial family.

Emperor Sujin (97-30 B.C.E.) built a sanctuary for the solar emblems given by Amaterasu to her divine son, and appointed his daughter to oversee their worship. Emperor Suinin (29 B.C.E.-70 C.E.), ordered his daughter, Yamato-Hime no Mikoto, to find an appropriate site for Amaterasu's glorification. Accordingly, a sanctuary was built in Ise province in keeping with the dictates of the oracle, through whose voices she heard the Great Goddess's commands.

> The province of Ise, of the divine wind, is the land whither repair the waves from the eternal world, the successive waves. It is a secluded and pleasant land. In this land I wish to dwell" (*Nihongi*, 176).

The carrying out of further instructions led to the building of an Abstinence Palace at Kawakami in Isuzu, for it was here that Amaterasu first descended from Heaven.

It was declared that when an Emperor acceded to the throne, an unmarried Princess of the Imperial House would be appointed to serve at the Shrine of Ise. If there were no unmarried Princesses at the time, then another Princess was selected by divination. She was to reside in the Worship-Palace for the duration of her tenure (*Nihongi*, 176). The sanctuary's sacred octagonal mirror, *shintai* (the object through which the Goddess's spirit enters), enabled Amaterasu not only to listen to the prayers of the faithful, but also to be present during the ceremonies. Cocks, considered sacred to Amaterasu since they greet the dawn, were also in the vicinity. Because Amaterasu is the weaver of divine garments and because she officiates in Heaven at ceremonies for the harvest, festivals honoring her are celebrated in April and September at the Ise Shrine. As the Sun rises between "the Wedded Rocks" on the seashore of Futami, pilgrims piously salute her ascension by clapping their hands. Prayers of great beauty are addressed to Amaterasu as, for example:

> More especially do I humbly declare in the mighty presence of the Great-Heaven-Shining Deity who dwells in Ise. Because the Great Deity has bestowed on him [the sovereign] the lands of the four quarters over which her glance extends as far as where the walls of heaven rise, as far as where the bounds of Earth stand up, as far as the blue sky extends, as far as where the white clouds settle down; by the blue sea-plain, as far as the prows of ships can reach without letting dry their poles and oars; by land, as far as the hoofs of horses can go, with tightened baggage-cords, treading their way among rock, beds and tree-roots where the long roads extend, continuously widening the narrow regions and making the steep regions level, in drawing together, as it were, the distant regions by throwing over them [a net of] many ropes—therefore let the first-fruits for the Sovran Deity be piled up in her mighty presence like a range of hills, leaving the remainder for him [the sovereign] tranquilly to partake of.
>
> Moreover, whereas you bless the Sovran Grandchild's reign as a long reign, firm and enduring, and render it a happy and prosperous reign, I plunged down my neck cormorant-wise in reverence to you as our Sovran's dear, divine ancestress, and fulfill your praise by making these plenteous offerings on his behalf (*Sources*, 23).

The Grand Shrine in Ise is even today one of the holiest spots in Japan for the Amaterasu cult.

The main deity of nature as well as of ancestor worship, Amaterasu is implicit in Shinto ("The Way of the Gods"). An indigenous animistic religion, Shinto has no official scriptures, no theology, and no code of ethics. Nor has it any structure, as do the organized religions of the west. Shintoists believe that a life force exists in all things, animate or inanimate, and everything in the world of phenomena is endowed with a spirit. Worship is based on the simple feeling of "awe" for all things in nature: a waterfall, a flower, a stone, an insect, a mountain, snow, an ancestor, a hero, the emperor, the sun, the moon. Such numinous forces are called *kami*, which is translated as "god," "superior," or "above." Human beings approach *kami* in reverence and friendship and without fear. Before doing so, however, they must purify themselves by washing their hands and mouths, and taking part in devotions, such as standing within a sacred enclosure (a quiet grove with a shrine) or before a particular stone or mountain.

Shinto worship requires "attendance," that is, physical presence, with focusing on the object of worship, and participation in ceremonial dances, processions, and rituals. Important also were the "offerings" to the *kami*: the first fruits of the season or the first fish caught.

High priestesses or shamanesses attached to various shrines understood the language of the *kami* and interpreted their will. The mediums translated the spiritual essence of what remained a mystery for others. Women serving in the various shrines as mediums and priestesses later enacted sacred dances (*kagura*). It must also be noted that belief in spirit or demonic possession, necromancy, black magic, and witchcraft were popular in Japan at this period (Bunce, *Religions in Japan*, 103).

Credible documentation, drawn from relatively late Chinese official instruments such as the *History of the Kingdom of Wei* (*Wei Chih*) (297 C.E.), refers to Japan (known then as Wa) not in terms of a matriarchate, but rather as a society characterized by equality between the sexes. "In their meetings and in their deportment, there is no distinction between father and son or between man and woman" (*Sources*, 5). Still, it was noted that men in the upper echelons of the hierarchy had four or five wives, while those on lower tiers had only two or three (*Sources*, 5).

Even more astonishing for our purposes was the fact that this same *History of the Kingdom of Wei* mentions the fact that the country of Wa, once ruled by men, had undergone so many upheavals that the people decided they wanted to be governed by Pimiko, a woman. She was depicted as follows:

> She occupied herself with magic and sorcery, bewitching the people. Though mature in age, she remained unmarried. She had a younger brother who assisted

> her in ruling the country. After she became the ruler, there were few who saw her. She had one thousand women as attendants, but only one man. He served her food and drink and acted as a medium of communication. She resided in a palace surrounded by towers and stockades, with armed guards in a state of constant vigilance ... (*Sources*, 6).

It is further recorded that Pimiko or the Queen of Wa sent an emissary to Tai-fang in China in 238 C.E., requesting permission to pay tribute to the Emperor at his court. That she had official stature and was much admired is evident from the Emperor's edict to the Queen of Wa which reads:

> Herein we address Pimiko, queen of Wa, whom we now officially call a friend of Wei. The Governor of Tai-fang, Liu Hsia, has sent a messenger to accompany your vassal, Nashonmi, and his lieutenant, Tsushi Gori. They have arrived here with your tribute consisting of four male slaves and six female slaves, together with two pieces of cloth with designs, each twenty feet in length. You live very far away across the sea; yet you have sent an embassy with tribute. Your loyalty and filial piety we appreciate exceedingly. We confer upon you, therefore, the title 'Queen of Wa Friendly to Wei,' together with the decoration of the gold seal with purple ribbon. The latter, properly encased, is to be sent to you through the Governor. We expect you, O Queen, to rule your people in peace and to endeavor to be devoted and obedient" (*Sources*, 6).

After Pimiko's demise, a mound over a hundred paces in diameter was raised and more than a hundred male and female attendants were buried with her.

No sooner had a king been placed on the throne of Wa than the people manifested their continuous dissatisfaction by murdering and assassinating over a thousand people. Seemingly, the inhabitants of Wa wanted to be ruled by a woman. When the thirteen-year-old Iyo, a relative of Pimiko, was chosen to be queen, bloodshed ceased (*Sources*, 6).

Women are again mentioned during the reign of Emperor Temmu (672-686 C.E.) who, for political reasons, appointed a committee to set down in writing his country's old traditions. One of his female attendants, Hieda-no-Are, endowed with an extraordinary memory, was ordered to memorize the ancient legends surrounding the Age of the Gods and the founding of the Japanese Imperial dynasty. In 711, Empress Gemmyo (707-715

C.E.) had O no Yasumaro commit to writing the tales told to him by Hieda-no-Are. His selection became the *Records of Ancient Matters* (712 C.E.), a collection of myths, legends, songs, poems, clan genealogies, and some historical accounts, beginning with the Creation—the separation of Heaven and Earth—and concluding with the death of Empress Suiko (592-628 C.E.). Mention is made of other women rulers: Kogyoku Tenno (642-645); Jito Tenno (686-697); Genmei (707-715); Gensho (715-724); Koken (749-758), etc.

Further details concerning the pantheon of Gods are to be found in the previously mentioned pseudo-national history, the *Chronicles of Japan* (720 C.E.), also ordered by Empress Gemmyo (714 C.E.) during the reign of Emperor Gensho (715-726 C.E.). Prince Toneri and O no Yasumaro were the compilers of this work, which so closely parallels the *Records of Ancient Matters*, despite the different versions of the myths and legends recounted (*Sources*, 13).

The information concerning the origin of the Gods and ancestors included in the *Chronicles of Japan* was seemingly compiled from a hereditary group of *Kataribe* ("reciters"), whose role was to recite "ancient words." Their recitations at great Shinto festivals, on important state occasions, and at banquets at the Imperial Court or palace of highly-placed families, were frequently accompanied by music. Whether or not Yasumaro's informant was a member of the group is unknown, but he was evidently conversant with the myths and legends recited by the *Kataribe* (W.G. Aston, *Japanese Literature*, 20).

Contact with China increased considerably in the early centuries, and the cultural interchange enriched Japan both scientifically and religiously. The continental civilization whetted the Japanese appetite for learning, expansion, creativity, and was also responsible for the introduction of Buddhism to the Yamato clan in 552 C.E. Dissension broke out shortly thereafter, when the sovereign asked his advisors whether they favored the worship of the Buddhist image brought to them from Korea. Understandably, Buddhism was considered a threat: if Buddha had greater powers than the *kami* from which they descended, they probably reasoned, then their authority would vanish. The Soga family, a branch of the Yamato clan, fought for the establishment of Buddhism in Japan, defeating the Shintoist Manonobe, who opposed the importation of the new religion. The Soga rulers dominated and arranged for the assassination of the Yamato chief, after which they proclaimed his niece, Suiko, Empress

(John Whitney Hall, *Japan from Prehistory to Modern Times*, 42).

Extraordinary changes took place in the Yamato court under the reign of Empress Suiko. According to the *Chronicles of Japan*, she was both unusually beautiful and intellectually competent.

> Her appearance was beautiful, and her conduct was marked by propriety. At the age of eighteen, she was appointed empress-consort of the Emperor Nunakura futo-damashiki. When she was thirty-four years of age ... the Emperor was murdered by the Great Imperial Chieftain Mumako no Sukune, and the succession of the Dignity being vacant, the Ministers besought the Empress-consort ... to ascend the throne (*Sources*, 43).

Twice she declined the great honor, as was the custom, and accepted upon the third request. Under her rule, the "Inner doctrines" [Buddhism] was promoted, as were the building of Buddhist temples, the collecting of relics, the establishment of priestly orders and nunneries, and the constructing of Buddhas, one of which was sixteen feet in height (*Sources*, 45).

Empress Suiko's nephew, Prince Shotoku, having been appointed "regent," effected numerous changes in Japan. Emulating the much-admired Chinese civilization, he imposed the adoption of the Chinese calender, the erection of Buddhist temples, and the reorganization of the government with the court becoming the central authority. An official embassy was sent to China in 607. A devout Buddhist, Prince Shotoku recommended that young scholars specializing in literature, philosophy, history, Buddhist theology and ritual, and artistic skills, be sent to China to study. Upon their return to the Yamato court, they were given positions which enabled them to impart their learning to the Japanese. It is said that Prince Shotoku turned to Buddhism for guidance in spiritual matters, and to Confucianism in secular matters.

Buddhism, founded by the Indian Shakyamuni Gautama (566-483 B.C.E.), preached the doctrine of Buddha, the Enlightened One. Happiness and salvation result from inwardness and are not dependent upon transitory exterior phenomena; life on earth is the product of imperfection and sorrow; the annihilation of desire leads to salvation and "perpetual enlightenment" (nirvana). After Buddhism was introduced into Japan it was modified by the Japanese and divested of most of its theology. It became a philosophy.

Confucianism also played a significant role in the growing patriarchate that Japan was to become. Confucius (551-479 B.C.E.), who preached a family-style morality based on the ethical wisdom of "superior men," on character building, learning, virtue, filial piety and ancestral piety, gave virtually no importance to women. For Confucius, "filial duty and fraternal duty" were "fundamental to Manhood-at-its-best." In the *Canon of Filiality* (3rd cent.), a collection of statements allegedly made by Confucius, we read:

> Filiality is the root of virtue, and that from which civilization derives . . . the body, the hair and skin, are received from our parents, and we dare not injure them: this is the beginning of filiality . . . filiality begins with the serving of our parents, continues with the serving of our prince, and is completed with the establishing of our own character (Laurence G. Thompson, *Chinese Religion: An Introduction*, 39).

Because only the wisest and most honorable men were capable of governing society, moral integrity was stressed. A "gentleman" alone was capable of governing, and it was incumbent upon him to elevate those he ruled by serving as an example rather than by exercising autocratic control. Civilization's continuity depended upon the moral fiber and rules of conduct of the central authority. The practice of paying homage to past generations in China was similar in some ways to Shinto belief in ancestor worship.

Shinto, Buddhism, and Confucianism were compatible. All three revered ancestors, and all three were based on purity of soul and ethicality of action. Only the latter two, however, preached asceticism and intellectuality. They also minimized, if not denigrated women, accounting to a great extent for the inferior place allotted them after the eighth century in Japan. Women's social and political dominance vanished, and they became the "handmaids," so to speak, of the male population—until the twentieth century.

* * *

Now that we have briefly examined the woman's role with regard to religion and history, let us glance at her creative contributions. The eighth-century *Collection of Ten Thousand Leaves* (*Manyoshu*), the earliest extant anthology of Japanese poetry (4,500 poems), allegedly includes verses attributed to the Empress Iwa-no-hime (d. 347). In another important work, the *Collection of Ancient and Modern Times* (*Kokinshu*, 905), the poems selected are grouped according to seasons and subject matter (Spring, Summer, Autumn, Winter, Partings, etc.).

One of the most lyrical and passionate poets of early times was the much-admired Princess Nukada (ca. 660-90), the daughter of Prince Kagami, and both wife and favorite of Emperors Temmu and Tenji. Her verses reflect the turbulent times in which she lived: the period of the founding and entrenchment of the Imperial clan. The musical impact and rhythmical qualities of her language were so impressive that she was considered not only of the stature of a shamaness, but a sort of spokesperson for the womankind of her era. "On Preferring the Autumn Hills," partly in the form of a *choka* (a long poem with an unfixed number of alternating lines of 5 and 7 syllables), takes the form of a debate on whether spring or autumn is the more beautiful season.

> When spring at last
> Is freed from winter's bonds,
> The silent birds
> Arrive in their full song
> And lifeless flowers
> Burst forth in brilliant bloom;
> Yet I cannot find
> The flowers on their luxuriant slopes
> Or appreciate the blossoms
> Hopelessly entangled in the grass.
>
> However, when I see
> The leaves upon the autumn hills,
> My eager hands
> Tremble with their load of crimson leaves
> And with reluctance
> Leave the green ones on their boughs—
> Yes, the green ones are the pity,
> And the autumn hills for me (Earl Miner, *An Introduction to Japanese Court Poetry*, 38).

Princess Nukada also wrote love poems which conflate eternal and universal thematics with a personal code of values. In the following poem, she identifies her subjective feelings with nature's own surroundings.

> Longing for you,
> loving you,

> waiting for you,
> the bamboo blinds were swayed
> only by the autumn wind (Kenneth Rexroth and Ikuko
>   Atsumi, *The Burning Heart*, 3).

Because the wind pushed aside the bamboo in the image of the "blinds," she is able to peer out of her room and into the world, searching longingly for her beloved. The use by ancient poets of bamboo to write upon is another indication of her need to convey her feelings in poetic form. That bamboo, an evergreen luxuriant throughout the winter, is also a symbol for longevity, represents the long duration of her passion. That his plant is also edible, suggests how deeply it courses through her being. Wind, which sweeps over the land in autumn—the poet's favorite season—represents the spiritual side of her love. Although the divestiture of these bleak months arouses melancholy, it also has a positive attribute: the wind, traversing her house as well as her heart, serves to link her with her beloved.

The brother of Emperor Tenji, Prince Oama (the future Emperor Temmu) approached Princess Nukada, his former wife. Although she is married to Emperor Tenji, Oama waved his sleeve, which according to the complex code of etiquette at the time indicated his wish to have sexual union with her. Such a gesture was not considered in any way indecorous; indeed, it inspired the Princess to write the following poem:

> As they go through the fields of Murasaki,
> As they go through the hunting fields,
> Will not the field-watchers have seen it?—
> The waving of my lord's sleeves!

The Prince responded:

> My love, delightful as the Murasaki flower;
> If I thought her hateful being the wife of another,
> Would I then still love her? (Shuichi Kato, *A History
>   of Japanese Literature*, 60).

Wife-stealing, as in the case of Princess Nukada, was undoubtedly due to the unsteady political situation of the time when power struggles were so rampant. Emperor Tenji put Prince Arima to death in 658, for example, with the hope of solidifying clan allegiance. Ten years later, Prince Otsu was put to death by the future Empress Jito for ostensibly the same reason. Prior to his death he visited in secret his sister, Princess Oku, at the Ise Shrine. Upon their parting she composed two poems, indicating a premonition of the tragedy to befall her brother.

Empress Jito (645-702), the wife of Emperor Temmu, ascended to the throne upon her husband's death in 686. She ruled for ten years, again suggesting that the Yamato clan might have been a matriarchate. Or was it that these Empresses were, in fact, shamanesses, representing and furthering Shinto within the clan?

Empress Jito conveys her sorrow "On the Death of the Emperor Temmu" in the following poem:

> Even flaming fire
> can be snatched up, smothered
> and carried in a bag.
> Why then can't I
> meet my dead lord again? (Rexroth and Atsumi, 7).

If the all-important complex fire ritual is carried out twice a year at the Imperial Palace by Shinto priests to placate the Fire God (Ho-Masubi), then the Empress wishes for equally difficult ceremonies to be enacted to bring her husband back to the land of the living. The Fire God, let us note, was deeply feared during windy seasons in Japan since most of the houses were built of highly flammable wood. The complex ceremony enacted at the shrines require that a pure fire—the embodiment of the God—be made by the priest through friction (by rubbing two pieces of wood, hard stone, or steel together). On New Year's Day, the faithful make their way to the shrine, receive the pure fire directly from the priest, which they then take home and use to light carefully the fire in their hearths, believing it will protect them throughout the year. The Emperor's food must also be cooked in this pure flame (*New Larousse Encyclopedia of Mythology*, 417). That Empress Jito identifies her husband with fire suggests that although redoubtable, he *is* flame, energy, power—possessor of those divine masculine forces which she worshipped.

Otomo no Sakanoe no Iratsume (8th cent.), one of the best women poets of the early Nara Period, was both aunt and mother-in-law of the famous poet, Otomo no Yakamochi. Wed several times and the mother of two children, this intellectually and emotionally superior woman was also strong and determined. When obliged to take over the rule of the Otomo clan, forever the butt of attack in the complex politics at court, she did so with aplomb.

Love, as evident in the following poem, impacted not only on Sakanoe no Iratsume's spirit and emotions, but on her physical being as well, causing her severe pain.

> My love hurts me because you cannot know it—
> Love like the maiden lily,
> blooming in the thickets of the summer moor (Rexroth and Atsumi, 9).

By using the metaphor of the lily to which she compares herself, the poet sees her body and spirit blooming in beauty. Her maidenhood is analogous to the flower's pristine whiteness. Just as the lily, standing stately and passive in the moor, develops to its fullest during the summer months, so her physical being and love also evolve in depth. The short lifespan of these two conflated images, drawn from the vegetal and human world, pursues its life-cycle, compelling them to wither and die after having fulfilled their destiny in the manifest world.

Another poet, Yosami, Wife of Hitomaro (8th cent.), seemingly was one of the three wives of the courtier-poet, Kakinomoto Hitomaro. Thematically sophisticated, subjective yet objective, imaginative but also adhering to the expressive and concrete vocabulary of her day, Yosami conflated opposites, adding to the intensity of her inner drama.

> Day after day I've longed for my husband,
> thinking each day he would return.
> Now they tell me that he lies buried
> in the Canyon of Stone River (Rexroth and Atsumi, 10).

Lyrical, yet controlled, she sings out her despair when her husband must leave home to fulfill his government missions to distant parts and even more poignantly when she learns of his death.

Yosami's use of the thematics of time in the above poem is intriguing. Her repetition of the noun "day," in view of the concision and restraint inherent in her poem, takes on cumulative power, giving an impression of prolonged and increasingly harrowing periods of loneliness and suffering. So, too, is the cyclicality of her recurring feelings of loss given amplitude in such words as "return." Unending, then, is her torment, ceaseless are her feelings of divestiture, reaching agonizing proportions upon learning of her beloved's death and his burial in a narrow valley between towering cliffs. Significant also, is the poet's antithetical "Stone River." By juxtaposing the hard, brittle, and eternal cohesiveness of rock with its counterpart, the liquidity, formlessness of water, she reveals the multiple obstacles and painful encounters she has experienced from the beginning to the end of her love experience. Blended in her lyrical lines are philosophical innuendoes: the temporality of daily life and the intemporality of the Great Whole.

Lady Kii (8th cent.), the consort of Prince Aki and one of Otomo no Yakamochi's many lovers, conveys her simple yet lyrical hurt in straightforward and conventional imagery.

> I know the reputation
> of the idle ways
> of the beach of Takashi.
> I will not go near them,
> for I would surely wet my sleeves (Rexroth and Atsumi, 12).

Instead of yielding to her desire as do others, she refuses to allow her pride to be sullied and the esteem she has for herself to be degraded. Unlike other women, she chooses to remain at home, unwilling to join them at the beach. The metonymy of the breaking waves at the beach and the splattering of her "sleeve" indicates the tears that would accompany the sadness that would follow her loss of the respectability which she so treasures.

The verses of Kasa no Iratsume (8th cent.), also one of Otomo no Yakamochi's paramours, are unique for their nuanced and subtly seductive note. Eroticism marks the twenty-nine love poems written to her beloved, each redolent with yearning.

> The Gods of heaven are irrational
> So I may die and never meet you,
> whom I love so much (Rexroth and Atsumi, 13).

Although seemingly irreverent, Kasa no Iratsume not only understood human nature, but also accepted the fact that Gods were neither omnipotent nor omniscient. That her earthly lot was marked with sorrow proved the importance of the Buddhist precept of detachment and strength in attempting to attain indifference.

In other verses, the poet turns to nature to help overcome those very passions that could smother her. Her use of the night hours, a paradigm of the unconscious, tightens the interrelationship between daytime and the rational sphere—between human and inhuman domains.

> When evening comes
> sorrow overwhelms my mind.
> I see his phantom
> that speaks the words
> he used to say (Rexroth and Atsumi, 13).

As evening approaches, her visual and feeling worlds are wrapped in sorrow. Yet, she longs for night, for it is at this time that her beloved speaks to her, that he, in "phantom" form, appears to her mind's eye. For disquieted souls, particularly in Japan where both friendly and destructive ghosts, demons, ghouls return to life, such a tremulous thought takes on ambivalent soundings. They haunt; yet these materialized and audible apparitions, viewed psychologically, are manifestations of previously repressed thoughts and sensations. For Kasa no Iratsume, the words spoken by her "phantom" lover, although perhaps traumatizing, are, nevertheless, comforting—companions that lull and diminish her misery.

Legend rather than fact surrounds Ono no Komachi (c. 850), one of the most famous of Japanese poets. We know only that eighteen of her poems appeared in the *Kokinshu*, and three more, in the *Gosenshu* (Kazuko Sugisaki, "Ono-no-Komachi—The Legend and the Reality"). Apocryphal and imaginative stories focusing on this extraordinary figure abound, and five intensely moving Noh dramas, including *Komachi at Sekidera*, introduce incidents in the Komachi legend which suggest that the poet had a plethora of lovers when young, grew ugly in her old age, and in time was forced into beggardom. Her poetry frequently deals with the transitory world, as in the following poem:

> The colors of flowers
> has changed and faded, in vain
> While so long I have lived
> In sad, idle reveries (Kazuko Sugisaki, 76).

What is not open for conjecture is the complexity and self-consciousness of her language, and the emphasis on the erotic in her verse. Komachi's poetic universe does not wax in stilled reverie. On the contrary, she prefers action, vigor, and increased momentum which she effects by her expert inclusion of "pivot-words." A technique used long before her time, pivot-words as manipulated by Komachi trigger multiple meanings in words and lines, depending upon how these are parsed grammatically. Pivot-words, then, underscore meaning, function, and interrelationships, thereby unifying the disparate elements within the poem. Komachi's skillful verbal technique includes the frequent use of associative words which enable her to set off multiple reverberations and sympathetic vibrations in her verse.

Thematically, Komachi's poetry centers most frequently on love: on man's abandonment of woman, and the erupting emotions suffered by the victim when passions are denied fulfillment.

> On such a night as this
> When no moon lights your way to me,
>   I wake, my passion blazing,
> My breast a fire raging, exploding flame
> While within me my heart chars (Earl Miner, *An Introduction to Japanese Court Poetry*, 82).

Although viewed as humorous, the sub-text yields a more painful meaning. The oxymoron of a moonless "night," juxtaposed to "passion blazing . . . fire raging, exploding flame . . . heart chars," conveys a sequence of images studded with body language. As momentum builds, the control and concision in the catapulting sensations inflates their power. The antithetical lighting effects, drawn from the blackness of the night, give birth to fulgurating currents which trigger her dream/sensation. As she longs for her lover's embrace, an entire inner topography becomes sensate. Erotic feelings set off fiery bursts of prismatic reflections. Cumulative, their charge and density increase as her passion becomes increasingly incandescent. Although flame lights her world and fuels her desire for his burning touch, what lingers of her love, now lost, are cinders—fine residue, ash-like memories.

The Buddhist notion of detachment and of the futility and deceptive nature of worldly pleasures was perhaps understood by Komachi as an intellectual concept, but certainly not experientially. The intensity of her passion links her more importantly to Shinto forces, to certain nocturnal and frequently transparent *kami* which appear to her as embodiments of living instincts. Emerging at night, in darkness, her irrational world seems to be taking on concretion, each form/sensation parading its pain before her. Although she recognizes, in keeping with Buddhist credo, the illusory and ephemeral nature of earthly love as well as man's unfaithful nature, she is drawn to him who was her love—bodily, instinctually, naturally.

In the following poem, Komachi uses the image of the flower metaphorically: its opening, blossoming, and dying mirror humankind's earthly existence as well as the individual's love and sexual experience.

> That which fades away
> Without revealing its altered color
>   Is, in the world of love,
> That single flower which blossoms
> In the fickle heart of man (Miner, 83).

Like the flower, so passion is born, reaches perfection, languishes, declines, and concludes. Komachi's paradigmatic use of coloration and decoloration enhances the growing, burgeoning, and declining emotions which embody a relationship—and life in general. The rhythmic beats of the heart in joy, followed by their slackening in sorrow, serve to increase the poem's dramatic pulsations. For Komachi, a "single flower" (referring to cherry blossoms), identified with that unique love, is destroyed by humankind's deceptive ways. On a cosmic scale, the continuously churning and transformatory processes interwoven into the theme also help to blot out ties with the transient world, thereby allowing the eternally detached collective sphere to prevail. Yet, the ephemeral flower lives on as an eternal metaphor in the *reality* of the poem itself.

Intense activity prevails in the following poem, in such images as endless running, uninterrupted footwork, in search of an abstraction—her dream.

> Although my feet
> Never cease running to you
>   On the path of dreams,
> Such nights of love are never worth
> One glimpse of you in your reality (Miner, 83).

The poet's nightly meanderings cause her feet, barely touching the ground, to carry her swiftly toward her beloved. The breathlessness of anticipation heightens her excitement. Used as a parallelism for the sexual act, the compressed rhythms and rapidity of the tightly etched images accentuate the sensuality of the verses. For the Buddhist, fantasies are illusions (*maya*), or entrapments. Like the flower's life span in the preceding poem, passion is, as all else in the cosmic experience, unvarying in the constancy of the universal law which is *change*. Urges are collective, albeit archetypal in dimension, forever repeated throughout empirical existence, always catalyzed by desire. For the poet, however, the sensations evoked in her dream are dim replicas, tarnished reflections of the *real* act. They cannot parallel the fervent violence she had experienced with her lover—for whom she longs. Nor could the poet have imbued her writing with authentic livingness had she not *known* it body and soul.

Komachi's Buddhism was not austere. On the contrary, her vision of Enlightenment resulted from an inner luminosity—or passion—born from the life experience itself. In this poem, she seems not to have fully accepted the basic doctrine of Buddhism which teaches that existence is suffering, caused by craving and attachment, and the path leading to the cessation of suffering is *nirvana*. Komachi gives the impression of struggling against the inevitable in her poems, of fighting fate, while yearning for fulfillment in love which she knows rationally to be illusory and, worse, an entrapment in *maya*'s cunning and seductive web.

Komachi's poetic voice was significant with regard to court poetry for having revealed the importance of women's passions, so continuously undervalued by men. Her poems suggest that their needs are not only superior, but more intense. Komachi's heaving emotions could no longer be cast aside or tread upon with ruthless indifference by her readers or entourage. The woman's world of feeling and sexuality had a place in society as well as in the larger cosmic plan implicit in the principles of Buddhist and Shinto thought.

As attested to in the following poem, empirical existence had imposed suffering upon the passionate Komachi. Jealousies, intrigues, deceptions, and cruelties, experienced rationally during her waking hours, reverberate with increasing intensity in the subliminal domain.

> In waking daylight,
> Then, oh then, it can be understood;
> But when I see you
> Shrinking from those hostile eyes
> Even in my dreams: that is misery itself (Miner, 83).

The most terrifying image in the poem, "Shrinking from those hostile eyes," uses explosive body language to increase the viscerality of her agony. The verb to *shrink*, expressing both action and event, suggests the very process of diminution and contraction in size as the aging process begins. It may also be associated with feelings of humiliation, lack of self-esteem, and fear, as in the act of recoiling, avoiding, drawing away from others into oneself. It suggests an abstract notion as well: a decrease in value and a depreciation of the individual by society.

What makes this poem unique is the intensity of the image of the "hostile eyes" focusing an everyday reality in a court filled with vying, hurtful, and hateful beings. Those orbs also encompass an invisible domain: the world of ghosts and revenants. Forever observing, prying, and angering in their savage power, these luminous powers watch her every move. When identified with Shinto, they may be understood as manifestations of Izanagi's eyes, the left one which gave birth to the Sun, and the right, to the Moon—symbols of synthetic as well as intuitive vision. For the Buddhist, the eye corresponds to fire, as in the searing trajectory experienced during one's contemplative and inward journey. Viewed as embodiments of feared forces living inchoate in the poet's subliminal domain, these integuments rise, unexpectedly and with explosive power, brutalizing the sleeper. Intent upon working revenge on their victim, they instill their venom more insidiously, as the beauty of youth withers into the ugliness of old age; as the love-feast begets a ghoulish palpable world in the very fabric of the unfolding nightmare.

Lady Ise (ca. 900), like Komachi, centers on her passion, but with less terrifying impact, less viscerality, less fierceness, in her animalistic intent. More structured and intellectual, her work reflects the relatively rigid mood of the court, newly moved to Kyoto. The daughter of Lord Ise, she, like some of the poets mentioned above, had also been the lover of various men and the Emperor's concubine as well. Her use of the traditional "pillow-word," an epithet or attribute which had become a kind of "formula" in verse, may be interpreted in its literal as well as in its abstract or figurative meaning.

> Since "the pillow knows all"
> we slept without a pillow.
> Still my reputation
> reaches to the skies
> like a dust storm (Rexroth and Atsumi, 17).

The pillow upon which the head rests evokes a most intimate world, where ears hear concealed conversations, and eyes pour tears of pain or gratitude. So in need of isolation were the lovers that they set the pillow aside, living out the experience in utter secrecy, far from the peering and envious glances of spies emerging from every corner of the outside world, who pride themselves on their ability to read pillowtalk. Unwilling to sully the esteem in which society holds the poet, and though her personal existence is far from serene, she remains aloof and distant. Her inner world, however, reminiscent of "a dust storm," is beset with chaos from the pull and tug of violent winds. Not always negative powers, they serve to propel into motion what might otherwise have remained static, forcing the creative power implicit in the dust to pollinate, to fecundate, just as the seed takes root in the work of art.

Increasingly secretive, Lady Ise wants to limit further the intensity of her joy—to the point of barring her lover from having access to *her* experience. Cutting him off from her fantasy world, she withdraws into her own sphere. Shy and embarrassed, she grows red with shame at the very thought of being perceived by another in the joy of a recklessly marvelous experience. Unable to *face* her *face* in the *mirror*, an instrument of temporality as well as of perception, she veers away from her own peering eyes as these focus on this very instrument of self-contemplation. Reflected in the image is both the world of the individual and that of the universe; surface and depth; reality and illusion; ephemerality and eternality; night and day; Sun and Moon; diversity and Oneness.

> Even in dreams
> I do not want him to know
> that it is me he is making love to
> for I am overcome with blushes
> when I see my face in my morning mirror (Rexroth and
>   Atsumi, 18).

* * *

Life was changing for women at court, as evidenced by the *Kokinshu*, despite the fact that in this anthology men poets outnumbered women four to one. Selections were not drawn, as in the earlier *Manyoshu* anthology, from various social classes. Only members of the aristocracy and court officials were represented in the *Kokinshu*, inasmuch as the Japanese court hierarchy was now based on birth and class. Given the complexity of marital ties and the role played by concubinage, the multiple offspring of so many relationships created a complex and frequently antithetical code of ethics.

Although women lived a sheltered existence behind walls and screens, poetry played a significant role in fostering amatory relationships. A maid, for example, might hand her lady a *waka* (poem) written on beautifully decorated and scented paper—an act that might prelude a long licit or illicit courtship. Poetry, when recited, chanted, or intoned in the presence of another or others, took on increasing importance in the ceremonies, events, and contests of court life. Verses became a means of communication for lovers and a way to further courtship. Poems were frequently tied to a spray of leaves on a wild plum, red maple, or willow tree, depending upon the season. No matter how the gentleman and lady correspondents felt about each other, an answer, in keeping with the complexity of the etiquette of the period, was mandatory.

Love also burgeoned frequently in other ways, without the man ever having seen the woman in question. An object or a detail of the woman's clothing, for example, might catch his eye as she passed by in her carriage. Or he might be mesmerized by the manner in which the exquisite designs of a lady's many-layered kimono sleeve hung over the side of the ox-cart taking her, perhaps, on a pilgrimage.

* * *

The rise of the warring ruling class and the increasing influence of the Confucian ethic led to the further denigration of women. While Buddhism also deprecated the female, its philosophy became a vital moral force in Japan. Confucianism, by comparison, seemed overly rational and dry, and its ethical code appealed more to the intellectual than to the ruling class. Buddhism, in its fascination with a life beyond, triggered the imagination. Shinto's intense sense of awe for sun, water, trees, and rocks, struck a responsive note in the Japanese psyche. Its mystery and warmth, identified with the sacrality of the *kami spirit* experienced in the very heart of nature's sanctuaries, encouraged serenity—and the participation of women in its rituals.

Despite the repression of the female sex, women writers, instrumental in the evolution of Japan's native literature, reached their apogee in the Heian era with Murasaki Shikibu's *The Tale of Genji*.

Chapter 1

Murasaki Shikibu's *The Tale of Genji*: Search for the Mother

The Tale of Genji (*Genji Monogatari*), the greatest of all Japanese novels, was written, it is believed, by a court lady, Murasaki Shikibu, who lived from ca. 978 to 1016. Not only does this spectacular work recreate human personalities of the ultra-refined and aristocratic world of the Heian dynasty (794-1185), offering insights into religious, social, aesthetic, and cultural vistas as well as personalities, but it also invites readers into the very heart of the woman's world.

The name Heian was adopted in 794, when the capital of Japan was moved from Nara to Heian-kyo ("City of Peace and Tranquility," Kyoto today). Reforms in mores and manners were effected by the rulers and regents of the time in an attempt to create a new Japan modeled on the Chinese T'ang prototype. Politically, however, the country lacked a strong, unifying central administration, and the "provinces," as they were referred to, were ruled by great families or clans, such as that of the Fujiwaras. Astute in every way, the Fujiwaras, as chancellors or regents, gained complete control over the imperial family. The puppet emperors—frequently children—were given in marriage to older women, perhaps unwittingly resulting in a cult for the mother which exists in Japan to this day. What was of crucial importance to the ruling clique was the maintenance of traditional government. Hereditary authority, already strong in Shinto Japan, grew even more powerful during Heian times, thus assuring the stability and continuity of Fujiwara dominance. Indeed, Fujiwara Michinaga (966-1027) was the great figure of the Heian period: it was he who set its tone, standards, mores, fashions, and taste (Edwin O. Reischauer, *Japan, the Story of a Nation*, 42).

As the T'ang dynasty in China declined, its influence upon Japanese political systems and aesthetics diminished. It was otherwise in matters of religion: Tendai Buddhism, introduced into Japan from China by Saicho (767-822), emphasized salvation through one's own efforts; and Shingon Buddhism, by Kukai (774-835), was esoteric in nature. Kukai brought to Japan, for example, a complete set of sutras containing symbolic codes, and instructions for making Buddhist images. The study of painting and sculpture became a virtual necessity for young priests and for those who sought to understand the scriptures involved (Noritake Tsuda, *Handbook of Japanese Art*, 74). Understandably, the role of the arts, both visual and literary, was significant in Kukai's teachings.

Both Tendai and Shingon, emerging as they did from Mahayana Buddhism, while teaching that everyone had the potential for Buddhahood, also emphasized rank and class, thus placing a hierarchic order in the religious perception of Truth. The stress upon magical incantations and pictorial representations, as in diverse readings of mandala images, impressed Heian aristocrats, as did esoterism, suggestive of élitism. The Pure Land Sect (Pure Land meaning Paradise) of Buddhism, on the other hand, offered eternal salvation to all who called the name of Amida, the Buddha of Boundless Light, with utter devotion. Such invocations, known as the *Nembutsu*, required fervent repetitions of Amida's name in a spirit of complete trust. Pure Land, far more emotional and less intellectual than Shingon or Tendai, allowed all people to understand it, thereby accounting for its growth and its mass appeal as a religious movement in Japan (*Sources of Japanese Tradition*, I, 118, 110).

The spread of the Pure Land doctrine had fascinating social and psychological ramifications. Whereas attainment of Buddhahood and Enlightenment had been stressed in Shingon Buddhism, the new belief underscored rebirth in a land of bliss. The criterium for entry into paradise was no longer dependent upon an individual's effort. Buddha's saving power was now of import. With the advent of the spiritual leader Honen (1133-1212), Pure Land Buddhism or Amidism became a separate sect. Because Shingon relied on individual endeavor, it was labeled "the difficult path"; since in Amidism "another" offered salvation to the devout, it was considered the "easy path" (*Sources*, 198).

Of extreme significance in Pure Land Buddhism was the inclusion of women's rights. Previously men alone had been accorded the possibility of salvation; now women were given equal opportunity to enter Buddha's Paradise. Nor had women, heretofore, ever been received in Japan's great monastic centers (Hiei, Koya, etc.), their presence in these holy sanctuaries being considered a source of defilement.

Whereas Confucianism played a minor role in Heian society, save for its extreme views on filial piety, Shintoism was of great importance. In that the imperial family claimed descent from the Sun Goddess, Amaterasu, and rituals associated with fertility and pollution played prominent roles in court ceremony, cults and sacred shrines in Japan attracted many believers. Ise, Kamo, Suma, and Sumiyoshi, to mention but a few, were crucial to worshippers in general and to the protagonists in *The Tale of Genji* in particular.

Lady Murasaki Shikibu

Little is known of Murasaki Shikibu's life. Even her name remains a mystery: Murasaki is derived from a root, "gromwell," used for medical purposes and for the extraction of a purplish die (Norma Field, *The Splendor of Longing in the Tale of Genji*, 161), while Shikibu combines "Bureau of Ceremonial," an office held by her father, and a nickname (Richard Bowring, *Murasaki Shikibu. The Tale of Genji*, 5). Murasaki is also the name of the heroine in *The Tale of Genji*. Although Murasaki belonged to a junior branch of the important Fujiwara family, which included poets and scholars, she was considered to be at only second level of the court aristocracy. Evidence leads historians to believe that she followed her father to the provinces of Echizen when he began his governorship there in 996. She undoubtedly returned to the capital shortly before her marriage in 998 to Fujiwara no Nobutaka, a considerably older man who had already several wives. Some scholars are at odds as to whether her marriage was a happy one. Her daughter, Daini no Sammi, a future poet of note, was born in 999. After becoming widowed in 1001, Murasaki began writing *The Tale of Genji*. She entered the employ of the chancellor Michinaga in the service of his daughter, the future Empress Shoshi or Akiko. Her seemingly intense attachment to Shoshi, whose love of learning was great, may account for Murasaki's unusual knowledge of ceremonies and institutions at the Kyoto court. Nowhere has it been determined how long Murasaki remained at court nor when she died (W. G. Aston, *A History of Japanese Literature*, 92-3). It is clear, nevertheless, that at court she greatly deepened her understanding of people and of the cultural and esthetic code of society. Her descriptions of the intricate religious ceremonies, the elegant processes of courtship, the complexities of the marriage system, and her disquisitions on the arts, reveal a unique understanding of the Heian world.

Since women of the Heian aristocracy lived, both physically and psychologically, in a *world within*, and refused an education except when related to comportment, manners, religion, and the arts, one may wonder how a woman like Murasaki Shikibu succeeded in writing her monumental work. Although many answers have been proffered, none is conclusive.

Although Lady Murasaki's genius was the most significant factor in the writing of *The Tale of Genji*, other elements and especially the linguistic situation in the Japan of her day are also important.

Japanese rulers and their advisors prior to and during the early years of the Heian dynasty believed that by emulating Chinese prose and poetry they would enhance the intellectual foundations of their society. To write in Chinese was believed to be a "great enterprise of statecraft, a thing of imperishable grandeur," and a requisite to political and social advancement which would allow the Japanese to enjoy equal prestige with their neighbors (Edward Putzar, *Japanese Literature*, 44). Written Japanese became a secondary language at this time. Serious literary works were written only in Chinese, men preferring to compose their treatises, histories, and official documents in this greatly prized foreign tongue. Disuse rendered their Japanese faulty. Women, on the other hand, denied most explicitly the learning of Chinese, had no other medium of expression but their own language. The many hours spent in study enabled them to perfect their knowledge of Japanese along with their writing skills.

Masters of their native tongue, some women worked on composing diaries, memoirs, poems, and narratives, examples of which are Mother Mitchitsuna's *The Gossamer Years*; Sei Shonagon's *The Pillow Book of Sei Shonagon*; Izumi Shikibu's *The Izumi Shikibu Diary; The Sarashina Diary;* Murasaki Shikibu's *The Tale of Genji, Poetic Memoirs,* and *Diary*. Murasaki notes the following concerning the woman's situation in Japan:

> When my brother, Secretary at the Ministry of Ceremonial, was a young boy learning the Chinese classics, I was in the habit of listening to him and I became unusually proficient at understanding those passages that he found too difficult to grasp. Father, a most learned man, was always regretting the fact: 'Just my luck!' he would say. 'What a pity she was not born a man!' But then I gradually realized that people were saying, 'It's bad enough when a man flaunts his learning: she will come to no good,' and ever since than I have avoided writing even the simplest character. My handwriting is appalling. And as for those classics, or whatever they are called, that I used to read, I gave them up entirely. Still I kept on hearing these malicious remarks. Worried what people would think if they heard such rumours, I pretended to be unable to read even the inscriptions on the screens. Then her Majesty asked me to read to her here and there from the *Collected Works* of Po Chu-i and, because she evinced a desire to know more about such things, we carefully chose a time when other women would not be present; amateur that I was, we read in secret the two books of Po Chu-i's *New Ballads* (Murasaki Shikibu, *Her Diary and Poetic Memoirs*, 139).

The mood reflected in *The Tale of Genji* suggests that Lady Murasaki was also the product of her time: hers was the ultra-refined Heian aristocratic sensibility which has been described as follows:

> It was an age of the "cloud gallants" and the "flower maidens," of the luxurious nobles and ladies who moved amidst the romantic and artificial surroundings of the Imperial court. It was an epoch of aestheticism and sentimentalism, in which free rein was given to emotions that were refined and cultivated by the somewhat enervating atmosphere of the Imperial capital. Every member of this picturesque society, man or woman, was a poet, sensitive to the charm of nature and eager to express every phase of feeling in verse. Their intimate feeling for nature and for the varied emotions of the human heart was expressed in the word *aware*, which meant both "pity" and "sympathy." This sentiment had its course in the tender romanticism of the age; it owed much, too, to the Buddhist teaching of the oneness of existences, of the basic unity that joins together different beings, and which persists through the changing incarnations of one individual. That conviction of the continuity of life, both in this existence and hereafter, deepened the sentimental note and widened

the sympathetic reach of *aware*. It is not strange that the reign of *aware* produced many romances of love, both in actual life and in the stories of the period (*Sources*, I, 172-73).

The protagonists, the events, the descriptions reflected in *The Tale of Genji* may be associated with the Japanese word *aware*, as defined, for it conveys a unique type of sensibility identified by many with the feminine gender. For example, the feeling of "a gentle sorrow," an ennobling but ephemeral love, a tender emotion or sensation aroused by a color or a perfume, a certain pathos engendered by the fall of a flower or the cry of a bird are associated with that mysteriously secretive world of women.

The Heian Aristocracy

The Tale of Genji mirrors a world marked with a penchant for the cultivation of the arts: architecture, music, dance, clothing, perfumes, poetry, elaborate religious rituals, and painting. Moral laxity, marital and pre-marital sex, acceptable and illicit love, jealousy and envy, indolence, and power struggles on all levels are likewise included in Lady Murasaki's epic novel.

Architecture was of basic importance in Heian Japan. The greater Imperial Palace, for example, located on three hundred acres in the center of the capital city, and containing both the palace buildings and the government offices, was modeled in elaborate Chinese style. The huge Palace of Administration, with a great stone base, red lacquered pillars, white walls, and a rococo roof with green glazed tiles contrasted with the emperor's residence in more ascetic Shinto style, made of plain wood, wattled roofs, and cypress floorboards. The gardens surrounding the Palace were simple, with raked white gravel, tubbed trees, and rocks placed in special formation (Ivan Morris, *The World of the Shining Prince. Court Life in Ancient Japan*, 40).

As Heian aristocrats, Lady Murasaki and Prince Genji, her great love, were both accomplished musicians.

> Then he [Prince Genji] sent for his zithern and asked her to play to him. But it was a big Chinese instrument with thirteen strings; the five slender strings in the middle embarrassed her and she could not get the full sound out of them. Taking it from her he shifted the bridge, and tuning it to a lower pitch played a few

> chords upon it and bade her try again ... She began to play very prettily; sometimes, when there was a gap too long for one small hand to stretch, helping herself out so adroitly with the other hand that Genji was completely captivated and taking up his flute taught her a number of new tunes. She was very quick and grasped the most complicated rhythms at a single hearing (*The Tale of Genji*. Translated by Arthur Waley, 138).

Dance, also featured in *The Tale of Genji*, was stylized. An outstanding performer, the protagonist Lady Murasaki describes Prince Genji as he executes with brio the popular "Waves of the Blue Sea":

> he seemed like a mountain fir growing beside a cherry-tree in blossom. There was a wonderful moment when the rays of the setting sun fell upon him and the music grew suddenly louder. Never had the onlookers seen feet tread so delicately nor head so exquisitely poised; and in the song which follows the first movement of the dance his voice was sweet as that of Kalavinka [the bird that sings in Paradise] whose music is Buddha's law. So moving and beautiful was this dance that at the end of it the emperor's eyes were wet, and all the princes and great gentlemen wept aloud.

The Heian court's gorgeous world of clothing in all its variety and symbolic meaning, particularly with regard to seasonal change, was described in detail in *The Tale of Genji*:

> Dress after dress was now brought in fresh from the beating room, and Genji would choose some robe now for its marvelous dark red, now for some curious and exciting pattern or colour-blend, and have it laid aside ... To Murasaki herself, a kirtle yellow without and flowered within, lightly diapered with the red plumb-blossom crest—a marvel of dyeing. To the Akashi child, a long close-fitting dress, white without, yellow within, the whole seen through an outer facing of shimmering red gauze. To the Lady from the Village of Falling Flower she gave a light blue robe with a pattern of seashells woven into it.

Sometimes seven to ten gowns were superimposed one on another on elegantly attired women, so that the contrasting colors, visible either in the hems, arm holes, or sleeves, would create a feast for the eyes. Refinement in color-effects encouraged purples and scarlet tones to be worn, along with a medley of greens and blues overlaid by gauzy materials which, when light was cast on them, offered the viewer a complex variety of impressionable tones. Images of snow falling on scarlet or prune color silks were woven into garments, with backdrops of pine trees in the distance. The combination of dark and lighter greens added a dramatic or poignant flavor to the mood of the event for which these magnificent costumes were worn. Despite the fact that brilliant blues and reds were reserved for the Empress and the Emperor's mistresses, some well-placed court ladies were at times given permission to wear these spectacular hues. Since the fabrics—brocades, silk damasks, satins, etc.—indicated a lady's class and rank, they understandably played an important role in court etiquette. During summer months, women wore lighter textures and always carried a fan as well as some folded paper in their pockets, serving them as both a handkerchief and as writing paraphernalia. If the occasion warranted it, ladies were prepared to compose a poem to a lover or to respond to his (Hidéko Fukumoto and Catherine Pigeaire, *Femmes et Samourai*, 20-26).

In sharp contrast to the colorful vestments worn by court ladies was the stark jet blackness of their long and silky hair. The longer a woman's hair, the more beautiful was she considered. Great care was accorded to hair, which was regularly shampooed with sea-weed and wheat flower. In that white skin was particularly prized, ladies used powder with a lead base imported from China. (Lead poisoning may account for the early demise of so many women of the time.) Thus was their skin's pallor accentuated. Eyebrows were shaven and redrawn in the form of a crescent thus giving the impression of elongated eyes (*Femmes et Samurai*, 20-26).

A woman was also judged by the perfume she used on her clothes, as well as the scent, the color, and type of flower included in a letter. The images embroidered or painted on her screens and fans, particularly those used for special occasions, served to place her with respect to character and class.

The higher the woman's rank, the more cloistered she remained, spending long hours in semi-darkness behind a screen of state (a curtain hanging from a wooden frame separating her section of the house from the others.) No man but her father or husband was allowed to look at her (Morris, 222). Since, with few exceptions, wives lived separately from their husbands (a wife remaining with her family after marriage received her husband in her own home, where their children were brought up), much of her time was spent waiting for him to appear. Likewise concubines and mistresses waited for their lovers, suffering the anguish of unrequited love, the revulsion of unsolicited passion, or enjoying, usually only ephemerally, a requited relationship.

Recipients of only those favors a man chose to bestow upon them, these forced recluses, who conveyed their disappointments and humiliations via tears and poetry, were looked upon by emperors and highly placed dignitaries as objects, playthings, and procreating devices. In some cases, a lady's forced isolation and remoteness from the world served to inure her to sorrow. Others, however, lapsed into progressively serious melancholia, became ill, and, understandably, let themselves die.

On the other hand, the outward passivity of some of these cloistered female protagonists as depicted in *The Tale of Genji* could be considered a mask, behind which lay a whole hidden realm of female deception and dissimulation. The stronger women planned ways of manipulating and dominating the weaker ones, vying for power even within their curtained areas. They spent their time plotting ways to hold their man, to occupy a place of honor in society, or to marry their children into the emperor's family. Jealously, they connived to guard whatever tenuous hold they may have had on the opposite sex, fomenting, intriguing, and ruthlessly crushing any other female whom they might suspect of usurping their prey. Deprived and depraved, many of these cloistered women focused almost exclusively on finding ways of gratifying their needs, desires, and longings. When thwarted in their intent, subtle and insidious acts of violence erupted among them. Those who were not fighters meditated on their earthly lot, accepting their incarceration and suffering in an almost martyr-like manner, relegating to the most secret areas of their minds whatever turmoil impacted upon them, frequently wasting away in the process, dying from the ordeal that was their lives. Many religious women became Buddhist nuns, spending the time allotted to them on earth in meditation and prayer.

Unless endowed with an inner life of their own or a creative bent, court women had little to do except to play games. Go was one of their favorites. They also enjoyed the company of cats. Because they had so little to live for, melancholia, as previously mentioned, was not infrequent, nor were related emotional illnesses. Along with continuous pregnancies which depleted their energies, women suffered from such diseases as beriberi, colds, tuberculosis. Their scant fare added to their physical vulnerability: two meals a day were eaten—one at ten in the morning, the other at four in the afternoon—the menu consisting mainly of cooked rice, a few vegetables, very little meat, but much fish. Eating copiously, according to Heian etiquette, was a sign of vulgarity. Since appearance played a large part in the esthetic sensibilities of the higher classes, a man's admiration for a woman rested on externals: her beauty, comportment, taste in dress, and etiquette.

Noble women were forbidden to take verbal initiatives. Rarely, if ever, did they speak directly to a man. Communication was possible through a hand-maiden, a letter, or a poem. Dialogue between lovers was expressed mainly in the poems they exchanged, for which finesse of calligraphy, use of proper paper, and the scent chosen for the message's theme, were as important as the tastefully chosen words.

Because distance between partners had to be maintained, poetry was one of the most popular pastimes, but also an important accouterment in a love relationship. A catalyst, it was instrumental in arousing desirability, eroticism, sexual passion, and could even be considered a kind of fetish. The writer of a poem took utmost care in the choice of graphology, writing paper, and perfume—details considered of crucial importance and symbolizing the *sign* of a person's identity, sex, age, status, and taste. Interestingly, the meaning and impact of a poem for many was even more important than the beloved's presence.

The classical *waka* was the preferred poetic form in Heian times. Its thirty-one syllables seemed best able to convey the highly emotional and frequently melancholy nature of Heian love relationships, particularly those depicted in *The Tale of Genji*. *Waka* poems served for official ceremonies, for marriages, and for expressions of sexual pleasure.

The subliminal and the occult—dreams, the supernatural, spirit possession—are interwoven into the very fabric of Murasaki's ambiguously alluring world. Nature becomes a protagonist; its moods and visualizations take on symbolic intent as manifested in calm or stormy weather, gentle rains or typhoons, gardens, lakes, mountains, islands, rivers, seas, and seasonal cycles. More than a novel, *The Tale of Genji* is an unforgettable prose epic which brings to life in the most subtle color-tones a world of emotion, secrecy, and harrowing pain—a universe in which fragile and vulnerable feelings reveal the inner workings of tender souls.

The Tale of Genji

The events in *The Tale of Genji* span seventy-five years and are set approximately three-quarters of a century before Murasaki's time, during the reigns of Emperor Daigo (897-930) and his son, Emperor Murakami (946-967). The hero of the first forty-one chapters—"the Shining Prince Genji"—was the son of a politically ineffective reigning emperor; and the chapters deal with Genji's many loves, the greatest of which was Lady Murasaki. So intricate were the politics of marriage and the bonds tying one member of the imperial family to another, that Murasaki's employer, Fujiwara no Michinaga (966-1027) was at once the brother-in-law to two emperors, uncle to another, uncle and father-in-law to yet another, and grandfather to two more. The intensity of the power struggle waged by Michinaga to obtain his lofty position required extreme astuteness in manipulating courtly life. Because conspiracies, intrigues, as well as the purest of love, were the rule of the day in *The Tale of Genji*, is it any wonder that passion reigned and that spirit possession was the means of gaining one's goal?

Passion

According to Buddhist doctrine, happiness and salvation are the products of inwardness and not dependent upon transitory exterior phenomena. Life on earth, therefore, with all of its passions, is the product of imperfection and sorrow. Only through detachment and the annihilation of desire can one experience redemption and "perpetual enlightenment" (nirvana). Such a discipline allows the individual to transcend the material world and experience timelessness and transcendence. It also encourages the expression of compressed feelings through symbols: a word, a color, design, brush stroke, a mood, impulse, gesture, facial expression, etc.

For the Buddhist, passion or desire of any kind—love, rage, jealousy—is the antithesis of self-discipline, control, detachment, and objectivity. To allow oneself to succumb to passion, therefore, is a sinful act, and, according to karmic law, the culprit is subject to retribution: he must bear the burden of negative reincarnations. Whatever the worldly joy experienced, it is viewed as illusion; whatever the love, be it between adults or between parents and children, it is considered inimical to detachment. Although some passionate relationships depicted in *The Tale of Genji* seem irresponsible and irreconcilable with Buddhist doctrine, in certain cases they may be viewed as learning devices: instruments on an earthly plane causing a protagonist to alter his or her focus, thereby experiencing a modicum of enlightenment.

The sophisticated, tasteful, and discriminating mood and manner in which Lady Murasaki spins her complex tale permits innumerable discussions revolving around a hierarchy of values associated with beauty, love, and political and religious obligations (Earl Miner, *An Introduction to Japanese Court Poetry*, 15-16).

The Mother Syndrome

A.   Fujitsubo

Prince Genji's love experience revolves to a great extent around his unconscious search for a mother figure, his real mother, Lady Kiritsubo, having died when he was but three. Because her rank was lower than that of the Emperor's chief wife and such favorites as Lady Kokiden, a Fujiwara with important connections, Lady Kiritsubo, their rival, became the butt of their intrigue which took the form of psychological torture. Growing increasingly unhappy, she wasted away and finally died. Disconsolate over his loss, the Emperor sought a surrogate Lady-in-Perpetual-Attendance who would treat him with the same warmth, tenderness, and profound love as Lady Kiritsubo, but was unable to find a replacement for several years. After meeting Fujitsubo ("Wisteria Tub"), a lady of high rank whom everyone tried to please, the Emperor, stunned by her strong resemblance to Lady Kiritsubo, transferred all of his affection to her.

Although Genji was too young to remember his own mother, when he was told that Fujitsubo, five years his senior, looked like Kiritsubo, his passion for this surrogate mother was instantaneous: her "fleeting beauty took its hold upon his thoughts." According to protocol, as long as Genji was under twelve, he had free access to the women's quarters and, therefore, could be with Fujitsubo as much as he wished. Once initiated into manhood, however, he was barred from these precincts. Deprived of his mother figure—his love object—Genji conjured up ways of approaching this beautiful, entrancing, and gentle power. Deeply frustrating was the fact that his coming of age forced him into marriage with Lady Aoi, a Fujiwara, considered by him to be an obstacle separating him from his beloved.

So deeply and passionately taken was Genji with Fujitsubo that there were moments when the mere sound of her voice, even from a distance, "dimly blending with the sound of zithern or flute," could calm his intense emotions. Aware of Genji's dangerous and obsessive passion for her, Lady Fujitsubo, on the rare occasions when they saw or spoke with one another, "met him with a stern and sorrowful countenance," adding "great coldness and disdain" to her otherwise tender and gracious demeanor. Rather than turn away from her, however, Genji only fell more deeply in love and even discovered a way of insinuating himself into her quarters one evening. Lady Fujitsubo, despite her firm resolve to repel him, yielded, allowing him to spend the night with her. Following their sexual encounter, only alluded to in Lady Murasaki's narrative, Genji whispered his poem to her—"would that we might vanish forever into the dream we dreamed tonight!" Tormented with guilt, she responded with a metaphor revelatory of the depth of her error and the terror of the punishment that might be meted out to her should her secret become known: "Though I were to hide in the darkness of eternal sleep, yet would my shame run through the world from tongue to tongue." Convinced that her ruination was imminent, Lady Fujitsubo grew melancholy, her tangled feelings replete with secret foreboding. Genji also dreaded the possibility that his father, the Emperor, might discover his sinful act—all the more probable since the outcome of that one night of love-making led to the birth of a son, Reizei.

Although Fujitsubo's passion for Genji never abated, the sin of the Heir Apparent's birth weighed heavily upon the two. She was convinced "that a day of disastrous reckoning might still be at hand." If her secret were kept, however, she would have "escaped more lightly than her *karma* in any degree warranted." Only after the Emperor's death could this highly moral and dignified woman come to terms with her sin: she took her vows, became a Buddhist nun, and spent the rest of her days in prayer, penance, and meditation.

Only when Reizei became Emperor did Fujitsubo's character suddenly alter, at least on the surface. She began planning and scheming for a marriage that would assure her son's continuous reign. The arrangement of such an alliance necessitated her meeting with Genji, but since she had already taken vows to become a nun, there was no longer any danger of involvement with him. So strong was her feeling of righteousness in her *way* that, upon meeting Genji, rather than adhere to protocol she took the liberty of speaking to him directly and without another person in the room. Having once succeeded in arranging for her son's marriage, Fujitsubo, the daughter and consort of emperors, and Genji's substitute mother figure, died at the age of thirty-seven. Only now, but still in veiled terms, does she reveal her unalterable love for Genji.

> Much had happened in the last years for which she had cause to be grateful to him, and she had often meant to tell him how sensible she was of his kindness, and there was another matter of which she had meant for some time to speak ... to the Emperor himself. She was sorry she had never ... Here her voice became inaudible, and tears for a while prevented him from making a reply.

Because Fujitsubo was not Genji's real mother, his sexual relationship with her, from a Westerner's point of view, was not considered incestuous. For the Japanese, however, it represented a sinful act: a violation of imperial succession. No longer a moral problem, except with regard to the Buddhist interdict of extreme desire, it had become a political crime since Genji's and not his father's son would become Emperor.

Genji's irrational obsessive passion for Fujitsubo, however, reveals a psychological need: for both a childhood he had lost or perhaps had never really known, and for a relationship with a feminine principle (*anima* or that unconscious image of woman) given to a child by the mother. When a boy child experiences his own mother as a nourishing force in his life, he learns how to deal with her and the problems emerging from their relationship in the world of reality. From three years of age until Fujitsubo's arrival, Genji had been divested of that positive and loving force; thus he floundered, never learning to face his many obligations in the empirical world. When, therefore, Fujitsubo, an impersonal surrogate maternal figure entered his life, he projected all of his emotional needs onto her and she became for him a larger than life archetypal figure (Jolande Jacobi, *Complex Archetype Symbol in the Psychology of C. G. Jung*, 26).

That a son sometimes desires a personal mother sexually, suffering the psychic consequences of his act, does not apply in Genji's case since we are not dealing with a blood tie. Since, however, Lady Kiritsubo had died when he was but three, his yearning for warmth, security, and understanding had been replaced by an overwhelming sense of loss, absence, and divestiture. When Fujitsubo entered his father's household, she not only filled that void within him, but also became the symbol of the ideal mother: a universal human and transpersonal power, alone able to fulfill his deepest yearning. Unconsciously he was seeking to recapture the paradisaical state of childhood—that state of unconsciousness where sheltering, nurturing, and loving are given lavishly without any demands upon the child and no sense of commitment or responsibility is elicited from him in return. Genji's psychologically regressive attitude may explain in part many of his licit and illicit love relationships. Never did he overcome his primordial passion for Fujitsubo, the archetypal mother; never did he succeed in liberating himself from the impress of this inaccessible fantasy figure. Had he done so, he might have been able to transfer his energy onto another woman and live as a psychologically independent soul in the world of reality.

Other factors concerning Genji's passion for Fujitsubo are also significant. That he fathers a son who will succeed to the throne under the title of Emperor Ryozen may constitute his way of dealing with his unconscious rage resulting from an act committed by his pusillanimous father when he was but a child. At the time, he had been told that a Korean soothsayer had warned the Emperor that if Genji were to inherit the throne, "confusion and sorrow would attend his [father's] reign." Genji was then removed from succession to the throne. One may question whether this prognostication had been the only reason for the Emperor's decisive act? Most probably not. Lady Kokiden, the Emperor's first wife, jealous of both Kiritsubo and Fujitsubo and their descendents, had most certainly worked behind the scenes in her attempt to convince her husband to make Genji a commoner. In that way, her own son would inherit the throne (Field, 29). Although Genji knew he was his father's favorite, making him a cuckold was his lethal manner of dealing with what he must have unconsciously considered an unconscionable act by a tyrannical and weak father. That he cringed lest the Emperor discover his sinful secret is also normal for a hero attempting to punish one who had so deeply hurt him.

B.   Lady Murasaki

Genji's relationship with Lady Murasaki, considered ideal because of its apolitical nature, was also psychologically mother-oriented. Not only was the mature Murasaki a paradigm of the nourishing, beneficial, and loving mother type; but when she, at age seven, first met Genji (he was the same age when he first saw Fujitsubo), she represented a pre-conscious component of the future mother figure. Even when Murasaki was a child, she was the incarnation of the helpful and delightful *anima* image which had been forever lost to him and which he attempted to resurrect in each of the women with whom he fell in love.

The little girl (to be known as Murasaki), the granddaughter of an unidentified "previous emperor," and child of a mother who had prematurely died, is being brought up in the mountains of Kitayama by her grandmother, a nun. (Since the introduction of Tendai and Shingon sects to Japan, esoteric Buddhists who enjoyed living in close contact with nature built their monasteries in natural surroundings.)

Genji met the little girl on his way to the region to seek a cure from a holy man for his recurring fevers. He was instantly entranced by her simple and spontaneous ways, and even by her petulance toward her playmate, Inu, for having let her sparrow out of the clothes-basket. Never had he been exposed to such direct and impulsive behavior. That Genji saw her as a helpful, consoling, warm, and loving force in his life is obvious: "He would dearly love to have her always near him, to be able to turn to her at any moment for comfort and distraction, as once he had turned to the lady in the Palace"—a reference to Fujitsubo. Thus did he conflate the older mother figure with the one-to-be. Aroused by the child, both psychologically and sexually, Genji reflected on this alluring and fascinating object:

> Never had he seen a child like this. What an astonishing creature she would grow into! Her hair, thick and wavy, stood out fanwise about her head. She was very flushed and her lips were trembling . . . Her features were very exquisite; but it was above all the way her hair grew, in cloudy masses over her temples, but thrust back in childish fashion from her forehead, that struck him as marvellously beautiful. As he watched her and wondered what she would be like when she

grew up, it suddenly occurred to him that she bore no small resemblance to one whom he had loved with all his being [her aunt Fujitsubo] and at the resemblance he secretly wept.

Genji decided then and there, despite the difficulties that might arise with regard to protocol, that he would adopt her when the proper moment presented itself.

Viewed archetypally, the pure, virginal little girl is perfect fare for the outwardly sophisticated hero. Indeed, she is ready to be plucked from her mountain habitat and violated by her prince charming. Genji, however, is all but valiant and heroic. On the contrary, he is the perfect paradigm of the anti-hero, the uncommitted *puer*, yielding to his desires and seeking to gratify his sexual drives. Irresponsible, this outwardly sensitive man has no understanding of the needs of others, nor is he imbued with a sense of morality. Flittering about like a butterfly, Genji, metaphorically speaking, alights here and there on a most beautiful flower, sucking up its nectar, only to fly to another court beauty moments later.

The appropriate moment for Genji to take the fearful, shy, and grieving child to his residence (Nijo-in) occurs following the death of Murasaki's grandmother. Fearing that her father, Prince Hyobukyo, might interfere with his plan to adopt the girl, Genji has her kidnapped and brought to his home.

At first fearful of Genji's household and its luxurious surroundings, the child is soon taken by Genji's persuasive ways, his charm, and his beautiful garden. Indeed, she who had been brought up in the country responds lovingly to nature's various personalities: its unmanicured forested or mountainous land or its highly stylized forms, as manifested in Genji's Japanese garden, with its artificial lake and island in the center, its two miniature hills, its rocks arranged in linear fashion, and its fine white sand spread in even designs on the earth, reflecting both the beauty of moonlight and the brilliant fiery rays of the sun (Morris, 45).

> As she picked her way among the trees and along the side of the lake, and gazed with delight upon the frosty flowerbeds that glittered gay as a picture, while a many-coloured throng of unknown people passed constantly in and out of the house, she began to think that this was a very nice place indeed.

Outwardly thoughtful when it suited his ends, Genji provides Murasaki with playmates and toys, and even lessons in music and calligraphy. Since in Heian times calligraphy was revered not only as an art but as a sign of one's breeding and character, Murasaki spent long hours perfecting the elegance of her handwriting.

As Murasaki begins to know Genji better, she reacts lovingly to the man whom she looks upon as her "new father." Seated on his lap, the two not only hold long conversations, but also play all sorts of games together. No longer shy, she is friendly in a childishly naive and utterly disarming way. The utterly restrained Genji becomes increasingly attached to her sensually.

Although he writes the following poem to Murasaki—"Too long have we deferred this new emprise, who night by night will now have lain with a shift between"—still he waits. Only after the death of his first wife, Aoi, does he initiate Murasaki, now fourteen, into the sexual world. Not knowing what to expect, the child is so surprised, hurt, and humiliated by his comportment that she turns her head aside, shyly and naively, thereby tantalizing him still further. The following day she refuses to see or even look at Genji, burying herself instead "more deeply than ever under the bedclothes." So smitten with her is he, so sexually aroused by her withdrawal from his embrace and by her rebuffs, that he spends the entire day with her hoping to win back her confidence.

Understated and subtle, the prelude to Genji's sexual act is only alluded to in the narrative; never described in detail, it heightens the mood of sensuality and mystery.

> The little girl was at first terribly frightened. She did not know what he was going to do with her and shuddered violently. Even the feel of his delicate, cool skin when he drew her to him, gave her goose-flesh. He saw this; but none the less he began gently and carefully to remove her outer garments, and laid her down. Then, though he knew quite well that she was still frightened of him, he began talking to her softly and tenderly . . .

That Genji was not only physically drawn to her, but also saw this mother/child as a positive, reassuring, and bountiful force in his life, increases his rapture. Time and time again, he marvels at her character, which forever radiates amiability and generosity. "The beauty of her disposition was indeed quite out of the common. The idea that so perfect a nature was in his hands, to train and cultivate as he thought best, was very attractive to Genji."

Nothing of Murasaki's charm and beauty escapes Genji's eye. That object of extreme desire—her glistening black hair—must be trimmed for her to be stylish. Genji takes up his knife, begins the ritual cutting, reciting the proper prayer accompanying the ceremony. After this symbolic act of violation, he notes: "What a lot of it there is! I wonder how much longer it would have grown."

After an absence from home, Genji returns only to notice, after pulling up the little "curtain-of-honor"—psychologically, another act of violation on his part—that Murasaki has not only grown and filled out, but that her once countrified clothes have been replaced by exquisitely elegant ones which enhance her natural beauty. As he observes her "in profile with the lamplight falling upon her face, he realized with delight that she was becoming the very image of her whom from the beginning he had loved best." His reference here to Fujitsubo, the mother figure, suggests that the child had now assumed this same role for him.

In Murasaki, Genji felt unconsciously, lives the beloved resurrected mother for whom he always longed. When Genji

> saw how astonishingly the one resembled the other, he fancied that all the while Murasaki had but served as a substitute or eidolon of the lady who denied him her love. . . . he wondered whether, if they were side by side, he should be able to tell them apart.

Genji's search for the personal or archetypal Mother in the child Murasaki may also be understood as an unconscious attempt on his part to seek out life anew—in all of its beauteous excitement. Through the innocence, purity, and cleanliness of the little girl—those pristine qualities inherent in an infant breaking out of the womb—Genji, too, would be born anew. Whether such an unconscious projection would have positive or negative ramifications is another question.

To be under the spell or dominion of any force, be it a mother figure or other, is to risk enslavement to one power, which paves the way to regression and stagnation. Be it Fujitsubo or the little Murasaki, or the host of other women who enter Genji's life, he will forever be attempting, unconsciously to be sure, to fill the void within him. That devouring and mesmerizing power which he seeks lies not in the women he courts, but is deeply embedded within his own psyche and, therefore, can never be satiated. Only by facing the loss of a mother figure and coming to terms with it will its power over him diminish. Unable to accomplish such a feat, Genji remains its slave, thereby inviting destruction which, in his case, prevents his psychological growth. Emotional maturity can never be his.

Genji tells Murasaki that he will marry her, and he does, in accordance with Heian protocol: Genji spends three nights with Murasaki and has small rice cakes ('third-night cakes') placed in her room, symbolizing the physical and religious binding of matrimonial ties. (The rice-cakes represent Izanagi and Izanami, that is, humanity's Shintoist progenitors). However, and well Genji knew this, because the ritual had been so unceremoniously undertaken and because Murasaki's mother had been of low rank, she, as already mentioned, could never aspire to become a legitimate consort, and would remain at best only a chief concubine.

That Murasaki, the child bride, was described as "unworldly" and reacted negatively to Genji's first sexual encounter, thus serving to tantalize him still further, suggests his psychological need to relive the archetypal struggle of the man trying to tame the wild animal (his own instinctual realm). Thus does Genji enjoy the final play with even greater glee. Despite the fact that sexual relations in Japan begin at an early age for the girl, Genji's rational decision of adopting Murasaki when she was but a child had been motivated not by altruism but rather by a strong instinctual urge. It may be suggested, then, that he was responsible, covertly at first, then overtly, for violating her innocence.

That he took her to live with him in his Nijo-in residence inherited from his mother rather than on another estate where he kept his other women, is also symptomatic of the unconscious fusion of the mother/daughter image he projects on her. He makes love first to the child, then to the adult.

Despite Genji's claim that he loves Murasaki more than anyone else, she is merely his property to do with as he wishes. Unlike Fujitsubo, to whom Murasaki is related and whom she resembles, she is neither politically nor socially well placed; her presence instills neither respect nor fear in Genji. Nor does she bear him a son, as Aoi had done, or a daughter, as the Akashi Lady would do in the future. Although she is very beautiful and talented both intellectually and artistically, Heian society will not allow her to climb the social ladder (Field, 173). In this regard, Murasaki is Genji's mirror image, since he cannot aspire to emperorhood, his father having demoted him to commoner status.

Murasaki's life with Genji, although happy on the surface, is fraught with difficulties. His philanderings are many and his absence of three years in self-exile on Suma island, where he undergoes purification rituals to wipe away his sins, are deeply painful. In keeping with custom, she has some outlet through conveyance of her loneliness and despair in poetic form: "Could my death pay to hold you back, how gladly would I purchase a single moment of delay." And again, in a letter, her tears and loneliness are metaphorically depicted: "Look at the sleeves of the fisherfolk who trail salt-water tubs along the shore: you will not find them wetter than mine were on the night you put out to sea." Grief-stricken, she spends much time in religious devotions, praying for her beloved's speedy return.

When next she sees Genji, she confesses the long days of suffering and isolation she experienced, remonstrating him for not having sent her the pictures he had painted during his stay at Suma. How comforted she would have felt in their presence. "Better had it been for me when I was alone to look at pictures of the realms where fishers dwell, than stare at nothing, as I did all day long!"

Murasaki's well-grounded jealousy concerning her many rivals is momentarily stemmed by Genji in a poem assuring her of his undying love. Her answer, nevertheless, was somewhat ironic: "On the bright mirror of these waters I see stretched out the cloudless years love holds for us in garden." Despite the fact that Genji was to live with Murasaki longer than he would with anyone else, she lived in dread of the day he would tire of her and cast her away.

Genji rarely took Murasaki's anxiety concerning his philanderings seriously. That he considered her anger and pain a mark of childish petulance downgraded her even more markedly. Only those traits in her personality that served his purpose and fulfilled his image of the ideal mother did he admire: integrity, intelligence, warmth, tenderness, and beauty. He also revealed his confidence in her administrative capabilities and in her maturity prior to his departure for Suma, when he entrusted the most important task, the running of his large household, to her. In turn, she proved herself to be a committed and capable administrator. Perhaps even more of a compliment was the fact that he entrusted to the childless Murasaki the raising and educating of his daughter by the Akashi Lady. Although jealous of the child's mother, Murasaki was delighted to accept the enormous responsibility of guiding and teaching the future empress. Her success in this endeavor earned her accolades when her ward, known later as the Akashi Princess, received great admiration in the court of the Crown Prince.

When, however, Genji informed Murasaki that for reasons of state he would marry Nyosan, known as the Third Princess, she repressed her reactions, as was the custom, remaining seemingly unperturbed. Her feelings of utter despair were conveyed, metaphorically, in the following poem: "Is autumn near to me as to those leafy hills, that even while I watch them grow less green?" The reference to autumn (*aki*) not only indicated the fleeting nature of time, but "less green" suggests being tired of or fatigued with. Was Genji tiring of her now that she was growing old? Despite circumstantial appearances, he tried to assuage her anxiety by pointing to the political motivations for his marriage. Furthermore, he kept reiterating the fact that although he had been living with her for many years, she was increasingly more exciting to him as a mature woman than when she was young. She knew just how to provide him with an element of "surprise," astounding him both intellectually and artistically, in her poems, her ways, her dress, "her clothes scented with the subtlest and most delicious perfumes, her whole person ever more radiant this year than last year, today than yesterday." Although the emotional cost of dissimulating her hurt was great, Murasaki forced herself to be strong, to the point of helping her husband dress himself and perfume his clothes for his impending marriage and for the first three nights to be spent with his new bride.

With aching heart, Murasaki watched Genji leave their quarters to go to the Third Princess's room. Her only consolation now was the thought that life is short and that she would take her vows to become a nun. On that particular night, however, she could not sleep. The wind was howling, a storm rose, and she felt "awkward and lopsided as she tried to arrange herself in bed." First she had visions of Genji away at Suma, then she saw herself dead. So profound was her distress that it elicited a parapsychological event: she found her way into Genji's dream.

At the very instant of Murasaki's vision, Genji, lying with the Third Princess, also had "a terrifying vision of her [Murasaki]." He "woke up with a start and hearing the cock crow" left in the dead of night, treading on snow, to go to Murasaki's room, desperately anxious for her welfare. Upon pulling back Murasaki's coverlets, he found her head hidden in the sleeve of her dress, wet with tears. The extreme tenderness of his affection at this moment, although comforting, did not allay her torment. She turned from him in sorrow.

That Murasaki's dream was experienced simultaneously by Genji is an example of a synchronistic event: that is, a meaningful coincidence, or coeval occurrence of two events in a space/time continuum. It was believed that human souls could travel by themselves. To explain such an acausal phenomenon psychologically, C. G. Jung suggests that there is a "middle region" in each individual's being which borders on both conscious and unconscious realms. In that they overlap, the one may be regarded to a certain extent as feeding the other. It may be said that during certain stressful circumstances the threshold of consciousness is diminished and elements in the form of archetypal images within the collective unconscious (the deepest layer within the psyche) rise spontaneously into the rational sphere. The diffused and intuitive knowledge recorded in Genji's dream, then, had reached out into the empirical realm and was read or interpreted by him, thereby giving utterances to his own deepest concerns. Phrased in another manner, one may suggest that when the eyes are closed during sleep, the inner eye, so to speak, conveys its truths in the world of dream, thus symbolically opening one's eyes (Jacobi, 62; Franz, 166).

Was this synchronistic experience to be interpreted as a premonition of Murasaki's death? That Genji, fearing the worst, went to her room in the middle of the night was in itself an indication of how seriously he took his dream. By way of explanation, we may propose that there is something within the collective unconscious which may be described as an "*a priori* knowledge or an 'immediacy' of events which lacks any causal basis," but comes to the fore whenever its help is needed to rectify an imbalance (C. G. Jung, "Synchronicity," par. 818, Jacobi, 63).

In that Genji had already expressed his concern over Murasaki's advanced years (she was thirty-seven, Fujitsubo's age when she died), he was unconsciously obsessed with the possibility of losing her. He may have also felt pangs of guilt for having married the Third Princess, knowing the pain he was inflicting on Murasaki. Perhaps he himself was unaware of the underlying motivations of his act.

Murasaki no longer cares about the world, nor does she expend her energy struggling to retain Genji's attention. Slowly, and perhaps unconsciously, she is preparing to withdraw from life. Increasingly detached from earthly illusions, she asks Genji for permission to take her vows, which he refuses. He will not be deprived of his mother figure, the one person who has always seen to *his* well-being before her own, who looks after him and loves him in all ways.

Murasaki's desire to take vows is in keeping with her personality. From her earliest days, she had revealed a natural inclination for religion. Brought up in a mountain retreat by her grandmother, a nun, and her granduncle, a bishop, she was familiar with incense, rituals, and rosaries. When Genji first took her to his palace, the Nijo-in, then moved her into his newly refurbished domain, the sumptuous Rokujo-in (the land having been given to him by Lady Rokujo), Murasaki reacted to her new environs with pleasure. To her he gave the metaphoric name "Lady Spring" and the garden located in the Southeast section of the mansion associated with the spring season, which she considered an earthly replica of the Pure Land paradise of the Amida Buddha.

> The Spring Garden, with its great orchards of fruit trees at the moment far excelled the rest, and even behind her screens-of-state Murasaki breathed an atmosphere that was heavily laden with the scent of plum-blossom. Indeed the place was a Heaven upon earth; but a Heaven adapted to human requirements by the addition of numerous comforts and amenities.

Gardens in Heian times were arranged to arouse emotions or to foster poetic associations (Joan Stanley-Baker, *Japanese Art*, 79). Seasonal identifications suggest cyclicality: the passage of time in the linear sphere, but also its suspension, its continuous and methodical repetition in a transpersonal dimension. Murasaki's garden put her also in touch with transcendent spheres.

Seeing that his beloved Murasaki is now growing sick, Genji takes her away from Rokujo-in, back to the Nijo-in where he had first brought her as a child and where she had remained throughout her adolescence. Nijo-in, let us recall, had belonged to Genji's dead mother and had been administered by Murasaki during Genji's three-year absence at Suma.

Recovering somewhat from her illness in this comforting atmosphere, Murasaki again asks Genji for permission to take her vows, which is again refused. Unable to comprehend his reasons, she may have wondered whether some sin on her part was retarding her spiritual evolution. To assuage her turmoil, she plans a religious ceremony which was deeply meaningful in Heian times: the Hoke Hakko. During its unfolding, the Buddha's sacred Lotus Sutra, which promises salvation to both men and women, is recited continuously during four or five days. The devout Murasaki had had occasion throughout her years with Genji to have a thousand copies of the Lotus Sutra made. The very process of the writing of this sacred work was, it was believed, helpful in creating a karmic relation between mortal and transpersonal spheres. The Sutras, along with the robes which had been created after Murasaki's own design for the ministrants, she now gave as offerings to the temple.

On the day of the religious ceremony, nature seemed to be working in harmony with Murasaki, responding empathetically to her deeply felt spiritual experience. The trees were blossoming and the weather was mild, as if paradise had installed itself on earth. As she listened intently to the recitation of the holy *Woodman's Song*, its images and lines depicting Buddha's death (Sakyamuni), she wondered whether it was not also a prelude to her own: "Though in life no prize awaits me, yet am I sad to know the firewood is burnt out and soon the flame will sink."

Spring turned into summer, and with autumn Murasaki's slow decline became evident. The Akashi Empress, once the little Princess whom Murasaki had brought up from infancy and loved so deeply, had left the Palace to come to stay with her beloved surrogate mother. Genji was also present. More than pleased at the sight of Murasaki sitting up, he was convinced she was regaining her strength, but he was living an illusion, once again putting his needs before her own. Fearing the anguish awaiting him, she pronounces an acrostic poem: "Hopes then the dewdrop upon the wind-swept grasses of the heath to build a safe abode?"

As the Akashi Princess held her hands, the dying Murasaki faded away "like a dewdrop from the grass." Genji was consumed with guilt, not because he had wrought havoc with Murasaki's life but because he had not allowed her, before her death, to fulfil her desperate wish to take orders. Yet, even here, the *puer aeternus* rationalizes, taking the easy way out: unwilling to accept the blame for his egotism, he maintains that he had not realized how swift her end would be.

Beautiful in death, Murasaki's lifeless being seems to be marked with the purity of childhood.

> Her hair lay spread across the pillows, loose, but not tangled or disorderly, in a great mass, against which in the strong lamplight her face shone with a dazzling whiteness. Never, thought Genji, had her beauty seemed so flawless as now, when the eye could rest upon it undistracted by any ripple of sound or motion.

Murasaki's cremation took place the day after she died, on the fifteenth day of the Eight Month.

Genji's tears came swiftly. Realizing that his beauty, talent, position had not raised him above his peers, nor had they brought him contentment, he understood perhaps for the first time that loneliness would now be his lot.

> And then as though Buddha feared that even now he might harbour some remnant of trust in life and its joys, loss upon loss was visited upon him, from all of which he had in the end recovered. But now at last this greatest of imaginable sorrows had indeed effected what all previous afflictions had failed to achieve.

Spirit Possession

That incidents of spirit possession in *The Tale of Genji* lead to the demise of some of the protagonists comes as no surprise in view of the strong belief of the Japanese in Shinto, Buddhism, and Confucianism.

Shinto ("The Way of the Gods"), Japan's indigenous religion, teaches, as previously stated, that a life force exists in all things, whether animate or inanimate. Everything in the phenomenological world, then, has a soul or spirit within it; each entity exists in a state of becoming. Shinto deities (*kami*) are many; they include spirits of trees, mountains, flowers, deified ancestors, heroes, emperors, the sun, and the moon. That ancestor worship is implicit in Shinto and Confucianism, and that reincarnation is one of the basic tenets of Buddhism, not only reinforces the cosmic nature of active energy in the universe, but also implies a moral and eternal aspect within the human being.

During the Heian and later periods, manifestations of supernatural phenomena were widely recorded in folk-tales and myths, as well as in literary and artistic works. It was said that mysterious human or animal voices (foxes, racoon-dogs, wild boars) could be heard at certain times. These voices, emanating as if from nowhere, acted either benevolently or malevolently, depending upon the psyche of the humans to whom they attached themselves. Some spirits, demons, or ghosts brought joy and pleasure; others, sickness, disease, hunger, lightning, storms, and fire. If ancestral spirits, as well as living family members, considered themselves neglected or mistreated, they were capable of bringing disaster to an individual or a community.

According to the *Kojiki* (*Records of Ancient Matters*, 712), a compilation of traditions and myths, the universe is divided into three parts: Takama-ga-hara (The Plain of High Heaven), the abode of heavenly deities; Naka-stu-kuni (The Central Land), the home of earthly deities; and Yomi-no-kuni (The Subterranean Land of the Dead), ruled by the dead (Stephen Addis, ed., *Japanese Ghosts and Demons*, 11).

Although the Land of the Dead, frequently identified with pollution and impurity, did not imply punishment during the early centuries, with the introduction of Buddhism into Japan, new points of view were forwarded. Under the influence of the Tendai sect (popularized by the monk Genshin, 942-1017), paintings and drawings were used to underscore the wretchedness of Hell and to point to the importance of prayer directed to the compassionate Amida Buddha, the Savior. In the *Jigoku-e* (Drawings of Hell), demons (*Oni*) carry out the will of Emma Daio, the ruler of Hell. The *hyakki yako* (Night Parade of One Hundred Demons), popular during the Heian period, featured all types of demons walking the streets on certain nights, only to disappear at dawn. The sixteenth-century "One Hundred Devils Out at Night" by an unknown artist, the eighteenth-century Hokusai and Okyo, and the host of works by the nineteenth-century Yoshitaki and Kuniyoshi all point to the terror aroused by the invisible world—those infinite spaces surrounding each human being (*Japanese Ghosts and Demons*, 11, 15).

In Taoist tradition, the supernatural Immortals were endowed with the gift of transcendence and the power to free a soul from the body of a mortal, or implant one, even their own, into humans or animals. As the souls of the Immortals hovered above the earth in their search for quietude, they enjoyed, so it is recounted, fabulous adventures about which mere mortals might only dream. Such artists as the eighteenth-century Masinobu, the nineteenth-century Kunisada, and a host of others, drew figures depicting a world beyond, in an attempt perhaps to face their own demons of the night. According to Japanese tradition, if one faces an image, as in a mirror, it reveals its true identity, and in the process, can be depotentiated. Once it loses its hold on an individual, it vanishes (*Japanese Ghosts*, 57, 63-4).

The association of women with spirit possession (*mononoke*) dates back to the earliest times. The Yamato rulers, some of whom were priest-chiefs, considered themselves to be descendents of the Sun Goddess, Amaterasu, and saw to it that her worship was supreme in the land. Her cult centered at the Grand Shrine in Ise, as already mentioned, and its fourteen subsidiary shrines, founded about 260 C.E. by the Princess Yamatohime no Mikoto, under the instruction of Amaterasu herself.

An "Abstinence Palace" was also constructed in Kawakami in Isuzu, to mark the place where Amaterasu first descended from heaven. Architecturally, shrines were usually simple, and the one at Ise was no exception. Made of wood, with whole tree-trunks used for beams, it consisted of a single or partitioned room, raised from the ground with steps in the front or side giving access to it (*Sources*, I, 23).

In that Amaterasu was the central figure of the Sun cult, her shrine at Ise became the holiest place in Japan. Nature's most important deity as well, she was revered for her powers over fertility and over the nation's good fortune. Shamanesses at the Shrine of Ise worshipped Amaterasu as well as other deities and ancestors in all of their infinite mysteries. Shinto *miko* became important sacral mediums who not only served at the shrines but acted as mouthpieces for Gods and Ancestors. As such, they were empowered, it was believed, to implant their souls into the spirits of others, either to bring joy or to wreak vengeance. As a bridge, like deities and ancestors, between the visible and invisible realm, the temporal and transcendental spheres, they could at certain moments function in a space-time continuum. Amaterasu, the *miko* prototype, is depicted as follows in the *Kojiki*:

> Undoing her hair she wrapped it in bunches, and in these bunches, on the vine securing her hair, as well as on her left and right arms, she wrapped long strings of beads . . .
> Shaking the upper tip of her bow, stamping her legs up to her very thighs into the hard earth, and kicking it about as if it were light snow, she shouted with an awesome fury (Geoffrey Parrender, *Sex in the World's Religions*, 117).

The benevolent or malevolent roving spirits or souls conjured by the shamanesses belonged not only to the realm of the dead but were vital forces among the living. In that these invisible entities could wander about and detach themselves at will from the body of living people or things inspired dread in many. Understandably, mortals took great care not to anger such cosmic forces. Indeed, they treated them with respect and awe.

Because High-Priestesses and/or Shamanesses at Ise were believed to possess special occult powers, they were given charge of the shrine. As mediums, they translated messages between a believer and/or a political ruler and *kami*. They performed their sacred ceremonial and pantomimic dances (*kagura*) before the *kami* on a platform designed for the purpose and to the accompaniment of a fife and drum (W.G. Aston, 197). Their fans of cypress wood, their long jet black hair tied with a vermilion ribbon, their white kimonos and vermilion divided skirts flowed to the soundings of rhythms and tones. Each movement of their gestural language was deeply meaningful. Finger, arm, torso, and leg work called into play a whole other dimensional realm. The sight of such flamboyantly colorful figures ambulating before the worshipper in their mysterious steps and designs transformed them into living symbols (Sokyo Ono, *Shinto the Kami Way*, 4-45).

Supplicators, that is, officers of the shrine, and ablutioners helped shamanesses to carry out other religious functions. Before entering the sacred shrine, worshippers purified themselves by washing their mouths and hands in a water basin built into the precinct's architectural construct. Only then were believers permitted to take part in devotions. Usually very simple, these consisted of standing within a sacred enclosure or within a certain area on a mountain and paying complete attention to the object worshipped. Ceremonial dances or processions were also included in Shinto ritual, along with symbolic representation of a *kami* or a substitute spirit in the form of a stone or a mirror. No image existed in ancient Shinto ritual (*Sources*, I, 23).

Because shamanesses and priestesses had the power of transcending their mortal limitations and of making the wishes of spirits comprehensible to earthly beings, the Japanese male might have felt inferior to these females. Women as procreating powers might also have appeared as a threat to men: they were able to bridge the gap between the uncreated and the creative world. How best to combat such a force? such a fear? Through repression. To repress women in all other domains would limit her power, degrade her reputation, and relegate her to a secondary position.

Lady Rokujo

Incidents of spirit possession in *The Tale of Genji* centered around the awesome and terrifying Lady Rokujo. One may wonder why this elegant and stately woman, daughter of a minister, married to a crown prince at sixteen, bearing him a daughter (Akikonomu), and widowed at twenty, came to be the harbinger of such malignant forces? Her destructive outerworldly acts most probably resulted from the bitterness of her disappointment. Because of her husband's premature death, which she believed had been caused by political treachery, her dream of becoming Empress was dashed to the ground. When Genji began his passionate wooing of her, his love not only filled an aching void, but brought her supreme elation. The relationship between the two continued as long as she spelled "mystery" for him: in a thrilling "mist" his ecstatic love for the lady enclothed remained "blind," "intoxicating" him in every way. When, however, the glow of passion waned and Genji became completely indifferent to her, Lady Rokujo was unable to face the rejection. Her attachment to him grew obsessive; wretchedness and a sense of humiliation gnawed at her from within; frenzy, mistrust, and suspicion took over her personality.

Genji's unconcern for Lady Rokujo caused him to have unconscious guilt feelings, which produced nightmares and/or hallucinations. One night, when lying with another mistress, the young and charming Yugao, he saw Lady Rokujo's tall and majestic form standing over him to pronounce:

> You who think yourself so fine, how comes it that you have brought to toy with you here this worthless common creature, picked up at random in the streets. I am astonished and displeased.

Although Genji had read and heard about such female apparitions and ghosts in ancient fairy tales and he was aware of their alarming power, he could not understand how Lady Rokujo could work her spell over him. In the nightmare, he sees Yugao being dragged away from his side by Lady Rokujo; he awakens to find the trembling young girl perspiring cold, and finally falling into unconsciousness. Was it a fox-spirit or a demon that had cast its spell on Yugao and tried to snatch her spirit away? Genji's anxiety for the girl was in vain: by the time help came, Yugao was already dead.

Other examples of Lady Rokujo's strange activities became evident after her fourteen-year-old daughter, Akikonomu, had been chosen to be the new chief priestess at Ise. Seeking self-purification and release from her passion for Genji, Lady Rokujo took the unprecedented step of accompanying her daughter to the holy shrine and settling there, using her daughter's young age (she was only fourteen) as an excuse. But prior to her departure, Lady Rokujo had inadvertently been humiliated by Genji's first wife, Aoi, during a ritual of investiture for the Virgin Elect of the Kamo Shrine. During this "spectacle of unparalleled magnificence," Genji arrived in all of his splendor to pay homage to his first wife, Aoi, now pregnant after ten years of marriage. Not once did he look at Lady Rokujo. Even more of an affront was the fact that Aoi's retainers, unbeknown to her, had pushed Lady Rokujo's carriage to the rear, thus hiding her view of the spectacle. Because her feelings of disgrace were beyond human endurance, it comes as no surprise to believers in spirit possession to learn of Lady Rokujo's revenge: everyone concluded that malign spirits were to blame for Aoi's sudden illness. "It seemed at times as though some hostile spirit entered into her."

Rituals of exorcism and divination were performed almost continuously in an attempt to rid Aoi of possession by the spirit of a living person. Indeed, Aoi felt as if "some alien thing had entered into her, and though she was not conscious of any one definite pain or dread, the sense that the thing was there never for a moment left her." Healers called in to cure Aoi were powerless, unable to eject this "tremendous accumulation of malice" that had been discharging itself on her.

As a result of the carriage incident, Lady Rokujo's inner rage and suffering reached such proportions that they disturbed her entire emotional system. "She felt herself indeed swirled this way and that by paroxysms that sickened her but were utterly beyond her control." Had she become prey to "violent and distracting emotions which continually assailed her and had in some subtle way unhinged her mind?" She was determined to seek spiritual healing as well because of the violence of the recurring dream assailing her.

> It seemed to her that she had been in a large magnificent room where lay a girl whom she knew to be the

> Princess Aoi. Snatching her by the arm, she had dragged and mauled the prostrate figure with an outburst of brutal fury such as in her waking life would have been utterly foreign to her.

So traumatically did the force of this dream impact upon Lady Rokujo that she began to believe it "possible for one's spirit to leave the body and break out into emotions which the waking mind would not countenance." If a person's ghost "should pursue his enemies," and is looked upon as a sign of the dead person's "venomous and malignant character," this could destroy a reputation. What would people think of her who, still alive, was "guilty of so hideous a crime?" Utterly perplexed, she wondered whether her spirit had actually left her body to pound out its hatreds? Whatever the answer, she would have to face her fate.

Meanwhile Aoi's emotional and physical condition was growing steadily worse. During Genji's visits he gazed on her beauty and swollen stomach, feeling attracted to her for some strange reason.

> The plaited tresses of her long hair stood out in sharp contrast to her white jacket. Even to this loose, sickroom garb her natural grace imparted the air of a fashionable gown! . . . she gazed at him, but through his tears he saw that there was no longer in her eyes the wounded scorn that he had come to know so well, but a look of forebearance and tender concern; and while she watched him weep her own eyes brimmed with tears.

In an attempt to comfort her, Genji draws near to Aoi, who begins speaking to him in a wistful voice which he realizes is not her own but that of Lady Rokujo: "I did not think that you would come. I have waited for you till all my soul is burnt with longing." Then she recites the verse: "Bind thou, as the seam of a skirt is braided, this shred, that from my soul despair and loneliness have sundered." Never had Genji experienced such moments of sheer horror: "Ghastly, unbelievable as they were, such things did happen in real life."

After the birth of a son, Aoi seemed to recover somewhat, only to fall into a trance-like state lasting three days until her death. Inner demons had won their battle.

A psychological analysis of Lady Rokujo's destructive power suggests that she represented a negative *anima* figure for Genji—a murderous feminine principle alive within his unconscious. In that Lady Rojuko represented raw instinct, undifferentiated emotion, the unconscious, irrational, sensual, and passionate realm, she was a fearsome force for Genji and a threat to his equilibrium. Such a view is particularly evident in Japanese society, where instinctual outbursts were and are shunned, and emotional repression is the rule of the day. What was and still is of crucial import for the Japanese, then, is the world of appearances: the *persona*.

As a negative *anima* image, Lady Rokujo represented those powers intent on punishing Genji for what he unconsciously rejected in himself, that is, his whole *puer* side: his adolescence, irrationality, inability to face commitment, his thoughtlessness, his need for immediate gratification. She was a living manifestation of that unredeemed, uncontrolled, and visceral side of himself which ran counter to the cool, restrained, ultra-refined attitude acceptable to Heian society. As a power of darkness, she was a punitive, vengeful demon, a murderous mother archetype, alive and lurking within his own unconscious alongside the sublime Lady Murasaki.

Genji projects onto Lady Rokujo his own death-dealing demonic power which lies inchoate within his subliminal sphere. Complex and paradoxical, he both loves and hates the world of vulnerable and loving women. He is attracted to it, but also fears enslavement by it. His pattern of abandonment of his concubines and paramours and his complete disinterestedness and indifference towards them after a brief time, may be regarded as an unconscious protective device on his part. He may be seeking security against their grasping and death-dealing tentacles and a release from their stranglehold on his life. He may have reasoned, subliminally, that Yugao, the wife of another, might have caused him trouble had their affair lasted. In Aoi's case, she had been antipathetic to him ever since he had first met her. Rarely did he go to see her. That Lady Rokujo harassed him palled on him. To be uncommitted and free to pursue his amorous affairs is the *sine qua non* of the adolescent.

As the time for Lady Rokujo's departure for Ise drew near, Genji, to assuage his conscience, attempted to retain her. The backdrop for their parting scene is a passionate outburst of nature:

> A cold wind was blowing. The pine-crickets in neighbouring trees were whispering in harsh despairing tones, as though they knew well enough what was toward. Their dismal voices would have struck a chill to

> the heart of any casual passerby, and it may well be imagined what cheer they gave to lovers already at the height of distraction and anguish.

Lady Rokujo recites a verse to Genji: "Sad enough already is this autumn parting; add not your dismal song, O pine-crickets of the moor." Finally realizing that the root of Lady Rokujo's misery lies in his neglect of her, Genji weeps with shame. Tears, which come easily to him and to other male characters in the narrative, assuage, at least temporarily, feelings of culpability and malaise.

Festive crowds draw up in their gala-coaches to witness the momentous event of Lady Rokujo's and her Virgin daughter's departure for Ise.

> The windows of those coaches were hung with an exquisitely contrived display of coloured scarves and cloaks, and among the courtiers who were to go down to Ise there were many who thought with an especial pang of one who in his honour had added some gay touch of her own to the magnificence of this unprecedented show. It was already dark when the procession left the Palace.

Six years later, Lady Rokujo and her daughter returned to the capital. Only once did Genji visit her thereafter, when she was near death. Trying to rectify a wrong, he somewhat reluctantly promised her to look after her daughter, Akikonomu, a future empress. He kept his word and saw to it that she occupied quarters on her mother's estate which came to symbolize a memorial, a consolation, and resting place for Lady Rokujo's soul. In return, it was believed that Lady Rokujo's traveling spirit would journey from the Realm of the Dead to bless the house and its occupants. The close relationship between the living and the dead, unbeknown to Genji, bode danger.

Eighteen years after Lady Rokujo's death we learn that her spirit was still not at rest. Her latest victim was to be Genji's greatest love, Murasaki. Even in this instance, Genji may be said to be responsible for the negative happenings about to occur. His philanderings have caused Murasaki untold pain throughout their years together. Since he never even considered altering his ways, it may be suggested that his decision to marry the Third Princess dealt Murasaki her fatal blow. Without wealth of her own, nor a family to back her, nor a position of high rank, she was at Genji's mercy. Indeed, throughout her years with Genji

Murasaki Shikibu's *The Tale of Genji*

she had dreaded the thought of her beloved's change of heart toward her, fearing she might be displaced by another woman or simply sent away. Her continuous anguish grew increasingly acute with the passage of years, depleting her energies and thereby making her vulnerable to mental as well as physical disease. Lady Rokujo's spirit entered her body during her last hours, speaking through the medium of a young boy, and wreaking havoc with Murasaki's mind and body.

> What I must now say, no one else but he must hear. You have plagued me this long time past with your spells and incantations. I do not love you for it, of that you may be sure. And I would here and now take my vengeance on you all; it is not that I lack the power ... rather, I have chosen of my own free will to postpone the task; for strange though you may think it, we ghosts love as we loved on earth; and when I saw Prince Genji frantic with grief, shattered by long days of watching and apprehension ... then I was sorry for him; I, that have become a foul and fiendish thing, pitied him as tenderly as any living creature can pity. That is why I have shown myself to you. I did not mean that you should ever know ...

Now aware of the fact that although she is near death powerful forces are still alive within Murasaki, Genji listens intently to the voice of the medium.

> Do not think that, even in my most distant wanderings, banished amid the realms of outer space, I have ever for a moment been ignorant of what was passing here on earth. All that in penitence you have done for my daughter, the Empress's sake, is known to me, and I thank you for it. And yet—it is strange—nothing now seems the same to me. She is mine, I have not forgotten her. But do not think that I love her as a living woman loves her child. Nothing, not one thought nor feeling, have I brought with me, unaltered into the world of death, save this insensate passion, that even on earth made my own nature loathsome and despicable to me. Rage, jealousy, hatred—they alone cling to my soul and drag it back each moment closer to earth.

The incantations, scripture readings, and liturgies which Genji has ordered to be intoned have seared Murasaki's soul "like tongues of flame," the voice warns, but do not think that the rage and anger elicited by hurt have been conquered. These will return over and over again to destroy its victim.

> Back I shall come and back again, till in your liturgies I hear some word of comfort for my own soul. Say masses for me, read them night and day. Tell my daughter the Empress to pray for me with all her heart; and bid her never for one instant, though she may fall from favour and another be set in her place, never so much as in a dream to let one envious or jealous thought creep into her heart.

Genji has no illusions about the effectiveness of the secret masses celebrated for the release of Lady Rokujo's soul. He realizes only too well that she carried over into the world of the dead the sinister nature and evil intentions which had marked her during her lifetime: "a thing devoid of all human pity or compunction, it was hideous to think that her malice towards him was still unappeased."

Was it her malice towards him that had caused the death of his paramours? Let us note the intriguing fact that ghosts in Japan are usually female; and that they belong to the group of dissatisfied, lovesick, and suffering women who have been wronged. Their intentions upon returning to the land of the living are to hurt their victims, thus exacting retribution. In that Lady Rokujo's ghost represents an emotional hurt, and thus stems from the irrational domain, it is uncontrollable and therefore terrifying to its enemies (Donald Richie's "Introduction" to John Stevenson, *Yoshitoshi's Thirty-Six Ghosts*, 3-6).

Despite all of Genji's loving care, Murasaki slipped slowly away from the world of the living. As a tribute to her, and in a mood of largesse, he found it in his heart—just prior to her death—to realize one of her greatest wishes: that of receiving the tonsure. Nevertheless, in this case, as it was in her pseudo-marriage to Genji, the ceremony lacked authenticity. Only five of the Ten Vows were ministered, including Genji's cutting of a lock from the crown of Murasaki's head. Believing that such a step would help her recover, and despite convention, he sat by her side, his eyes brimming with tears during the vow-taking ritual. No cure was forthcoming and, as we know, Murasaki died. (One may be reminded that another parallelism comes to mind here: Genji cut Murasaki's hair himself prior to her initiation into womanhood.)

Not long after Murasaki's demise, Genji, deprived of zest for life, takes his vows and later dies.

Spirit Possession and Schizophrenia

Lady Rokujo's irrational reactions not only were not under the control of her conscious ego, but were disproportionate to the reality of the circumstances. Given the sexually permissive nature of Japanese society, her reaction to Genji's rejection of her verged on the pathological. Since she was aware of his philanderings, her need for a faithful partner not only seemed unrealistic—even morbid—but also destroyed the normal interrelationships to her mental processes, thereby paving the way for a schizophrenic split in her personality. Her obsessive jealousy, compounded by hate and rage, created a sub-personality dissociated from the total personality. As the center of consciousness, her ego was unable to exert any control over the split-off portion of her psyche—as in cases of hysteria, sonambulism, and schizophrenia.

In that Buddhist tradition preaches detachment, renunciation, and discipline over one's emotions, Lady Rokujo's heaving energies were looked upon as sinful; hers was a polluted soul. Instead of renouncing her passion for Genji, thus detaching herself from its power, she allowed it to control her. Her impassioned spirit, now separated from her organic world, seems to be moving out of her body into that of her rivals. Indeed, Lady Rokujo confessed to feelings of estrangement from herself. She even asked herself why her body was playing tricks on her: "Often she felt as though her whole personality had in some way suddenly altered." That she was always elegant in her manner, ultrarefined in her ways, implied great will power to stem her excessive nature; it also indicated enormous strength of character which could also be used aggressively. Of the nine exchanges of letters and poems with Genji, seven were initiated by her. Such comportment in Heian times was considered to be a transgression of the boundaries of good taste. Furthermore, that Lady Rokujo chose to accompany her daughter to Ise rather than allow her to face the ordeal herself as was customary, could also be considered in part a hostile act. Although rationalizing her decision by using her daughter's young age as a pretext, her unconscious intent could be considered a desire on her part to live through her daughter—projecting her own aspirations upon her kin.

If Lady Rokujo, who had dreamed of becoming Empress, could, through identification, experience vicariously the immense honor of being the future Priestess of Ise, she would have reached her goal. Let us examine the obligations of such a priestess: she must remain chaste as long as she is involved in a religious relationship with Amaterasu. That Lady Rokujo identifies at this point with chastity indicates a comportment diametrically opposed to her life at court and her passion of Genji. Was she, then, attempting to repress her whole instinctual sphere, hoping perhaps to still what she considered to be those negative instinctual energies in her personality?

Incidents of spirit possession, states of trance, and altered states of consciousness (leading to a diminution of reactions to external stimuli), such as those experienced and induced by Lady Rokujo, may be included under the general rubric of dissociative disorders. In Lady Rokujo's case, her psychic energy (*libido*), as evidenced by her excessive bouts of hatred and jealousy, eclipsed her ego (center of consciousness), allowing her instinctual domain to become fully operational. At this juncture, her subliminal depths hold full sway, weakening any possibility of adapting to either inner or outer worlds. Blinded by excessive charges of libido, her ego falters, stumbles, rendering an already unbalanced existence even more precarious. A psychological cripple, she becomes unable to distinguish between reality and fantasy.

So cut off is Lady Rokujo from reality and so imbued is she by her overpowering *libido* that she feels herself to be endowed with supernatural powers that divest her increasingly of any sense of obligation to, or connection with, her surroundings. Since she most frequently lives inwardly, her repressed *libido* explodes every now and then in the form of affects. Only when dissociated—unconsciously harming her rivals—does she find any semblance of solace from the abrasive world of reality. She is fire; she is flame; thus can she burn and sear her enemies.

Lady Rokujo's victims are all vulnerable: they suffer either from apathy, passivity, lack of self-esteem, or inferior class status. As long as they had been able to cope with their pain or were esteemed or loved by the object of their desire, a certain semblance of psychological equilibrium was maintained. Because Yugao felt herself so socially inferior to Genji; because Aoi understood that she had never been loved by him; and because Murasaki's future was threatened by his marriage to the Third Princess, hurt and anxiety set in, leading to increased spiritual compression and a further erosion of their already enfeebled ego. The split occurring within their psyches, as it had in Lady Rokujo's, resulted in a redistribution of values with which neither of the victims could cope. Illness resulted.

Since the Japanese maintained a close relationship with the souls of the deceased, indicating a free interchange between the living and the dead, barriers between these two worlds no longer existed. On the threshold of both life and death, Lady Rokujo's victims, already weakened by an insufferable emotional ordeal, were not strong enough to maintain the bridge between the living and the dead, the real and the unreal. Emotional confusion was followed by physical destitution, depletion, and death.

In well-adjusted and relatively normal persons, the ego may be said to be made up of many complexes—of a "whole mass of ideas" pertaining to it. The ego complex, defined as the "highest psychic unity or authority" within the personality, is not only able to cope with most problems relating to the individual in question, but it also gives direction to associations and to ideas. When a person is deeply disturbed, however, the psychic totality may become fragmented and split into various complexes. When such a split-off occurs, each complex may be looked upon as a kind of "miniature self-contained-psyche which . . . develops a peculiar fantasy-life of its own." When a complex becomes virtually autonomous (as in Lady Rokujo's case), the resulting fantasies may assume abnormal proportions. They become a kind of "vassal" no longer willing to give "unqualified allegiance" to the suzerain. Generally speaking, when an individual is asleep fantasies are manifested in dreams, but they pursue their course in actions, attitudes, writings, frequently under the dominion of "repressed or other unconscious complexes" when the individual is awake. Autonomous complexes may, therefore, be looked upon as "toxins" because they are unable to fit into the conscious mind harmoniously. They may, again as in Lady Rokujo's case, resist all attempts on the part of the will to cope with them (C. G. Jung, "The Psychogenesis of Mental Disease," 4, 45, 46, 87, 240; Erich Neumann, *The Origins and History of Consciousness*, 288).

Because complexes have a type of electric current running through them, they are replete with affective charges and feeling-tones. The affects given off are sometimes so great as to be capable of acting physically upon the person experiencing the complex. Respiration, blood pressure, the circulatory system may all be altered, leading to a variety of diseases, depending upon the power of the complex over the individual. When certain exceptionally deep-rooted complexes break through into consciousness, they can erupt with such extreme violence that they invade the entire personality. This kind of situation occurs in cases of psychosis and may be applied to Lady Rokujo, who complains of personality changes in herself; and to her victims, who speak in voices that are not theirs, or suffer from nightmares or hallucinations, thus indicating a split-off from the ego complex. When this occurs, one may say that their personalities have literally fallen apart and become reorganized under two distinct autonomous complexes: a rational system, and that other, uncontrollable complex within the collective unconscious. When schizophrenics allude to voices that they alone hear, or strange apparitions that suddenly appear to them in dream form or in the blackness of night, it suggests that the ego is no longer the center of consciousness.

Genji is also troubled by nightmares and hallucinations and alarmed by their impact on him. He could not, for example, understand how the image of Lady Rokujo dragging the defenseless Yugao from his side had come into his mind. Nor could he explain her subsequent trembling and cold perspiration when it was he who had had the vision. Nor did he fathom his immediate response to Murasaki's nightmare, which had become his own. Genji's guilt feelings toward her and others, and his inability to live his religious principles which taught detachment, self-control, and spiritual discipline, were so strong as to arouse him affectively. Such a condition may account to a great extent for his frequent indulgence in religious rituals, his three year exile, and his hyperemotional reactions—his tears and sobs.

An autonomous complex, like a virus, if allowed to spread throughout the body and disturb the emotions, can destroy its very lifeline. Thus does the infection spread from the mind to the body, and destroy a life—as Lady Rokujo accomplished with her victims.

Face-saving Devices

Lady Rokujo's excessive affective reaction to the loss of her love object—Genji—may have resulted from an early narcissistic injury accompanied by a loss of self-esteem and compounded by her ego's former and unrealistic sense of omnipotence. Let us not forget that when she married, as previously stated, she envisioned herself as a future Empress; with her husband's untimely death, she had to face the obliteration of her dream. Her intense humiliation after Genji tired of her fomented antibodies of hate and rage—energies powerful enough to supplant her lack of self-worth.

How best can one fight disgrace, debasement, and ignominious dishonor? Lady Rokujo chose to operate sadistically. Such a means of destruction is an example of the killer instinct: it demonstrates a need to annihilate the forces responsible for the hurt.

Sadism suggests a sensual and psychological need to inflict pain and violence, either directly or indirectly, on the love-object. Since Genji had been Lady Rokujo's lover and was also a prince, he was the perfect paradigm for her emotional and political grievances. Because she needed to humiliate her humiliator but could not murder such a highly placed individual, her killer instinct had to find other means of discharging and gratifying its destructive bent.

Lady Rokujo found the perfect foil to vent her ire on her weaker rivals. A demonic and fearful force, this authoritarian, devouring, and castrating feminine principle—a *vagina dentata* type always lurking in the Japanese psyche—lay in wait to terrorize the unsuspecting female and male.

Because many Japanese males were and still are unconsciously terrorized by the feminine, they frequently portray women both in the visual as well as the literary arts as a fearful force whose powers must be restricted. Thus for centuries has the male attempted to curtail women's activities and rights, believing this to be the way to keep them in check.

In compensation, the Japanese male nurtures his psychological need for an all-encompassing and ideal mother figure. Genji, the *puer aeternus*, spent his life searching for her and found her in the gentle and loving Murasaki, who accepted his childish ways, his hurts, and his perversion of her worth.

* * *

Nevertheless, women in *The Tale of Genji*, forced into reclusion, hidden behind a wall, screen, or curtain, guard the secret of their existence. Although much of their lives were spent passively, that is, waiting for their lover's approach, such an existence denotes enormous inner reserves and great strength on their part. We are astounded at the ways women find to function and cope under such restrictive conditions, and under the most insidious of circumstances. The result is a double-edged sword; forced withdrawal from the outside world increases the aura of mystery surrounding women, which in turn arouses the male erotically, thrusting him into their power.

In the eyes of the male, woman, a sexual force, is transformed into a *fetish*: an impersonal object with magical powers, a charm, a votary. Longing for the chase, the male lusts for this inaccessible and collective creature whose allure grows all the more potent as she sits or lies behind her veils, curtains, or screens of state. Once the conquest is over, and the male inseminates the female, after which the child is born, the woman, paradoxically, transcends her earthly and degraded condition. She takes on the contours, for certain men, of an elusive illusion, an archetype, and thus enters the domain of the sacred and awesome.

Just as *The Tale of Genji* has never ceased to fascinate readers the world over, so, too, has its hold over Japanese artists also never abated. Only nineteen paintings of what had once been a large twelfth-century series of illustrations of Lady Murasaki's work survive. In typical Heian style, the multi-layered broad blocks of flat color, with their carefully detailed multiple inklines, referred to as *tsukuri-e* ("made-up painting"), all point up the drama of each scene. In keeping with Heian conventions, the roof was removed in the drawing, allowing viewers to see into the rooms, disclosing seated figures in their robes, with their stylized white faces, all suggested by lines, dots, and hooks. Emotions and moods were revealed by a variety of signs and symbols: a silver, tarnished, or blackened moon was associated with night time; a flute suggested musical tones in the air; silks and satins hanging over a veranda aroused unconscious associations of ephemerality and human frailty (Yoshiaki Shimizu and Susan E. Nelson, *Genji: The World of a Prince*, 10).

Inspiration was drawn also from *The Tale of Genji* in later centuries, as, for example, some fourteenth-century handscrolls; paintings attributed to Tosa Mitsuyoshi (1539-1613); designs of ink, colors and gold on paper for a pair of sixfold screens by Tosa Mitsuoki (1617-1691); those made by members of the Kano school in the late seventeenth-century; and the portrait of Lady Murasaki Shikibu by the woman artist, Kiyohara Yukinobu (1642-1682).

* * *

Perhaps considered overly lengthy by Western standards, the fifty-four books making up *The Tale of Genji* (1145 pages) is written in a language which reaches the highest tone of excellence, beauty, and artistry. Its innovative nature and extraordinary sensitivity to social, philosophical, and aesthetic aspects of a society, suggests affinities with Marcel Proust's monumental *In Search of Lost Time*. Both are works of genius. They excite by their penetrating and perceptive observations concerning art, music, clothing; the use of metaphor, image, symbol, and gestural language; the roles played by nature and the subliminal realm. Mention must also be made in both cases, but for different reasons, of the element of mystery generated in the hidden, veiled, and masked world within which protagonists exist and cohabit in an insalubrious and frequently festering climate. The multidimensional canvases of both Proust's and Lady Murasaki's novels are unique—treasures of two civilizations, East and West—conflating in the eternal and universal work of art.

Chapter 2

The Heian Art Diary:
Hidden Behind the Screens

The diary (*nikki*) flourished as an art form in Japan from the tenth to the fourteenth centuries. Rather than a mere chronicle of events, the art diary focused on style and technique, as well as on mood tone. Art diaries, containing letters, narratives, and poems, dealt with the realities of daily life, although a special happening was frequently singled out for imaging and characterization. Thus did an event convey the quintessence of the feelings experienced at a particular moment; it both dramatized while also arresting a fleeting time span, thereby setting it apart from the rest of the literary work (Earl Miner, *Japanese Poetic Diaries*, 6-9).

Although the dates of the earliest written diaries are unknown, the practice of keeping personal records began in the middle of the seventh century. During the Heian period, an official office was created for the safekeeping of public diaries. Imperial and travel diaries were also valued, as, for example, monk Ennin's record of his pilgrimage to China (ca. 847). Such journals, although quite useful, were simply factual accounts of daily activities (Edward Putzar, *Japanese Literature*, 53).

Women of the Heian aristocracy as, for example, Lady Murasaki, wrote not only narratives, but personal diaries as well—a genre they transformed into an art form. By recording their feelings, thoughts, and yearnings during their seemingly endless hours of leisure, they gave body to a whole subliminal world of dreams and fantasies.

A comforter and companion, the diary enabled them to *secrete* their most *secret* thoughts in symbols, signs, and archetypal images. A friend whose fidelity could always be counted upon during periods of loss, whose rectitude and integrity were always pristine, the art diary offered its aristocratic authors a modicum of emotional security and of well-being. It made the absent present; it comforted against a hostile environment.

The art diary stimulated its introspective authors to develop insights into themselves and the world around them as well as to evaluate these in the verbalizing process. While affording court ladies an escape from the rigors or distress of daily existence, it also enabled them to distill *feeling* into *form*. By resurrecting a happening, within a cyclical time scheme, and adorning it with the crystals of feeling—beautified or uglified via memory's mirrored images—the writing procedure itself empowered authors to *enter* an eternal present: that transcendent sphere or *meta-reality*.

Like a curtain of state (*kicho*), the portable frame supporting opaque hangings designed to protect women in the home from being seen by men, so the diary may also be considered a protective mask behind which creative women lived their lives. The seat of their individuality, the art diary encouraged these isolated women to develop their *inner eye* so as to better peer into their depths and teach them to separate the dross from the purest of elements within their beings. They were, to be sure, like live-in companions.

The events transcribed by many of the diarists may seem at first diffused and scattered to the Westerner, appearing as a medley of disparate situations or isolated segments depicted in a variety of time schemes. It must be noted in this regard that the Japanese not only do not limit themselves to a single visual center in their writings, but interrelate and enmesh occurrences interlinearally. Events are not bound together as a Westerner thinks of them, according to a so-called logical pattern. For the Buddhist, existence consists of a series of fleeting moments which authors as well as artists seek to arrest. Mind, matter, and time, conceived by the Westerner as something tangible, is *unreal* for the Buddhist. Because "continuity" and "duration" do not exist, nothing is permanent for the Buddhist. Life is not a whole, but a series of agglomerations. Linear time, then, is a concept devoid of meaning—a figment of the mind. The only past and future that exist are those associated with incarnations; the only concrete reality is the single *moment* or *actuality*. To flesh out this span in the diary is to transmute the intangible into the work of art.

The Gossamer Years (974), unlike *The Diary of Lady Murasaki* or *The Sarashina Diary* and *The Diary of Izumi Shikibu* which will be explored in this chapter, is autobiographical in nature. In keeping with Heian practice, the woman author of *The Gossamer Years* remained anonymous and was referred to simply as "the mother of Michitsuna." Considered one of the most beautiful women of her day, she could not reconcile herself to being merely the second wife of the young, handsome, and highly placed Fujiwara Kaneie. Her diary begins in 954, with his love letters to her, and concludes twenty years later, with their estrangement. What is fascinating in *The Gossamer Years* is the openness of the author's jealousy, the candor with which her rage and outrage at her husband's philanderings manifests itself. She wanted a husband of her own, "thirty days and thirty nights a month," and not to be shared by others. Unlike Lady Murasaki or Sei Shonagon, the author of *The Gossamer Years* was not a court lady. She lived alone, isolated from the stimulation of those with whom she might have conversed. She did have a sister who visited her on rare occasions. Most fascinating is the realism with which the author conveys her hurt, her low regard for men, and her lack of confidence in their promises. Nor did she look upon her rivals with kindness, going so far as wishing them ill and hoping that they might suffer as she did. Written in the third person, her diary may be regarded as the work of a social nonconformist, an objector to the Heian marriage system.

> These times have passed, and there was one who drifted uncertainly through them, scarcely knowing where she was. It was perhaps natural that such should be her fate. She handsome less than most, and not remarkably gifted. Yet, as the days went by in monotonous succession, she had occasion to look at the old romances, and found them masses of the rankest fabrication. Perhaps, she said to herself, even the story of her own dreary life, set down in a journal, might be of interest; and it might also answer a question: had that life been one befitting a well-born lady? But they must all be recounted, events of long ago, events of but yesterday. She was by no means certain that she could bring them to order (*The Gossamer Years*, 33).

The Diary of Lady Murasaki (1010) is an account of her social life at court. Like *The Tale of Genji*, her diary drew heavily from her virtually scientific ability to observe both the world of nature as well as that of the human spirit and psyche. She singled out specific events for scrutiny, describing them in a realistic style. She made much of the delivery of the Queen's baby and the multiple ceremonies this happening elicited, including the Prime Minister's examinations of the breasts of the wet-nurses considered for the post—a duty to which "he very naturally devoted himself with utmost care." Detailed descriptions of complicated court dances and musical interludes are delineated in the painterly fashion of the day and are rendered with excitement and with Lady Murasaki's usual finesse. Nor does she omit portraits of well-known court ladies. With discretion, she includes only those whom she likes, with notable exceptions: Sei Shonagon and Izumi Shikibu. Did jealousy and/or disdain color her usual objectivity and obscure her lucid views and critical judgments?

One of the most arresting aspects in *The Diary of Lady Murasaki* are her insights into her own personality. Although cognizant of her identity and worth, she underplays her talents and achievements and emphasizes her inadequacies, as though she were willing to tempt or offend the celestial powers in charge of her *karma*.

> Having no excellence within myself, I have passed my days without making a special impression on anyone. Especially the fact I have no man who will look out for my future makes me comfortless. I do not wish to bury myself in dreariness. Is it because of my worldly mind that I feel lonely? On moon-light nights in autumn, when I am hopelessly sad, I often go out on the balcony and gaze dreamily at the moon. It makes me think of days gone by. People say that it is dangerous to look at the moon in solitude, but something impels me, and sitting a little withdrawn I muse there. In the wind-cooled evening I play on the Koto, though others may not care to hear it. I fear that my playing betrays the sorrow which becomes more intense, and I become disgusted with myself so foolish and miserable am I (*Murasaki Shikibu. Her Diary and Poetic Memoirs*, 131).

The Pillow Book of Sei Shonagon (ca. 965-1024) includes 325 short notes or sections focusing on nature (mountains, rivers, trees), listings of beautiful as well as humorous statements or situations, random thoughts on life at court, views on human activities and people's characters, and narrative sections concerning the author's own experiences. Unlike the modest and humble Lady Murasaki, Sei Shonagan is aware of her fine intellect and attractive physique, playing them up to the fullest as she seeks to entice men to her fold. To the already long list of her attributes, she proclaimed to one and all her knowledge of Chinese—no mean achievement for a woman of her time, nor ours. She did not, however, as had Lady Murasaki, probe the inner recesses of her heart and psyche nor those of whom she depicted. Superficial by comparison, she set down her nonlinear impressions in disconnected segments, as if purposefully breaking sequential connections in order to lend more reality to her writings even while allowing full play to her imagination. Her fragmented style works in her favor as an artist in that it adds spontaneity and capriciousness to her vivid and exciting work (Armando Martins Janeira, *Japanese and Western Literature*, 131).

> In the Fifth Month I love going up to a mountain village. When one passes a marsh on the way, a thick covering of weeds hides the water and it seems like a stretch of green grass; but if anyone gets out of the carriage and walks across one of these patches, the water spurts up under his feet though it is quite shallow. The water is incredibly clear and looks very pretty as it gushes forth.
>   Where the road runs between hedges, a branch will sometimes thrust its way into the carriage. One snatches at it quickly, hoping to break it off; alas, it always slips out of one's hand.
>   Sometimes one's carriage will pass over a branch of sagebrush, which then gets caught in the wheel and is lifted up at each turn, letting the passengers breathe its delicious scent (Janeira, 78).

The Diary of Sarashina (Sarashina Nikki, ca. 1059)

In keeping with the anonymity of the Heian diary form, the name and the particulars concerning the existence of the author of *The Diary of Sarashina* remain unknown; she is simply "Takasue's Daughter." The writer injects a sense of intimacy into her work, but her confessional tone was divested of personal details. Her innermost thoughts were expressed in the *tanka*, a poetic genre enabling the author to capture the essence of a feeling or moment in space. Unlike the diaries of Lady Murasaki and Sei Shonagon, who spent much of their lives either in court or in Heian-kyo (Kyoto), the capital of Japan at the time, Lady Sarashina lived her early years in the provinces where she joined her family on multiple pilgrimages to distant shrines. After returning to the capital to live, she spent relatively little time in court.

The uniqueness of *The Diary of Sarashina* lies in the dream sequences, which are approached as journeys into transpersonal (unconscious) spheres. Significant also are the author's pilgrimages, which afforded her the possibility of depicting a variety of landscapes in emotive and painterly fashion. Because of her emphasis on pain and loneliness, Sarashina's *Diary* may be viewed as a verbal transliteration of a soul in distress.

The author of *The Diary of Sarashina* was born in 1008 into a middle class family. Her father, Takasue, boasted of ancestors who had succeeded in combining literary with political careers. Sarashina's mother belonged to a minor branch of the important Fujiwara clan. Until the age of nine, Sarashina lived in Heian-Kyo, after which her father, appointed Assistant Governor of an eastern province, moved with his family to this faraway and, at the time, primitive area. Sarashina begins her *Diary* with a depiction of herself as a twelve-year-old girl setting out on a journey back to the capital, which in Heian times took three months (Ivan Morris, *As I Crossed A Bridge of Dreams*, 11-38).

Heian-kyo, in Sarashina's day, was both a spiritual and artistic center embracing a Buddhism that emphasized inner spiritual discipline. The beauty of its temples was remarkable, architecturally and spatially. The Byodoin temple (completed in 1053) of the Pure Land Paradise cult inspired worshipers ceaselessly to recite the name of Amida, Buddha of the Western Pure Land Paradise. The harmony of the temple's setting among manicured lawns, trees, ponds, gravel and stones, blended religious élan with an unsurpassable sense of the aesthetic, paradoxically fusing light and clarity with the ineffable realm of shadow and mystery.

The main building of the Byodoin—the Phoenix Hall—set on a small island at the center of a lake, housed the all-important statue of Amida by the master sculptor Jocho (d. 1057). Made of gilded and lacquered wood blocks modeled in human proportion, Amida, seated on a golden lotus in meditation, inspired feelings of awe as well as of approachability and compassion, taking the meditator on a journey from terrestrial to celestial spheres, from problematic preoccupations to sublime serenity (Joan Stanley-Baker, *Japanese Art*, 71).

Journey

That Lady Sarashina devotes so much of her *Diary* to traveling has great symbolic and psychological import.

Because of her ultrasensitivity, Sarashina felt emotionally drained when a person dear to her died. Deeply did she suffer at the death of her nurse, and of her sister after childbirth. She experienced intense anguish even at the death of people whom she did not know personally, but whom she admired—a Fujiwara lady, for example, whose calligraphy was "remarkably beautiful." Perhaps even more significant than her inability to accept loss was her psychologically complex attachment to her father. Whenever he left on a government mission that took him to distant and dangerous areas of Japan for a long period of time, Sarashina's life seemed empty. When, at the age of sixty, he was sent to a far-off eastern province to fulfill an appointment, she felt cut off from the vital source of energy of her father, whose strength, wisdom, and determination had guided her always. Four years later, when Sarashina was twenty-four, her father's return filled her with a sense of well-being. At twenty-eight and unmarried, she still lived at home with her family (Morris, 16).

Sarashina's life was far from sedentary. Various visits to shrines, including Hae, Kurama, Ishiyama, Uzumasa, and Kiyomizu implied all the difficulties and dangers of traveling in those days. Distant, unsurveyed areas in the forests and mountains, where shrines were so frequently located, were infested with brigands and outlaws of all types. When Sarashina's father was absent from home, her desire to travel alone was thwarted by her mother's more realistic fears, and although she yielded to the interdict, she took umbrage at what she considered her mother's lack of comprehension of her needs.

Why the necessity to travel? Certainly, the young girl had important spiritual reasons. Her worship of Amida Buddha was primary, as was her devotion to her father, her human role model. But such dedication does not tell the whole story. The concept of travel may be viewed as a paradigm—a quest for truth, a desire to understand the surrounding world of imponderables, or at least connect with that which surpasses comprehension. It was Sarashina's way of finding a link between the individual's mortal existence and the immortality of the collective cosmic sphere. Each time she set out on a trip, frequently with her father, he played the role of spiritual guide and mentor. She was, then, unconsciously attempting to emulate him by venturing into the unknown with courage.

Nevertheless, traveling cannot be considered merely an escape, nor a metaphor of life's journey, nor a healing device that would bring equilibrium to soul and psyche. It combined the multiple memorable factors of living that might help to untangle a network of chaotic emotions lying heavily on mind and heart.

By seeking her spiritual orientation, Sarashina hoped to discover the *center* of her being, which would allow her to cope with her deep sense of inferiority. Timid and fearful, she considered herself awkward and unattractive; in the society of others, she frequently withdrew into herself. Court life, with its overly rigorous and hostile environment, must have presented particularly noxious problems; her shortcomings were singled out in comparisons with other girls of her age.

The opening lines of Sarashina's *Diary* are telling: "I was brought up in a part of the country so remote that it lies beyond the end of the Great East Road" [the province of Hitachi]. The above statement indicates the unbridgeable distance between her "remote" inner world and her still unknown outer sphere "beyond," identifiable with the much-feared social realm. As a child, she enjoyed reading *The Tale of Genji* and other stories; and reading in general was a source of great joy during her early years spent in the wilds of Japan. During the family's move to Imatachi in preparation for the return to Heian-kyo, when she was twelve years old, the dismantling of her house is depicted in terms of a "great disorder"—a replication of her own inner psychological chaos. Her actual departure reveals the tenor of her inner climate: "As I stepped into the carriage to leave for the last time, the sun had just set and the sky was shrouded with mist." The setting sun, the ensuing darkness, and the fogginess of the picture obliterate clear thinking on her part. Emotions of bereavement set in. Her last and most searing glimpse is of the "Healing Buddha standing there alone—that Buddha before Whom I had prayed so often in secret. At the thought of abandoning Him I began weeping quietly." That she had been wrenched from her Divine Father, He who had promised her health and long life, left her facing an abyss. To abandon Him meant stepping away from that pleasing world she knew, into a terrifying unknown. Yet, it was just this unknown, paradoxically, that catalyzed her need to wander.

Sarashina passes from the light and warm world within the home to the "dark" and "wet" outside domain. So drenching was the rain "that our cottage was almost afloat, and I was far too frightened to sleep." The very image of the floating house replicates the directionless drifting of her new life: too young to choose, she is swept up by the current, rootless and rudderless. A more positive image emerges as she looks onto land: "I saw a hillock rising from a bare plain, and on it grew three isolated trees." The verticality of the hill, like that of the mountain, represents solidity and continuity linking earth and heaven. The same is true of the Tree: its branches look toward the sky; its trunk stands upon the terrestrial sphere; and its roots are implanted deep within the earth's surface. That there were three trees may suggest the three aspects of the Healing Buddha: essence, potentiality, and manifestation—still alive within her psyche despite the fact she had left It behind.

The ferry ride "across a deep river" reveals another connection with Buddha. Known as the Great Navigator, He was the one to take people from the bank of life to the other—death. So, too, would her direction in life change, both empirically as well as subliminally. On the beach that evening, her verbal designs took on sensual allure, focusing on "the white dunes stretched out far in the distance"; while the "bright moon," hanging over the dense pine groves, excited her aesthetically. An identification between her pristine but fragmented earthly existence, as replicated in the crystalline sloping hills, is also evident. That she sees the Moon as a father figure is understandable since this celestial body, Tsuki-yumi, as already indicated, is male. Continuous mention of the Moon throughout the diary suggests a dual need in Sarashina: of a personal as well as an impersonal father, the latter in the form of the immortal Buddha.

Traveling, then, was not only an emotional experience for Sarashina; it was a religious one as well. The change of pace and space was an indication of her wistful yearning for the Buddha Paradise of the world beyond. Her approach to nature, always delicate, was now endowed with increasingly ethereal analogies, tonalities, rhythms, and palette. Her discreet verbal distillations of trees, sea shores, mists, seem painterly in essence, giving the illusion of remoteness and awe as well as of proximity and intimacy by the simple brushing of her phonemic canvas with flat or wet casts.

> The range of hills known as Nishitomi was like a row of folding screens decorated with beautiful paintings. I

was charmed by the beach where the great waves beat down and drew away. For several days we walked along the pure white sand of Morokoshi Plain. I heard someone say that in the summer this plain was covered with Japanese carnations of all shades and looked like a great expanse of brocade...

The journey back to the capital required ascending steep hills and mountains in thickly forested areas: "how much more terrifying it became as we made our way into the depths of the forest, going higher and higher until we were stepping on the very clouds!" Although high mountains terrified Sarashina, she was also awed by them. Their heights dizzied her; their proximity to celestial spheres dazzled her. Nor did she feel comforted by the undisciplined and unpredictable forest, a paradigm of Mother Nature's raw and instinctual side. Its blackness blinded her, leaving her vulnerable to dangerous animals and brigands along the way. So, too, is the unconscious at times divested of light or inner vision, obscuring the primitive, irrational pulsations within the psyche. The unpredictable, when identified with the subliminal sphere, like the forest, has its fearsome aspect; while the rational domain, the handmaid of the thinking process, can be manipulated by the intellect.

One of the most sacred mountains for the Japanese, Mt. Fuji, was the gathering place of the Gods. This immutable force is, paradoxically, volcanic, and thereby unpredictable, as are all divine acts. A manifestation of sacred powers, Mt. Fuji became a hierophany—a living and breathing power—representative of Divinity and of transcendence. Shrouded in clouds and mists during most of the year, it represented then, and still does now, the very heart of mystery. In keeping with Shinto tradition, pilgrims ringing bells as they ascended its slopes wore white clothes and broad straw hats. Sarashina depicts Mt. Fuji as follows:

> There is no mountain like it in the world. It has a most unusual shape and seems to have been painted deep blue; its thick cover of unmelting snow gives the impression that the mountain is wearing a white jacket over a dress of deep violet.

Sarashina's veneration of Mt. Fuji, which in Chinese characters means "No-death," included the hope of ascending to the top of the "sacred mountain" to greet and worship the Sun—Amaterasu. To perceive the radiance of the progenitrix, intensified by direct and intimate contact with Her light as she rises from the waters of the Pacific, ushers in the greatest of all harmonies: a cosmic *conjunctio* of opposites (*We Japanese*, 307-9).

Sarashina's metaphorical projection through time and space during her imaginary ascent of Mt. Fuji encapsulates the numinosity of the moment, thereby enabling her to share her solitude with the ineffable—in Buddha's Pure Land. The day would come when she, too, would wander up Mt. Fuji, ritually, in keeping with the disclipines of the sequenced ritual purifications. Her ascension into primordial and nondifferentiated spheres would lift her out of the morass of earthly existence and into the dream.

The Dream

"I lived forever in a dream world," Sarashina wrote. Unable to cope with sorrow, loss, and separation, particularly from her father, she was enveloped in protracted periods of despair. Reading such works as *The Tale of Genji* far into the night, undisturbed, behind her curtain of state, not only relieved her of increasingly burdensome feelings of doom, but also nourished and enriched her unconscious.

Sarashina's familiarity with the characters in *The Tale of Genji* allowed her to project her own unlived feelings—her world so sorely lacking in tender affection—onto passionate love affairs and tragic heroines.

> One night I dreamt that a handsome priest appeared before me in a yellow surplice and ordered me to learn the fifth volume of the Lotus Sutra as soon as possible.

That Sarashina did not obey the dream's dictates indicates a reluctance or fear on her part to approach greater understanding, which requires a certain detachment and objectivity—a collective rather than a personal view of people and life in general. She was, evidently, not yet ready to assume the disciplines required to bring about her spiritual and psychological evolution, from concentration on self to expansion throughout the universe. She was not prepared for the bonding of the individual with nature, the cosmos, and the dynamic synthesis of her fragmented and chaotic inner world.

Why did the priest tell Sarashina to read the fifth book of the Lotus Sutra, the most popular and important Sutra of Saicho's Tendai sect and of Mayahanna Buddhists? Why was it so crucial to Sarashina's emotional well-being? What is the significance of the Lotus, that one of the Sutras should have taken on the image of this flower? Representative of the purity, truth, and beauty which may emerge from muddied waters, each of the lotus' petals reaches out into the many Buddha-realms, thus symbolizing the Universe as One and Infinite.

The Lotus Sutra narrates Shakyamuni's last discourse on Vulture Peak before his entry into Nirvana. As he is revealing a vision of the infinite Buddha-worlds to his disciples, the Buddhas, in their supernal sphere, are disclosing the Truth to their disciples. That Shakyamuni is but one manifestation of the Eternal Buddha was revealed in the Lotus Sutra, as was the fact that He becomes visible in the infinite realms when humanity, overcome by evil, is in need of Him. That Buddhahood is accessible to all and not merely to a few—to women as well as to men—focuses attention on the compassionate earthly bodhisattvas who are the keepers of Buddha's Truth, and on the *Sutra* in which It is disseminated.

> Should one wish to dwell in Buddhahood
> And attain to intuitive Wisdom,
> He must always earnestly honor
> The keepers of the Flower of the Law.
> Should one wish quickly to attain
> To complete omniscience,
> He must receive and keep this Sutra
> And honor those who keep it.
> Should one be able to receive and keep
> The Wonderful Law-Flower Sutra,
> Let him know he is the Buddha's messenger,
> Who compassionates all living beings (*Sources of Japanese Tradition*, I, 123).

Although Sarashina's Healing Buddha had been her antidote to loneliness and isolation and she had been overcome with sorrow and guilt when "abandoning Him," she nevertheless failed to act upon her dream and upon the priest's advice. The dream showed her *the way*, but it was unable to oblige her to pursue the *path*.

That Sarashina projected onto a priest suggests a fusion of two basic needs: love and religion. Her sense of homeliness triggered conflict within her psyche, which may have been accentuated by Lady Murasaki's excessively beautiful characters in *The Tale of Genji*. Yearning to be comely is, moreover, a violation of Buddhist doctrine, which considers the world of appearances to be illusion.

What did Sarashina's projection onto a priest indicate? Projection (a "process whereby an unconscious quality or content of one's own is perceived and reacted to in an outer object") is assignment or attribution of characteristics one loves or hates onto others (Edward Edinger, *Melville's Moby Dick*, 148). Sarashina is unaware of the fact that the qualities she projects onto others are potentially hers. The priest, as spiritual guide and father figure, is also a love object and therefore a source of fulfillment.

Sarashina's longing for love expresses recognition of primordial energetic power that promotes, on a personal or cosmic level, a *conjunctio oppositorum*. Love insures both the continuity of life and the internal cohesion of the Cosmos. As a sign, love stands for relatedness—union between animate and/or inanimate worlds. Like a magnet, it attracts to its fold. Love's psychological counterpart, *libido* (psychic energy), is a catalyst promoting everything in the universe to realize itself, to actualize its virtualities, to pass from a condition of inertia to activity.

In the following dream, Sarashina mentions certain characters from *The Tale of Genji*:

> I dreamt that a man came to me and said, "I have just finished building a stream in the Hall of Six Sides. It is for the Princess of the First Order, the daughter of the Empress Dowager." When I asked for an explanation, he replied, "Offer prayers to the heavenly Goddess Amaterasu!" But his words were wasted on me; I neither told anyone about the dream nor gave it further thought.

Additional clues to Sarashina's involvement in Buddhism are yielded in this dream: a nine-year old Princess had ordered the building of an artificial stream in the garden of The Hall of Six Sides (Part of the Chobo Temple of the Tendai Sect) (Morris, 132). Sarashina's identification with this fantasy figure indicates her desire to help restore a temple for the purpose not only of furthering Buddhism in the empirical world, but of applying experientially the power within her being as well.

Sarashina's synchretistic approach to Tendai Buddhism, with its emphasis on the male, and Shinto, with its devotion to the female through Amaterasu, indicates a psychological need to reconcile disruptive opposites within her. Thus could be healed the wound separating masculine and feminine principles, which might otherwise tear her apart. How could the dichotomy between these polarities be breached in sacred spheres? A solar myth tells us that when Amaterasu was insulted by her brother, she retreated into her cave to brood over her hurt. The world, deprived of Sun, was plunged into Darkness. The laughter she heard outside the cave provoked her curiosity, drawing her out into the world, thus permitting her glow and warmth again to shine on humankind. (See Introduction.)

Psychologically, one may suggest that Buddha, meditative and absorbed in contemplation, as opposed to Amaterasu, whose incandescence warms and comforts as well as illuminates, were active forces in Sarashina's psyche. The former, identified with introversion, and the latter with extroversion, were not working in harmony in Sarashina's psyche. Had she listened to the messages implicit in her dreams, her intense timidity and lack of self-worth, rather than finding expression within (Buddhist meditation), would have been exposed to the light of consciousness (Amaterasu's sunlit realm) and possibly transformed into more positive channels. She would learn to approach what she considered to be her inadequacies with discernment and animation, eloquently and in cheerful anticipation.

The building of the stream in the hall of the temple links profane and sacred worlds through the fluid element, an indication of the importance of bridging the two polarities in Sarashina's psyche. Water contains everything *in potentia;* it stands for a world of possibilities and of transformation. The building of the stream, then, serves to dissolve old routes while also forming new ones. As a symbol for the unconscious, water represents that non-formal active feminine sphere within the psyche, once again emphasizing Sarashina's underlying schism between feminine and masculine principles. That she is told by the man (similar to the priest in the first dream) to pray to Amaterasu indicates clearly a need to develop her feminine nature—to exteriorize her feelings, be more sociable, and show understanding of others. But again, Sarashina neglected to take the dream's advice.

Sarashina's negative relationship with her mother also comes to the fore in her dream. When, for example, she announces her intention of going on a pilgrimage, her mother, a very "old-fashioned woman," aware of the dangers involved in such a project, tells her she must await her father's return. "She obviously regarded me as a great nuisance and unfit for normal society," Sarashina wrote angrily. Unconsciously projecting onto her mother the traits of timorousness and withdrawal which she despised in herself, she further rejected these as well as identifying them with 'feminine' characteristics. So troubled was she that when she actually went on a pilgrimage to the temple in Kiyomizu, the only one to which her mother would allow her to go, she found herself unable to pray sincerely. The entire experience proved unsatisfactory.

Nor were Sarashina's other dreams revolving around Buddha and Amaterasu acted upon. Meanwhile, time was passing; she had reached the age of thirty-one and became a lady-in-waiting to an Imperial Princess; but her inability to relate to people isolated her from society, increasing her grief and solitude. Her father's letters urging her to return home played on her sympathies, particularly when he described his feebleness and his loneliness. "When you were here, the house was full of visitors and attendants, but during the past days it has been completely silent and we have not seen a soul. It has been terribly sad and lonely. What will become of us if you stay at Court?" Nevertheless, Sarashina waited before complying. Her mother, on the other hand, had fulfilled a long-time wish: she had become a nun and had been granted permission to live in her home, but in quarters separate from the family. Finally Sarashina did return home, where she had an archetypal dream about a previous incarnation.

> A man, evidently the Intendant, appeared before me and said, "In a previous incarnation you were a priest in this temple. As a carver of many Buddhist images you accumulated great merit, and in your next incarnation you were born into a much better family than before. It was you who carved the sixteen-foot statue of the Buddha in the eastern wing of this chapel. In fact you were covering it with gold foil when you died."
> "Dear me!" I said. "In that case I had better gild it now."
> "No. Someone else finished the job after your death. And it is he who dedicated the image."

Although Sarashina neither explored nor followed up the indications of this dream any more than the others, she admitted that her future would have been happier had she done so.

That she (in the dream) had once been a carver of Buddhist images indicated a potentially creative nature, as well as a powerful spiritual center within her psyche. Her identification with the sixteen-foot Buddha which she had carved in a previous incarnation is reminiscent of her projection onto the Healing Buddha which she had left behind as a child. In both cases, she had turned her back on powerful religious urges within her being. She had allowed passivity to dominate, her weakly structured characteristics to prevail, and continued to consider herself ill-equipped to deal with virtually everything in the empirical world. In that *gold* symbolizes Enlightenment, the highest of spiritual values, and that in her dream she died during the gilding process, suggest an inability to evolve. Gold is also associated with the Sun, Amaterasu, and Her radiance and energy. Had Sarashina succeeded in blending the masculine (Buddhist) with the feminine (Shinto) principles within her psyche, she might have been able to heal the spirit. Her death prior to the completion of her task cast a shadow on her future *karma*.

Unchanging in her ways, when Sarashina again returned to court, she remained aloof and so inconspicuous that, she noted in her diary, hardly anyone saw her. Nevertheless, at the age of thirty-four, she fell in love with a handsome courtier. Marriage, however, was impossible because of his high and her low rank. Unlike so many Heian court ladies, she refused him as a lover, and their unconsummated relationship apparently ended some months later. Sarashina married at the age of thirty-six. Her husband, a member of the middle class, was six years older than she, but further mention of him and their three children is only occasional.

Even after her marriage, Sarashina's pilgrimages—or *wanderings*—continued. Nature's colors, values, and rhythms were for her carriers of energy and magic. Everything she saw in the landscape was an intercessor from transcendental spheres. Lakes became mirrors, replete with crystal markings; their endless reflections encouraged her to peer into their infinite depth. Mountains, bearers of mystery, motivated her to probe their geological folds experientially. Awe-inspiring Sun and Moon, though fugitive in their cyclicality, lit her way in gleaming rays by day and in subdued tones at night. Captivated by Nature and its world of enigmas—its silences, reveries, and erotic aspirations—she entered into close touch with the continuously unfolding scapes before her.

It was on one of Sarashina's pilgrimages, during a stay in a temple at Yamanobe, that the image of a woman appeared to her for the first time in a dream. "A very beautiful and impressive-looking woman" asked her: "Why have you come here?" Sarashina answered: "How could I possibly not have come?" The beautiful lady then questioned: "You are hoping to become a lady-in-waiting in the Imperial Palace. For this purpose you must look to Lady Hakase for help."

Upon awakening from her dream, Sarashina felt happy and encouraged for the first time. The feminine image was no longer absent or repressed, nor did it represent a negative mother figure. It had taken on the form of a beautiful court lady who greeted her with warmth and understanding, and who sought to guide her along the right path. Such an identification indicated that a positive part of Sarashina's personality was emerging, no longer angry or self-deprecating, but perceptive, harmonious, and sharing. A partner and not an enemy.

Other dreams, retreats, and pilgrimages followed. Sarashina now could pray sincerely and deeply. Her rapport with Buddha and Amaterasu worked in unison with spirit and psyche, enabling her to accept herself wholeheartedly and embrace all of nature as a living and breathing force within her being:

> ... we reached the Bay of Sumiyoshi just as the sun was sinking over the mountain top. I have never seen a painting to equal the beauty of this scene—the pine branches and the sky all shrouded by mist, the surface of the sea, the waves breaking on the beach,
>
> *How shall I describe it,*
> *To what shall I compare it—*
> *This Bay of Sumiyoshi on an Autumn eve?*
>
> I gazed about me as we rowed along, after we had passed, I kept looking back and felt that I could never have enough.

Unlike earlier images which were so emotionally debilitating and upsetting to the point of depleting Sarashina's energies, she now experienced a sense of fulfillment in the very act of taking nature into her. The absorption of its endless bounties and unfoldings not only divested her of feelings of loss and displacement, but also enriched her spirit and psyche.

Sarashina was fifty when her husband died. That his passing elicited lamentations from her—she "lost him like a dream"—was surprising, inasmuch as she seemed indifferent to him during their life together. Her one and single great love had been her father: his needs, his wishes, and his moods. We know nothing of Sarashina's later years nor when she died. The last dream included in her *Diary* was about a woman who had lived deeply, suffered intensely, and who, at the end of her days, finally found harmony of being.

> Then I had dreamt that Amida Buddha was standing in the far end of our garden. I could not see Him clearly, for a layer of mist seemed to separate us, but when I peered through the mist I saw that He was about six foot tall and that the lotus pedestal on which He stood was about four foot off the ground. He glowed with a golden light, and one of His hands was stretched out, while the other formed a magical sign. He was invisible to everyone but me. I had been greatly impressed but at the same time frightened and did not dare move near my blinds to get a clearer view of Him. He had said, "I shall leave now, but later I shall return to fetch you." And it was only I who could hear His voice. Thereafter it was on this dream alone that I set my hopes for salvation.

That Sarashina came face to face with Deity in the form of a six-foot tall Buddha seated on the sacred lotus, and that a "golden light" radiated from His being, may be viewed, psychologically, as an image of the Self. This central archetype, the Self/Deity, is an expression of wholeness or totality of the personality. For within this paradoxical unity polarity exists—in Sarashina's case, the schism between masculine and feminine principles, the individual ego and the transpersonal Self, the introvert and the extrovert. That Sarashina saw the Buddha of the Western Paradise in the far end of her garden suggests an identification with an ordered and oriented aspect of nature rather than a disorderly forested domain of fearful storms and nature's cataclysms. The Buddha was welcoming her into peace and eternal bliss, into His Pure Land—His Paradise.

Unlike those in Lady Murasaki's diary, Sarashina's descriptions are brief, like flashes of insights or miniatures. Never does she elaborate her visions; nor are there emotional highs or moments of intense drama, except after her nurse's or her sister's deaths. Although Sarashina's travels entailed physical displacements, her depictions of these expeditions are not geographically recorded. She is not a *thinker* but rather a *feeler*. Incapable of finding and maintaining that delicate balance between the two, as had Murasaki, she found herself unable to evaluate her situation objectively. Nor had she learned detachment. An overidentification with her father, the ideal masculine type, and with the Buddha, as she understood him, prevented her from healing a deep breech within her psyche. Is it any wonder then, that the image of the misunderstood little girl so in need of love should take first place in her diary? Only later, via the dream process, do we know that she developed a *modus vivendi*.

The Diary of Izumi Shikibu

Unlike *The Diary of Sarashina*, which was the work of an introverted personality type who concentrated on her solitary inner world, *The Diary of Izumi Shikibu* focuses on the author's love experience. The peripeteia of her great passion, with its hopes and disappointments, its alternating yearnings and indifference, all framed within the courtly rituals, is strangely contemporary. The suffering of both lovers, although subjective and personal, conveys a feeling of universality and of eternalness (Kazuko Sugisaki, "Darkness of Passion: The Diary of Izumi Shikibu," 43-51).

Unlike the diaries of Lady Murasaki and Sei Shonagon, Izumi Shikibu's is based on an exchange of letters and poems written by the lovers. (Its style has been compared to the *utamonogatari*: *wakas* linked by prose passages. Kazuko Sugisaki, "Darkness of Passion: The Diary of Izumi Shikibu," 41.) Suspense-creating devices, such as the objective voice of a narrator dialoguing the events, is reminiscent in many ways of high drama. The tensions provoked by the information gleaned from the missives serves to intensify or slacken emotions, thereby playing up the theatrics of the lovers' meetings and/or separations. That each of the lovers presents his and her points of view and reactions to their encounters lends greater authenticity to the text, while also increasing the depth of an unfolding and evolving passion.

The use of indirect discourse by the narrator, who sets the tone and structures the peripeteia, and the words of the protagonists, serve at times to foster an enigmatic climate in the reader's mind, which mirrors the protagonists' doubts. Is the narrator or one of the protagonists speaking, repeating, or rethinking a given situation, feeling, or description? Like the protagonist mulling over a conversation, letter, or poem, so the reader pauses to reflect, thereby increasing the complexity and excitement of relationships and the personalities involved. Although seemingly straightforward, both imagistically and emotionally, *The Diary of Izumi Shikibu* is far from being clear-cut and precise.

As the preceding ones, *The Diary of Izumi Shikibu* is also anonymous. "Shikibu" means a lesser court office; and "Izumi," the name of Izumi Province, is where the author's first husband, Tachibana Michisada, had been governor in 999 (Miner, *Japanese Poetic Diaries*, 32). Nor has the question of the authorship of her *Diary* been solved. Theories abound, but none is conclusive.

Little is known about Izumi Shikibu's life. Even her birth and death dates, generally given as 970-1030, are uncertain. Her marriage (probably prior to 999) was arranged, it is believed, and was no love match. Some scholars suggest that the year of her marriage also saw the beginning of the first of her two great love affairs, both with bloodline princes: Prince Tametaka, the son of Emperor Reizei (967-969), who died at the age of twenty-six in 1002; and Prince Atsumichi, who lived only to the age of twenty-seven (981-1007). The void left by the demise of her first lover might have been instrumental in encouraging Izumi Shikibu to seek solace in a new love affair and the recording of its perepeteia in *Diary* form (Miner, *Japanese Poetic Diaries*, 33).

Izumi Shikibu, like Lady Murasaki Shikibu and Sei Shonagon, served at the court of Empress Akiko (Shoto Mon'in, 988-1074), herself noted for her literary pursuits. Certainly Izumi Shikibu must have sparkled with wit as well as with beauty and talent. She also knew how to lure men to her orbit and was criticized by the author of *The Tale of Genji*, perhaps for drawing so much attention:

> She does have a rather unsavory side to her character but has a genius for tossing off letters with ease and can make the most banal statement sound special. Her poems are quite delightful. Although her knowledge of the canon and her judgments leave something to be desired, she can produce poems at will and always manages to include some clever phrase or other that catches the eye, and yet when it comes to criticizing or judging the work of others, well, she never really comes up to scratch; the sort of person who relies on a talent for extemporization, one feels. I cannot think of her as a poet of the highest quality (Murasaki Shikibu, *Her Diary and Poetic Memoirs*, 131).

Although Murasaki's thoughts concerning her rival's proclivities may have elements of truth, her deprecating remarks about her rival's poetic talents were, seemingly, motivated by envy.

It is not known whether Izumi Shikibu's second marriage, to Fujiwara Yasumasa (958-1036), was any happier than her first had been. That she had other lovers after her betrothal is deduced from the names mentioned in headnotes to her poems. As far as we know, she had one child, Koshikibu, on whom she lavished affection. Her daughter, who followed her mother's footsteps on the path of lovers and poetry, died prematurely in 1025.

Love

Love, the focus of Izumi's diary, is for the Buddhist a conflictual and paradoxical concept inasmuch as earthly attachments were frowned upon. Such entanglements were considered impediments to spiritual fulfillment, and the very notion of sensual desire bound one to the world of suffering, yearning, and rebirths—*samsara* (Diana Y. Paul, *Women in Buddhism*, 5).

Early Buddhism, misogynist to the extreme, considered the feminine as a source of Evil, as attested to by the following examples. It was written that when Buddha-Sakyamuni was on his way to complete enlightenment, Mara, the tempter, called upon his three *daughters*, Thirst, Sexual Pleasure, and Carnal Desire, to appear before the Buddha. As temptresses, women were not only personifications of Evil, but were also considered pollutants and contaminants, forever impeding man's rise toward pure spirituality (Paul, 52). In "The Tale of King Udayana of Vatsa," a Buddhist text, sexual intercourse was looked upon as vile and animal-like:

> Those who are not wise,
> Act like animals,
> Racing toward female forms
> Like hogs toward mud....
> Because of their ignorance
> They are bewildered by women, who
> Like profit seekers in the marketplace
> Deceive those who come near (Paul, 9).

The Buddha, as transcendence, was above feminine attachments. Meditation, centering on the evanescence of all things and the selflessness of all elements (*dharmas*), helped him attain the bliss of Nirvana. To diminish and finally obliterate any lustful thoughts or yearnings in man was one of the most significant of disciplines. In Buddhist scriptures on meditation we read:

> No distractions can touch the man who's alone both in
>   his body and mind.
> Therefore renounce you the world, give up all thinking
>   discursive!
> Thirsting for gain, and loving the world, the people
>   fail to renounce it.
> But the wise can discard this love . . . (Edward Conze,
>   *Buddhist Scriptures*, 100).

For some, meditative ecstasy replaced the elation of orgasm (Paul, 8).

With the coming of Amidism, derived from Mahayana Buddhism, such texts as the *Lotus Sutra* (100-200 C.E.) and *The Sutra of the Perfection of Wisdom in Eight Thousand Verses*, gave equal opportunity to both sexes for salvation. A woman was no longer looked upon solely as a temptress and a force of Evil, but could also be considered a good friend to a man. To be a helping force, the woman must adhere to Buddhist disciplines. Indeed, she could even, under quite extraordinary circumstances, become a Bodhisattva (Paul, 113).

Although Buddhism had come a long way from its misogynist beginnings, the Japanese man, with the help of Confucianism, still deprecated the feminine. That Shintoism cohabited with Buddhism and Confucianism in Japan, however, helped to improve the lot of women. Women helped in Shinto ceremonies, becoming priestesses, shamanesses, and mediums in their own right. Shinto emphasis on animism and fertility cults, the worship of nature and the belief that Amaterasu, the Sun Goddess, was not only the progenitrix of the Japanese Emperors but the one who saw to the nation's prosperity, not only suggested the acceptance of the feminine, but implied its importance for the people's well-being (*Sources*, 22-23).

Courtly love in Heian times, encompassing Buddhist, Confucian, and Shinto concepts, had its strictures as well as its permissivity. Because Japan's society was clan-oriented and polygamous, marriage demanded that women bear children; if they were barren, shame was heaped upon them. In that a husband could have several wives, in addition to concubines and mistresses of various ages—some young enough to be their children—not only provoked feelings of jealousy and envy among women, but encouraged certain transgressions. Incest, as well as deep resentment and insecurity in love relationships, were rather frequently to be found in Japanese society (Haruo Shirane, *The Bridge of Dreams*, 101).

Insights into the lot of Heian woman may be gleaned from the code of etiquette which obliged the man, if his love were not legitimized, to visit his paramour only at night and leave at dawn. The following day, the man and woman would convey to each other their reactions to the preceding night, frequently in delicate love poems replete with metaphors, images, symbols, personifications, and metonymies. Such figures of speech were not only part of the prescribed formula, but also served to mask personal feelings as well as to universalize the individual. To lay one's heart bare in any overt and obvious manner was unacceptable in Heian society (Kazuko Sugisaki, 43-51).

Izumi Shikibu, if she is the Lady depicted in the *Diary*, is a *hetaira* type: a courtesan similar to the Western Aspasia, Pericles' beautiful and brilliant paramour who eventually became his wife. Self-composed and a poet in her own right, the Lady of the *Diary* knew she was devastatingly appealing to men. Although of the middle class, her positive view of herself, her learning, physical attributes, and seductive manner increased her standing and allure. It is no wonder that Princes of blood were drawn to her, fascinated and obsessed by her elegance, sensitivity, and, above all, her mystery.

Although experienced in the domain of love, the Lady of the *Diary* suffered moments of intense grief, as attested to by her despair after the death of the first of her two great passions, Prince Tametaka. Her "world of love" had vanished; the evanescent and illusory relationship of love had "proved more fleeting than a dream."

The Lady of the *Diary* became attached to her former lover's younger brother, Atsumichi, the following year. His first wife, it was rumored, had gone mad, and his second, of the highest class, was arrogant and frigid. Certainly, they had been all but the right companions for the handsome, dashing, and tender Atsumichi. The various phases of the passion experienced by the two protagonists follow the complex rules and regulations of courtship etiquette. The Prince, unseen by prying eyes, visits his Lady at night and in disguise, thereby protecting her reputation. She fearfully questions the use of his sumptuous carriage to visit her. Might it not attract attention? Another problem arose: would it not be contrary to protocol to begin a new relationship so soon after the death of Prince Tametaka?

Although the Lady felt ill at ease, superbly cognizant of her ability to entice, she permitted a first meeting during which, in keeping with the love-ritual, "nothing except conversation" took place. Remaining quietly behind her curtain of state, she was duly impressed by the Prince's "unusually distinguished" demeanor. He, however, grew dissatisfied at the distance separating them and promised he would maintain his reserve if she would allow him to join her and talk face to face. In keeping with the dictates of courtly love, not to respond negatively to his advances was to acquiesce. Behind the screen, the two talked long into the night. A poem followed.

> I have not possessed
> Anything even so fleeting as a dream,
> And now dawn breaks—
> What is there left for me to recall
> In conversation on a later night?

> The Lady answered in verse:
> As the night comes
> My sleeves grow wet in recollection,
> And first and last
> I know this world holds no future chance
> For me to have a peaceful dream of love.

Leaving at dawn, the Prince had high hopes that his Lady would respond favorably to the poem he sent her as soon as he returned to his palace.

> Perhaps you think
> That as I spoke of love I intended
> Only what others mean,
> But my heart is filled this morning
> With an unrivalled truth of love.

> She responded:
> I do not think
> That this love can only signify
> What others mean by love:
> This morning I have learnt at last
> What it truly means to be in love.

When she heard nothing from the Prince, she felt confused and humiliated. Was she being punished for having betrayed Prince Tametaka's memory? Or, for her own immodest behavior? "My heart anguishes in yearning," she confessed.

Unworldly when it came to love, the Prince was at a loss to deal with his jealous Consort. He allowed days to pass before sending his lady love the next poem. "If you tell me / That you wait with all your heart," he writes, he will visit her every evening. No, he is a serious person, not one to trifle with her feelings. Attributing their amorous relationship to *karma*, the Lady knows that their love had been determined in a previous incarnation: "For, from other worlds, you and I / Have been fast bound by fate to love."

Delighted at the prospect of entering into an intimate relationship with his Lady, he was, nevertheless, at a loss as to how to deal with her overt passion. Once again he stopped writing. After a month of silence, she informs him of her longing in the metaphors the day.

> Oh, my wood thrush,
> Your endearing voice is hidden
> From our busy world,
> And if again today I miss you,
> When can I hope to hear your song?

Birds, as flying creatures, symbolize agents divested of dross or connecting principles which link heaven and earth. The ability of birds to ascend to airated spheres identifies them with spiritual values and a lightness of being. That the Lady makes reference to the wood thrush, already mentioned in the Prince's first poem, associates him in her mind with this idealized creature and with its mellifluous tones—like so many love poems she longs to hear.

> If its low voice
> Is one that brought you anguish,
> Listen now again,
> For from today the wood thrush
> Sings in a louder voice and true.

Either playing coy or actually hurt because of the Prince's lengthy absence, when he finally returns to her home in his customary disguise, she informs him of her imminent departure for a pilgrimage. The purification rituals required prior to the event leave little time for conversation between the two. He conveys his distress in a poem. She replies, expressing her yearning for him: "To bring that loving meeting of the eyes / To one whose vows have made her wife." When will she return? the Prince inquires. Her answer:

> The month is passing—
> Let be the waste of time, as now

> The slow rains come;
> Tonight I shall pick me iris bulbs
> And resolution for an agitated heart."

A month. A change of season. Time is fleeting. Nature points the way in the image of the iris, the flower mentioned in the Lady's poem. The Japanese believe it to be endowed with great virtues: it protects against physical illnesses while also keeping perverse spirits from contaminating the innocent. In that the iris blooms in spring, it suggests that the Prince's visits will, like the iris blossom, resume their course at that time—in beauty and love.

According to the rules and regulations of courtly love, impediments lie along the lovers' path. Upon the lady's return, she receives a letter informing her that when he went to the temple to be with her during her pilgrimage, he did not find her there. He suspects infidelity. The coldness of their last meeting intimated just that. Moreover, when he knocks at her door at night after her return, he is not admitted and is obliged to leave. Jealousy lurks. Had he listened to the insidious rumors circulating about? the Lady wonders. The Prince again conveys his pain: "Of what can hurt the trusting heart." Her reaction to his assumption is overt: "I very much dislike your unjust suspicion."

The rainy season advances. Although the Prince fails to call on his Lady, he does send her poems which stir in her "an endless reverie of love." Other gallants call on her, but she accepts none of them. Images of rain, identified with tears and pain, disclose his feeling world ("With the tears I shed in love of you.") and hers ("That these rains are really mingled / With your tears of love . . . "). Depression encourages the Lady to harbor suicidal thoughts of throwing herself into the lake. He, too, weeps during this seemingly endless rainy season.

After nature's tears have subsided, the Prince returns to his Lady, despite the advice given him by his "wet nurse": he must not continue this affair with someone "of no importance." So conscious was Heian society of class hierarchy that even a lowly creature like the Prince's wet nurse, devoted to tradition and to family structure, was permitted to speak out against such "pointless excursions." Her statement was motivated not from a moral point of view, but from a psychological one: to protect him from degrading himself, a factor to be considered in Heian society.

The Prince pays no heed. Increasingly impatient to see his Lady, he invites her to his secluded palace, explaining that he is ill at ease in her house because women of different ranks entertain their men there. Furthermore, he assures her that no one will see her either entering or leaving his palace. Gossip will be stemmed. She acquiesces. Sadness encloses itself upon her each time they part.

That many of the love interludes in the *Diary* are bathed in moon imagery is not surprising since this body's continuously altering hues and shapes—bright or dim, full or partial—mirror the highs and lows of human feelings. Unlike the Sun (Amaterasu), the Moon, her brother (Tsuki-yumi), sheds his silver radiance and shadowy self through both outer and inner worlds. That each of the Moon's phases marks the passage of time is attested to by his name: Tsuki, meaning moon, and Yumi, counter, that is, the "counter of months." In that Tsuki-yumi acts upon tides, waters, and rains, metaphorically he elicits tears, melancholia, moments of tempestuous rapture—or rage. Because the Moon shines only when the Sun's rays are cast upon it, its light is subdued, indirect, reflective, never blatant or brash; it symbolizes the mystery of the human heart.

On another evening, the Prince attempts to visit his Lady; the door remains closed, despite his knocking. In the few letters that follow, he accuses her of infidelity. Musing on her relationship, she observes the moon, whose soft glow opens her heart to dream.

> Looking on the moon
> I fall into a tender reverie
> In my ruined house,
> Wondering whom I might tell of its beauty
> When I know that he would fail to come.

Parallel actions and reactions are implicit throughout the *Diary*. So, too, are hurtful sequences. To punish him for his neglect, the Lady had once before informed him that preparations for a pilgrimage prevented her from seeing him. Now the Prince seeks her out on a day of abstinence and therefore cannot, according to the rituals, remain the night. Yearningly, she writes, "If the moon that passes through the sky / Would pass my house or linger here. . . ."

Gossip. Suspicions. The Prince stops writing. Tears flow. Something has gone awry. To increase tensions, another technical device of courtly writers is used: a visit to Ishiyama Temple for a week will clear her mind, she feels. Unaware of her departure, the Prince arrives at her house to find her gone. He waxes in despair and bemoans her cruelty.

Days fly by. One season fades into the next. The lovers continue their epistolary relationship, reiterating their feelings of sadness. Autumn winds and shattering storm clouds encourage both reverie and anxiety. The Lady can no longer sleep, so profound is her distress. Regret intrudes as the transience of illusory love impacts upon her.

The Prince resumes his visits. As he watches her intently in her half-sleep, he is aroused by the sight of this langorous figure. He then speaks to her "most tenderly and lovingly." Touching her, he whispers:

> There is no drizzle,
> There is no dew that falls tonight,
> But as we lie here,
> A strange wetness glistens softly
> Upon the sleeve of the pillowing arm.

She made no reply. Inert and deep in thought, so deep in thought was she. Tears fill her eyes. Each sparkles, as if touched by moonlight. As he looks at her langorous form with utmost tenderness, he asks her: "Why don't you reply? I know that what I said was unimportant—I must have said something wrong." She questions:

> What should I say? . . . My thoughts are lost in a maze of feeling, and your words have scarcely entered my ears. But this much I hope you believe—your poem about 'the sleeve of the pillowing arm' is one I will never forget. You may put me to the test on *that*.

With that, a smile covered her countenance.

The traditional poetic formulae which abound in the above scene underscore the whiteness, purity, and beauty of the moment. The Lady's withdrawn and secretive ways and her helplessness, verbal meanderings and reveries, catalyze the Prince's passion. A memorable night. One he would always recall.

The frost settling on the land increases the brilliance of the mobile and contrasting Sun's rays, each falling on the whitest of scapes. Unvitiated feelings reign.

> Fallen everywhere,
> The frost lies too upon the sleeve

> Of the pillowing arm,
> And looking on it in the morning light,
> I see it white like hempen sleeves.

Months of epistolary deliberation follow, after which the Prince brings his Lady to his palace to live. Although vowing to shield her from intrusive eyes, she still hesitates to remain, and asks again to be taken home at dawn. Letters of recrimination ensue. The fear of discovery and of deception make inroads in her moods. He insists, begging her to stop vacillating. Her distress is conveyed in violent and stark images: winter winds, autumn's bareness, frost, and snow.

The year is drawing to a close. Would she remain at his palace in spring? he asks her. Against a background of falling snow, he informs her of his intention of becoming a monk. Was it a ploy? She weeps: "rain mingled with sleet was slowly falling outside." When she finally yields to the Prince's wishes, she does so without any illusions as to the duration of the relationship. Love for her is a fleeting dream, and, like all painful attachments, cannot bring happiness, but only passing moments of joy in an eternity of sorrow.

> What was said last night
> Was of a sadness far too great
> To think to treat it as a dream
> To be forgotten as we wake.

The land, now blanketed in whiteness, encourages the Prince to send his Lady a poem attached to a snowflake-encrusted branch.

> As the snow falls,
> Even before the spring the leaves
> Of every kind of tree
> Without exception blossom forth
> With the white flowers of the plum.

The Lady finally complies and makes her home at the Prince's palace. When the Prince's Consort learns that the Lady has been installed in the most luxurious of chambers in the palace and that he visits her three or four times a day, her humiliation is complete. She will leave for her sister's home: "Our position as women is never what it should be."

The lovers remained together to the great chagrin of Heian readers who were shocked that a Prince should reject his Consort while esteeming and loving a socially inferior woman.

* * *

Izumi Shikibu, considered one of the finest poets of her time, knew exactly how to verbalize the palpable side of passion. She conveyed sensuality, for example, through figures of speech: images, sensations (touch, taste, sound, odor, sight), tones, and rhythms. Each served to heighten or diminish the intensity of the physicality that came into play in the lovers' ardor. Her ability to manipulate the suspense factor in her *Diary* enhanced its artistry. The Lady's identification with nature's moods, autumnal frosts, winter's icy glaze, spring's mists and fogs, and summer's burning blaze, served to usher in feelings of hope and renewal. The personal and deeply subjective manner in which Izumi Shikibu's *Diary* was written lends it authenticity even while injecting it with universality and eternalness.

Both *The Diary of Sarashina* and, paradoxical though it may seem, *The Diary of Izumi Shikibu*, may be considered religious works. The former, also exquisite in its artistry, deals not with a love episode, but with the progressive spiritual evolution of a psyche. The author's deep faith is attested to by her many journeys to religious shrines and by the importance of Buddha and Amaterasu in her dreams. Izumi Shikibu's faith is attested to by her understanding of Buddhist notions with regard to the illusory nature of empirical existence. Although unable to detach herself from her great love, she is lucid when decrying the pain resulting from this bonding. Each relationship, each attachment, is bound, as all else, to the wheel of *karma*. It runs its course, intensifying in momentum until it reaches the incandescence of ecstasy, diminishing in potency after a time frame, and finally concluding in indifference.

Chapter 3

Women's Mysteries:
Poetry and Noh in Feudal Japan

Although the ultrarefined and effete Heian Period saw the authoring of a rich body of narratives, diaries, and poems by women, it also witnessed the increased domination of the powerful Fujiwara clan, the Buddhist priesthood, and was partisan to the growth of feudal and military systems.

When the powerful leader, Minamoto-no-Yoritomo, established the Shogunate in 1192, he moved his military dictatorship to Kamakura (Kamakura Period, 1185-1333). The once flourishing Kyoto, seat of the Imperial Court during the Heian Period, had become nonfunctional. Emperor Daigo II, who attempted to reestablish imperial rule by displacing the Shogunate, invited a rebellion that brought about the downfall of the Kamakura regime. With the take-over of the Shogunate by Ashikaga Takauji, Kyoto once again became the capital of Japan. During the two-hundred and fifty years of civil wars that followed, feudal barons (*daimyo*) attempted to extend their power by increasing their domains and their private armies, and Buddhist monks, their monasteries.

The succeeding Shogun, Ashikaga Yoshimitsu, was not only a military power, but was also a patron of the arts. The Ashikaga Shogunate saw to it that painters, architects, and craftsmen were invited to Kyoto to provide its luxury- and pleasure-loving population with the most aesthetic of atmospheres (Peter C. Swann, *A Concise History of Japanese Art*, 175). Gardens, tea-houses, and pavilions were built; palaces constructed, including the celebrated *Gold Pavilion*, in 1394. Yoshimasa, the eighth Shogun, was highly regarded for his great collection of Chinese paintings, an inspiration to many Japanese artists of the time. The *Silver Pavilion* was built under his rulership. Zen monasteries, favored by shoguns in general, became cultural centers.

Painting flourished. Zen black and white painting was very much in favor because it attempted to and succeeded in transcending the visible domain, thereby allowing the essence of reality to emerge intuitively and spontaneously.

Ink paintings on hanging scrolls, such as *The Hermitage by a Mountain Brook* attributed to Mincho (1352-1431), depicts a Zen retreat within a Chinese-type landscape. The combination of trees, streams, and a cottage nestled in tranquil and misty scenery implied a natural communion conducive to enlightenment (Swann, 183). The priest-painter Shubun's *Landscape* scroll also reveals a hiddenness and mysteriously evanescent quality in the outer forms delineated. In *Winter Landscape* by the Zen priest Sesshu (1420-1506), the greatest water-ink painter of the time, snow was made to appear even more realistic than in life by leaving sections of the paper untouched. The thick black sheen of his ink gave the illusion of wetness, making the other elements in the depiction superfluous. What remained was "bone structure," a Chinese term for skeleton (Swann, 188). Zen painters on the whole, but each in his own manner, sought to capture life eternal as it exists throughout the world of phenomena (Noritake Tsuda, *Handbook of Japanese Art*, 146).

Other schools of painting, the Kano in particular, were also popular at the time. Kano Masanobu (1434-1530), who was not a Zen priest, began the school which continued to increase in reputation when his son, Kano Motonobu (1476-1559), entered the family business. Rather than adhering to Zen Buddhist inspiration, they drew on their own native stylistic elements. An appreciation for the actual landscape they observed around them became the basis for their art work, as in Kano Masanobu's *The Sage Chou Mao-shu in a Lotus Pond*; and Kano Motonobu's *Landscape with Flowers and Birds* (Swann, 194).

Woman's rights, unlike the arts, did not flourish. Indeed, they diminished.

Women's Rights

During the Heian period, women were allowed to inherit both property and money. The Ashikaga Shogunate subverted this right, in the belief that it would lead to the splitting up of family wealth.

Confucianism, with its patriarchal philosophy relegating women to subordinate positions while also severely restricting their freedom, gained in popularity in Japan's increasingly military-oriented male society. While the Heian period was lax in its attitude toward sex, and promiscuity was not considered sinful any more than homosexuality, Confucianism was puritanical, at least insofar as the woman was concerned.

Girls of higher classes in feudal Japan were married most frequently between the ages of fifteen and twenty-five. Because marriages were arranged for financial and/or political reasons, not infrequently a girl divorced one husband to marry another if it suited the family's needs. A husband could divorce his wife by simply writing down seven reasons for wanting to do so. For a woman, a divorce was far more difficult to obtain. If she found marriage intolerable, she might go to a temple of divorce (sanctuaries which helped women with good reasons to obtain a divorce); otherwise she had only to yield to her husband's will. A wife had no power. Her adultery, if discovered, was punishable by death. Nor was it considered a transgression for a husband to kill both his adulterous wife and her lover. Virtually a prisoner in her home, the wife even needed a permit to leave town (Joyce Ackroyd, "Women in Feudal Japan," 53).

The life of women of the peasant, merchant, and artisan class was less restrictive. Frequently working alongside their husbands on the farms, peasant women were necessary as laborers and were highly regarded in their capacity as partial breadwinners. Their rights, therefore, were not to be subverted. The same was true of merchant class women. Indeed, some proved to be so business-minded and so hardworking that they became powerful entrepreneurs in their own right. Shuho, for example (1590-1676), proved herself to be so brilliant a manager of her husband's pawnbroking and sake business, that she is considered the founder of the Mitsui family fortune (Patricia Fister, *Japanese Women Artists 1600-1900*, 11). Because successful merchant-class women had both money and leisure, they went to the theatre frequently, and some even became fine artists.

Women on the whole, however, were not encouraged to improve their minds; rather they were motivated to spend their time at household duties, including the bringing up of their children. Although reading was not forbidden to them, only certain books of classical poetry and narrative, such as *The Tale of*

Genji, were permitted. Some husbands and Zen monks felt that the reading of Lady Murasaki's work encouraged frivolity and mental meanderings into dangerous areas. If women achieved literary skills, they were advised to keep these to themselves, for in no way were they allowed to reveal their superiority.

The fate of women in aristocratic Samurai families was unique. The Samurai (warrior-aristocrats) based their rigorous military code of ethics on bravery, honor, self-discipline, and the ability to accept death with equanimity. If they faced defeat or humiliation, honor bade them to commit ritual suicide of *seppuku* (*harakiri*)—the cutting open of the abdomen.

Women, interestingly enough, were attracted to the Samurai's concept of *bushido* ("The Way of the Warrior"). Although Samurai husbands kept their wives under virtual bondage in the home, they expected them to be as strong and brave as they in the acceptance of death. Such strength, in their view, demonstrated a sense of loyalty to both the feudal lord (Daimyo) and to the Samurai's family. Whenever a Samurai husband left home to serve the Daimyo, the wife had to always prepare herself for the worst: her husband's death (Reischauer, *The Japanese*, 58). Thus, the wives of Samurai warriors developed into selfless, austere, heroic women, indifferent to their own pain, and prepared for any alternatives.

Tales abound of their heroism, self-sacrifice, virtue, and selflessness. One famous example is that of the fourteen-year-old No-Hime (1535-1582) whose father had her marry the fifteen-year-old Nobunaga of the Oda clan in order to secure his fiefdom. Fate willed it otherwise. A year after his daughter's marriage, Nobunaga told his wife in secret that he was planning to take over her father's land and have him murdered during the military coup that would effect the change. Aware of the Samurai's credo of loyalty to one's parents, but also intent upon insuring the secrecy of his project, Nobunaga had his wife placed under tight surveillance. To test her fidelity, but also to make his conquest that much easier, he resorted to the following ruse. He had his wife's guards withdrawn on one occasion, fully prepared to have her inform her father of the plan afoot. She did just that. His ruse worked perfectly. Although No-Hime failed in her endeavor to save her father's land, she triumphed as a daughter, having risked her own life to warn her father of the danger in store for him (Hidéko Fukumoto and Catherine Pigeaire, *Femmes et Samourai*, 198).

Nobunaga did not stop with this first victory in what was to be his continuous thirst for conquest. His sister, Oichi (1574-1583), one of eleven children all from different fathers, was deeply attached to her brother. To serve his interests, she married Asai, whom she grew to love. Although treachery on Nobunaga's part brought Asai's defeat, Oichi, ever loyal to her brother, sided with him, causing Asai to take his own life as his wife looked on. The ambitious Nobunaga, intent upon leaving his stamp on his country's history, pursued his warring ways until he was finally killed in 1582.

Poetry

As in the Heian period, women still practised the art of poetry, although perhaps less overtly. The traditional *tanka*, 31 syllables, remained fashionable, while others, although not new, continued to develop. The *renga* (linked verse), was highly esteemed during the fourteenth to the sixteenth centuries. The subjective themes of the *renga*, its exquisite beauty and complexity, and its courtly elegance, were implicit in verse in general, but also in the poetics of Noh theatre. Not only was fresh artistic vision evident in both creative forms, but the new vocabulary which also came into being seemed more suited to the changing ideational and emotional needs of the ruling society.

Poetics, in keeping with the new importance accorded self-reliance, self-understanding, and the rigorous Zen disciplines involving this new vision of life, banished flamboyant colorations and images and divested the poem of clutter. Instead, it singled out a bird, a branch, a leaf, a blade of grass, or a vague landscape as the fitting focus of the poem (*Sources*, 256).

Nature, for example, is the central point of a poem by Lady Eifuku Mon'in (ca. 1310). Eye-movement and emotions invite her to concentrate her gaze on a setting sun, leaves, trees, and grasses; encourage her meditation, thereby generating an ever-increasing flow of energy between the author and the scene which she is absorbing and recreating in her verse.

> As it grows weaker,
> The setting sun among the branches
> Does not tint the leaves;
> Under the trees the grasses on the hills
> Withers lightly in the dimming rays (Miner, 127).

So active and intense does the interchange between the poet and the objects of her gaze become that Lady Eifuku Mon'in seems to enter into the very essence of the Zen Buddhist doctrine. Becoming *one* with the sun, branches, leaves, trees, and objects of her gaze, be they small and/or infinite, sets the stage for the sudden—and overwhelming—intrusion of enlightenment and with it, the experience of cosmic unity. Under her ever-vigilant mind, the poetic process is never disorderly. On the contrary, an even greater order infiltrates itself in the very progression of her verbalizations.

The reader is ushered into a subjective world in the poem by Lady Junii Tameko (ca. 1290). No longer replete with metaphors or images, she conveys her powerful feelings in non-representational distillations drawn from her deep involvement. Abstract language, in keeping with the depth of her emotional commitment, is conveyed in a variety of diapasons and rhythms, reflecting the intensity and gradations of her experience and its ensuing revelation in language.

> O my heart,
> If you are turning to resentment,
> Do so to the limit,
> For if you turn to weaker sorrow
> It will be impossible to bear (Miner, 127).

Although readers are introduced to the mundane rather than the esoteric side of life in both poems, be it in the visualization of a landscape or the generating of the emotional impact of pain caused by an unfulfilled love, they experience the stilled event in all of its beauty and anguish. The very act of being able to transmute the powerful, sometimes even violent, impress of sensation into the word marks the poet's collective scene or emotion with its own individual stamp.

The love poem written by Empress Eifuku (1271-1342), although reflecting a fervent inner climate, also indicates great discipline in dealing with heightened emotions.

> Though I alone am anxious
> And do not wish to hate myself so much
> That I lose hold of life,
> There is nobody who understands
> How far I suffer as I love (Miner, 130).

That she is able to deal with such volatile emotions as anguish, self-hate, and depression, which cohabit in her world of unfulfilled love, suggests the presence of a higher principle in her soul/psyche. The intensity of her sorrow will not allow her to wax in morbidity, nor will passivity set in. Her frequently vaporous phonemes seem to cleanse her language of all superfluities, be they verbal, visual, or psychological. Such a sublimating or cleansing process, marked as it is by increasing discipline, encourages her feelings to condense. Order stems the tide of what could have been heaving hyperemotionalism. Unwilling to become enslaved to the facile world of yearning or allow herself to fester inwardly, she refuses to be destroyed by her sorrow. Instead, she uses it to enhance her stature. Rigorous self-control when staving off despair is also evident in the following poem:

> In my grieving heart,
> Weakened now by your betrayal
> To the point of death,
> Even misery takes on pathetic beauty
> And my bitterness is gone (Miner, 131).

Alternating rhythms, ranging from stasis to an intense flow of vertical images, mark the linear and mythical time sequences in Empress Eifuku's seasonal poem. As perceptions bore deeply into that unique moment which the poet singles out for scrutiny—when the rays of a dying evening sun flicker—the diminishing intensity of the lighting effects offer her the paradoxical luxury of duration and ephemerality.

> The evening sun
> Flickers upon the cherry blossoms
> With a moment's light,
> And though it does not seem to set,
> Its glowing melts away (Miner, 131).

The contrasting impressions of immobility and motion are accentuated by the fixity of the poet's gaze, centering as it does on an "evening sun" and "cherry blossoms," set against a "glowing" sun in the process of disappearing. The depth of her meditation makes her privy to the poignant drama involved: the irremediable erosion of linear time, and its concomitant resurrection in her unique verbal vision—the singling out of that sudden moment when enlightenment erupts, which she arrests for all eternity in her poem.

In "A Moor in Late Autumn," Lady Jusammi Chikako (ca. 1300) delineates her overview of nature's wistfulness and ephemerality in light and delicate touches. While encapsulating and concretizing that exquisite instant in the phoneme, she also experiences its depletion in the veering away of the elements, the movement affording her heightened awareness.

> The wind blows,
> Swelling in the pampas grasses
> Wide cross the moors,
> And in the cold of the evening sun
> Autumn darkens to its close (Miner, 132).

The agitated wind sublimates earthly entities, such as the grasses in the moors. Although the wildness of the image represents both the inconstancy and instability of the material world, it also symbolizes the Primordial Spirit or Cosmic Breath, the harbinger of Light and Illumination. Bearing the poet from an infinitely abstract space to concretion and back again, suggests a parallel movement from the uncreated to the created world; psychologically, from the unconscious to consciousness; and empirically, from personal to collective spheres.

In "Love Promises Broken," Lady Jusammi Chikako reveals the trauma involved in a love experience. Its intensity was so fulminating that it enabled her to transcend the human sphere. By transforming a subjective into a universal experience, the single form into the syncretistic, the opaque into the transluscent, she universalizes and debanalizes a mundane occurrence.

> In recent days
> I can no longer say of wretchedness
> That it is wretched
> For I feel my grief has made me
> No longer truly capable of grief (Miner, 133).

The impact of the Zen Buddhist's mind-altering meditation is also evident in "On the Full Moon of the Eighth Month" also by Lady Jusammi Chikako. She is no longer the slave of pain or emotion; those debilitating forces have assumed their rightful place in her newly ordered and enlightened universe.

> Long since clouded over,
> This heart of mine has now cleared up
> Of its own accord—
> It is good to gaze continuously
> Until one has absorbed the moon (Miner, 133).

Noh Theatre: Matsukaze

Although Noh drama, performed for the first time during the Ashikaga Shogunate, was written, acted, and directed by men, males even portraying female roles, the manner in which this patriarchal theatrical form envisaged and conceived of womankind is fascinating. Certainly the very concept of Noh theatre was indicative of a whole attitude toward the feminine principle, of interest to us as we attempt to unravel the need of the Japanese man to increasingly subvert woman's rights, to force her *behind the scenes*!

That Noh banishes women from performing in the theatre is all the more paradoxical since "poetic dance-monodrama," or Noh, along with Japanese performing arts in general, originated from the mythical conflict between Amaterasu, the Sun Goddess, and her brother. Let us recall that on one occasion he so terrified Amaterasu that she withdrew into a cave in heaven, placed a boulder in front of it, and thus deprived the world of sunlight. (See Introduction.) When the Gods failed to entice Amaterasu out of her isolation, Heavenly-Alarming-Female decided to perform her dance and removed her clothes upon reaching a state of ecstasy. Amaterasu's curiosity was peaked when she heard the Gods burst out laughing. When she peered out of her cave to see what had happened, light was returned to the world.

Noh is a composite art that includes dance, song, and poetic recitation. Shinto dance forms (*kagura*), Buddhist sacred incantations and pantomime (*shushi*), popular songs (*imayo*), and rustic type variety shows accompanied by music (*sangaku*) all served to create Japan's unique theatrical art form.

Taoism, Shintoism, and Buddhism are also basic to Noh theatre. According to the tenets of these sects, the transcendental and not merely the individual sphere must be experienced; the eternal and not only the mortal; the life force (cosmic energy or breath) and not just the concrete deity. For the most part, therefore, Noh plays do not bathe in linear time, but in cyclical schemes.

Archetypal in nature, Noh participates in a mythical world beyond the space/time continuum: only the month of the year or the season is mentioned. Decors and accessories are likewise vague. Never representational, they do not mirror the exterior world, but symbolize an inner spiritual emotional climate. Since most Noh plays have been rewritten countless times throughout the centuries, they purposely lack the stamp of individuality which is characteristic of occidental endeavors. The impersonal and the universal are emphasized by the Japanese Noh writers and performers.

Matsukaze, one of five categories of Noh plays, is defined as a "woman" play. Its imagery is just that. *Matsukaze* ("Wind in the Pines"), written by Kan'ami Kiyotsugu (1333-84) but reinterpreted by his son, Seami Motokiyo (1363-1443), takes place in autumn at Suma Bay, an area just outside of the modern city of Kobe. The imagery reflects a mood of sadness. Nature is preparing to face the difficult winter ahead. The drama tells the simple story of an itinerant Buddhist priest (*waki*, secondary actor who introduces the story), who stops in front of a pine tree. A poem slips from its branches. The priest reads it, and then questions a Villager (*kyogen*, comical clown), who happens to be passing by, about the meaning of the poem. The Villager informs him that it refers to two sisters long since dead: Matsukaze (*shite*, the principal character, a departed human soul), whose name means "Wind in the Pines," and Murasame (*tsure*, a shadow figure), whose name may be translated as "Autumn Rain." The two girls suddenly appear. They are gathering salt, their means of livelihood. The sisters, singing and chanting their litanies, recall the poetry of their memories: they had been loved by and had loved Ariwara no Yukihira (818-893), an exiled poet, scholar, and courtier. Dawn breaks. The image vanishes. The Priest hears only the murmur of the wind in the pine trees.

Water is the prevailing image in *Matsukaze*. Since it is associated with *yin*, the feminine principle, audiences know that the woman's world is to come into focus. A sublimated condition is to be evoked as the blending and cleansing of past experiences is integrated into a present reality through the spiritual encounters between the sisters, the Priest, and their beloved Yukihira. The residue of an earthly relationship has been purified; its essence emerges in the stage proceedings. In the heating and distillation of the emotional process, water is transformed into vapor, into a memory, a misty reawakening, leaving the Priest alone in the phenomenological realm, to pursue his wanderings, enriched by the beauty of the vision he has just experienced.

Matsukaze takes place in the ninth month of the year. Although the information given is specific, it takes on timelessness because it could be any autumn of any year. Autumn thus becomes a symbol for an eternal return, while also mirroring the notion of perpetual death and renewal. Changeless unity in the world of infinite variety becomes the focal point of the drama. Even the stillness of silence can be heard by the viewer as the Priest makes his way on stage: the "mind within the mind," which is the source of all energy, life, and breath, takes hold (Emma Hawkridge, *The Wisdom Tree*, 444).

After the Villager tells the wanderer about Matsukaze and Murasame, their unhappiness in love and their poverty, the priest says a prayer before proceeding on his journey.

> It is sad! Though their bodies are buried in the ground, their names linger on. This lonely pine tree lingers on also, ever green and untouched by autumn, their only memorial. Ah! While I have been chanting sutras and invoking Amida Buddha for their repose, the sun, as always on autumn days, has quickly set. That village at the foot of the mountain is a long way. Perhaps I can spend the night in the fisherman's salt shed (Donald Keene ed., *Twenty Plays of the No Theatre*, 22).

In few words, the Priest gives the impression of infinite distances, continuity of movement, parallel rhythms, and the ever-changing density of existence. Audiences are projected into a fourth dimension where time cannot be taken into account without referring to space, as in Einstein's theory of relativity. The Priest experiences the Buddha Breath and the concomitant vibrations or music of the spheres in a timeless and spaceless dimension, in fluid terms, as an active purification ritual.

The solitary pine tree to which the poem referring to the two sisters was attached, is inhabited by a *kami*. It is immortal and timeless, since it is ever green. The older the tree, the more experience it has had in the phenomenological world and the greater is its universal knowledge. Its agelessness suggests feelings of antiquity as well as wisdom. It stirs pity and longing for bygone days, when life was young and hopes ran high. The Japanese pine tree is very special because its branches are not regular and its trunk is gnarled. Asymmetry and the curves of its trunk set the mood for the events to come. As this force of nature stands strong and proud, it mirrors through contrast the solitude of humankind and the desolation of autumn. To the Japanese, the pine tree represents energy since its needles are always green. Unlike much of nature's greenery, which dies and is reborn yearly, the pine tree remains a perpetually consoling force, always ready to befriend those in need. When drenched in the misty and rainy atmosphere of Suma Bay, it evokes a mood of melancholy; its watery surroundings are reminiscent of tears, while the salt spray with which it is permeated purifies feelings and cleanses sensations.

The green of the pine tree recalls jade, considered by the Japanese (even more so by the Chinese) to possess very special virtues and mystical powers. Pine flowers, it has been stated by alchemists, are as pure as jade. The tree with its branches reaching toward the heavens is filled with *yang*, that is, male energy; it is strong, indestructible, and regal. Because pine trees are, the Japanese believe, endowed with magical and mystical powers, their wood is used frequently in the construction of Buddhist and Shinto temples as well as in the making of ritual instruments. The Priest stops before the pine tree at the outset and conclusion of the drama, after which he will set out on another divine pilgrimage.

The Priest mentions a mountain at the beginning of *Matsukaze*. A vaporous quality invades the scene immediately afterwards: form vanishes; the concrete disperses into its component parts. Mountains, seemingly unshakable and immovable, are in fact an accumulation of infinitesimal particles which reach into the clouds, blending with the universe in slow but forceful stages. Zen priests frequently ascend mountains for purification purposes. On their heights humans rid themselves of dross and experience the purity of the sublimated condition.

The Priest, who sees the mountain in the distance and the city lying at its foot, knows that he is not yet prepared to experience this transcendental force. Like the alchemist who must not pursue his experiments unless he is knowledgeable in both spiritual and physical domains, he understands that purification is necessary before one ascends such a mountain. Otherwise, tragedy may strike. Evil spirits in the mountain could turn the acolyte away from his goal, ensnare him, and then destroy him. The water image, associated with *yin*, takes precedence at this juncture (as a prelude to the sisters' entrance) over the *yang* force implicit in the mountain reference. The Priest kneels down, indicating his withdrawal from the action. The stage grows darker as the feminine element takes over: the woman's world, the dream, the unknown, the land of mystery comes into view.

Dusk descends; a somber note ushers in melancholy. Dreams take on form; fantasies are promoted; the unconscious dominates in preparation for the dream sequence to follow. The stage assistant places a pail of brine on a cart. Murasame enters wearing the *tsure* mask. Matsukaze, having donned her *shite* mask, walks down the bridgeway. Although they are ghosts, both sisters are very real for the Japanese audience.

Matsukaze and Murasame pull the brine cart along the beach. The salt-saturated water of oceans and tears suggests the emotions associated with vast expanses of these entities—sorrow, loneliness, and pain. Water has three main functions: it is the source of life; it paves the way for rebirth; and it is essential to purification rituals. In that water is an undifferentiated mass, it represents virtuality, a world of possibilities which dissolves conflict, immerses differences, and solves problems. Despite its apparent homogeneity and fluidity, it has been considered by alchemists and mystics to be double; and therefore in keeping with the universal forces of *yin* and *yang*. Water may be divided into superior (rain) and inferior (streams, oceans, etc.) principles. The waters mentioned in *Matsukaze* emanate from the heavens, as mist and rain, and from terrestrial regions in the form of Suma Bay, dew, and the vaporous haze on the pine tree.

Salt, from the brine from which the two sisters eke out their meager living, is a condiment, a preservative symbolizing immortality. Rock salt, mined from mountains in blocks has been associated with strength, power, and the clarity of crystal. After the brine has been left to evaporate, it is considered purified of all dross. Salt plays such an important role in Shinto ritual that, in Japan, small piles of salt are placed at entrances of houses to protect their inhabitants and purify the surroundings. It is also scattered in areas where fighting may take place and where funerals or ceremonial functions are held, with the hope of aiding the forces of good and tranquility.

The characteristics attributed to salt are inherent in the personalities of the two sisters: courage, strength, purity, and sensitivity. Psychologically, we may note that just as grains of salt dissolve in water, so the individual ego becomes absorbed into the Self, the person into the universe, the sisters into the collective. For Matsukaze and Murasame, whose lives revolve around water, salt is a life-saving force, not only because it allows them to eat, but also because of its potential for what alchemists term *purificatio* and *sublimatio*.

The moonlight mentioned with the water images plays an important role in *Matsukaze*.

> The waves shatter at our feet
> And even the moonlight wets our sleeves
> With its tears of loneliness.

Symbol of transformation, the moon, as we know, represents biological rhythms and other cyclical states. Its association with tides, water, and rain makes the moon important in vegetation and fertility rituals. An image so frequently evoked by Japanese poets, it represents indirect rather than direct experience: knowledge, passivity, receptivity, and the dream. As it makes its way in the night world or the poet's unconscious, it conjures up spirits and images of bygone days.

For the sisters, the moon evokes the past, those moments of joy now reintegrated into the present. A constant and lonely traveler through the heavens, the moon is a visual replica of their own feelings of isolation and exile. Delivering her soliloquy, Matsukaze looks upon the moon, whose rays are reflected in the water before her, as a companion.

> The autumn winds are sad...
> Salt winds blowing from the mountain pass...
> On the beach, night after night,
> Waves thunder at our door;
> And our long walks to the village
> We've no companion but the moon.

Like the moon receiving the sun's rays, the sisters passively accept their lot.

The mysterious light with which the moon shines suggests a dim, insinuating, shaded world. Never brilliant nor filled with glaring lights, its luminosities are remote, as if they had already been lived. Objects lit by moonlight are not individualized, but blend into the hazy and essentially obscure environment. As the moon, poetized by the Noh dramatist, casts its rays through the branches of the pine tree, feelings are stirred; its soft light falls lovingly on the complex forms which inhabit the stage. For Matsukaze, moonlight encourages a shadowy realm to come into being; ghostly forces—and she is one of them—make their presence known.

Matsukaze tells the audience that no boat can take her across the sea, nor can a dream alter her circumstances. Both she and her sister are compelled to toil alone and in poverty, to weep always "from our hearts' unanswered longing." As she speaks, the members of the Noh chorus echo her pain and reflect her shame of poverty. In so doing, they look down "as if catching a glimpse of their reflections in the water." Unity of theme, gesture, and mood prevails. Reinforcing the atmosphere of melancholy and dishonor are words such as "shrink," "timorous," "withdrawn," "vanish," "stranded," "discarded," "useless," "withered," and "rotting." The chorus repeats "Like our trailing sleeves," as if chanting a litany, thus indicating the disdain they feel for themselves. They are pariahs, isolated in their sorrow. The chorus chants the complaint in musical overtones; then each member of it hides his face in shame.

> The fishermen call out in muffled voices
> At sea, the small boats loom dimly.
> Across the faintly glowing face of the moon
> Flights of wild geese streak,
> And plovers flock below along the shore.
> Fall gales and still sea winds;
> These are things, in such a place,
> That truly belong to autumn.
> But oh, the terrible, lonely nights!

Images of water, night, autumn, and wind underscore the coldness and bleakness of the scene. Nature is divested of its color, warmth, and life. Yet Matsukaze's abject poverty and solitude are desirable states, according to Zen Buddhists. To be homeless and poor is to enter into timelessness, where subject and object become one and dichotomies present in the manifest world are wedded—good and evil, body and soul, spirit and matter, mortal and immortal. Despite Matsukaze's intense pain a sense of belonging to and of participating in nature's cosmic flow imbue her with quietude and a sense of belonging. In contrast to such sensations of metaphysical serenity is the turmoil she describes: the sea washes onto the shore, the winds howl, the trees blow their anguish.

Wind, which represents the breath of the universe or Buddha Breath, is significant, symbolically: it is transparent, vaporous, blends and penetrates the concrete world. Wind stands for the world of intuition, immediacy, and communication. It transcends the world of the senses and enters into the timeless domain of eternity. In contrast to the howling wind, however, is the stillness of the clouds, endowing the scene with a far more frightening and sinister character. Wind arouses tension because of its sound; as the water splashes up against the shore, the tree branches crack. Wind is also a creative force; it deposits fresh attitudes and alters nature's seeming stability, spreading vapor and water spray and dispersing clouds, mist, and matter. It is a powerful instrument, a spiritual agency which points to a world embedded in mystery. As the wind forces the water to wash against the bank, it suggests a purification ritual. The moisture of the air, the previously subdued and delicate atmosphere, is now endowed with power and dynamism; images of softness and tenderness have disappeared as mounting anguish takes hold in cyclical rotations, spreading rain water about in an incessant flow, immersing Matsukaze and her sister in a passionate climate.

The world of mass, solidity, and tangibility is unleashed; concreteness grows soluble. Water and wind pound away as they invade the poetic world of Noh: so nature's waters, in the form of human tears, dissolve problems and compel them to vanish, like salt crystals which disappear in water. A blending into a larger frame of reference arouses fresh views, more comprehensive attitudes, and a certain detachment. The ego no longer dominates the scene; the Self prevails.

Matsukaze's mind has been cleansed of pain and freed from the defilement of the senses. The chorus intones a description of wild geese streaking across "the faintly glowing face of the moon." The geese represent those who are forced to leave their homes, the exiled who weep when departing into lands unknown. In their flight they mourn their past, their land, and the warmth and security of their home life. The shadows of the geese in flight in the waters below prepare for the evocation of memories and dreams.

> While the rough breakers surge and fall,
> And cranes among the reeds
> Fly up with sharp cries.
> The four winds add their wailing.
> How shall we pass the cold night?

The wailing of the cranes adds to the sharp and piercing overtones of the scene. The night is cold, the moon's rays subdued, the atmosphere remote and mysterious.

Nature becomes a giant symphony of howling wind, pounding rain, and the shrill tones of the birds in flight. Even greater desolation, solemnity, and reverence pervade the scene. Matsukaze, who lives in the world of particulars and knows anguish, is encouraged, as she reiterates references to water, wind, and salt, to experience transcendental values. Her world of pain evaporates before the dazzling universe of sounds and reflected lights. The waters of Suma Bay replicate a heart throbbing with pain as it beats against the rocklike harshness of an immutable situation. Primal relationships exist in the collective domain in which Matsukaze has now immersed herself: the world of irreconcilable opposites present in the existential domain diminishes in importance.

Fire, the *yang* force, appears. "The smoke from the salt fires," the chorus says, activates emotions still further. According to Japanese alchemists, fire and water do not fight each other. Although they seem antithetical, each possesses its own sphere of energy and activates rather than subdues the other. Fire, in its redness harmonizing with the moon's rays, symbolizes passion, love, anger, and anguish. Fire is also spirit which burns with intuitive knowledge; it is part of the divine Buddha Essence. For the Shintoist, it expresses the spirit of renewal, rebirth, and purification.

Wood also participates in Matsukaze's drama: "Humble folk hauled wood for salt fires." Burning wood dries out the waters and prepares for further cleaning and whitening, encouraging spirit to reign supreme, unsullied in its crystal clarity. Wood emerges from the earth and in this condition is *yin*; when it grows into a tree, its branches reach out toward the heavens. In this position, it takes on *yang* qualities of ascension and sublimating. Matsukaze mentions "pine groves"; these "stand hazy" and "cut off the moonlight," thus disrupting the smoothness of the vision and adding a note of frustration to the beauty of the scene.

The mood alters once again and "rushing seas" dominate; passion swells; a limitless expanse becomes visible. Matsukaze's lonely cry of anguish cuts the atmosphere. Then she adds, "I have the moon in my pail!" Once a solitary force in an empty sky, the moon has now touched below surfaces, partakes of earthly waters, and becomes contained in a pail. The sense of infinity which had prevailed moments earlier now gives way to emotions of constriction and worldly existence. "The moon above is one; / Below it has two, no three reflections." A union of heaven (one) and earth (two) occurs; and subliminal spheres make three.

The pail is placed on the cart and rides along the road of life: "And on our cart we load the moon!" Like the traveler who wanders during his earthly existence, so the moon traverses the heavens in reflected grandeur, in a pail filled with brine. Yet Matsukaze realizes that life is not all misery as she sits on a low stool while Murasame kneels beside her. This pose represents two women seated in a hut, withdrawn into an inner realm, removed from the external world, as is the moon now circumscribed by the pail.

The Priest comes forward. He sees the sisters and asks them for a night's lodging. Although Matsukaze is humiliated because she considers the hut too wretched to house any stranger, the priest understands her shame but states that "poverty makes no difference" to him. For the Zen Buddhist, to be poor indicates the experiencing of inner riches and higher values—an aloofness amidst a world of multiplicities. The Priest must accept little in life: a hut and a tatami, the sparsest of goods. He is such a being. He lives life in primitive spiritual and physical simplicity. Only in this state can he reenter nature, experiencing its pulsations, breath, and cosmic rhythms. Artifice is nonexistent in this realm.

Matsukaze invites him to enter:

> I see in the moonlight
> One who has renounced the world.
> He will not mind a fisherman's hut,
> With its rough pine pillars and bamboo fence.

The Priest comes in and warms himself next to the "sad fire of rushes." He tells of his encounter with the Villager and the story he heard about the "solitary pine on the beach" associated with the two sisters. At the mention of their names, "Matsukaze and Murasame weep." The Priest is perplexed. The sisters explain that his reference to them

> Filled us with memories which are far too fond.
> Tears of attachment to the world
> Wet our sleeves once again.

The Priest wonders about what he has just heard and seen. They speak, he says, as though they were no longer alive. Together they chant their story and tell him that they have long been dead but yearn to reenter the world of the living. They feel "the sting of regret" for the joy they had once known.

Matsukaze and Murasame relate the story of their beloved Yukihira, who had chosen them above all others to receive his favors. During his three-year stay at Suma Bay, the sisters no longer wore the poor clothes of the salt-maker, but damask robes; no longer did they smell of brine, water, and earth, but of perfumes. Shortly after Yukihira's departure, the two sisters learned of his death. Their world was shattered. He was so young, they chant.

> Pine Wind and Autumn Rain
> Both drenched their sleeves with the tears
> Of hopeless love beyond their station. . . .
> Our love grew rank as wild grasses;
> Tears and love ran wild.
> It was madness that touched us.
> Despite the spring purification,
> Performed in our old robes,
> Despite prayers inscribed on paper streamers.
> The gods refused us their help.
> We were left to melt away
> Like foam on the waves,
> And, in misery, we died.

The hunting cloak and court hat which Yukihira had left the two sisters as a remembrance of his love are concrete objects which recall the past, never allowing the sisters to forget their beloved. They have become objects of worship. The hat, representing the head, spirit, and wisdom—the ultimate goals in the initiatory quest—radiates life, thought, ideas, and memories. When donned by Matsukaze, the cloak hides the inner being, covers emotion, acts as a screen which cuts off the outer world, masks poverty and pain, and instills sensations of dignity, wealth, and power. As Matsukaze holds the keepsakes, however, her pain deepens. She stands utterly still, as if she were in a trance, and then cradles the cloak in her arms, holding it tightly. Wherever she turns, she weeps her agony.

The stage assistant removes her robe and places the cloak and hat on her. Endowed with a new identity, she is overcome with joy. She stares at the pine tree. From its branches she hears her beloved call to her and she goes to him. Murasame tries to break her fantasy by instilling a harsh note of reality: Matsukaze has gone mad. It is not Yukihira who is calling to her but a pine tree, she tells her sister. Yukihira will never return. As Matsukaze nevertheless continues her reverie, Murasame weeps, kneeling before the flute player. Her sobs are echoed in the soft tones of the instrument. Matsukaze walks toward the first pine tree on the bridgeway, then returns to the center of the stage and begins her dance. She speaks to the pine tree, to the mountain, to the distant lands; she talks of the "curving Suma shore" where her "dear prince" had once lived. Tenderly, she tells of her love and "circles the tree" as she expresses her sorrow.

> Through the frenzied night
> We have come to you
> In a dream of deluded passion.

Matsukaze "presses her palms together in supplication" and retreats from the stage as the waves recede from the bank and the wind blows offshore.

> Your dream is over. Day has come.
> Last night you heard the autumn rain;
> This morning all that is left
> Is the wind in the pines,
> The wind in the pines.

The beauty of the concluding image remains ever alive within the viewer's mind and psyche: the washing away of pain through the reenactment of an awakening and burgeoning love. The recollection of a great passion has now distilled and crystallized, experienced in harmony with a pulsating universe.

Noh drama reflects Zen-Buddhist calmness of mind and oneness with nature; it is a manifestation of the Shintoist's beliefs which endow inanimate objects with life, thereby enlarging the scope and the depth of the dramatic spectacle. The intensity of its sustained emotion moves audiences to tears; its sublimated passion, with its exquisitely nuanced poetry and its cosmic purpose and design also impacts powerfully on the viewer. Divested of personal elements, the collective spheres of love, rage, and jealousy are instrumental in the creation of this dazzlingly rich, yet refined and ceremonious art form.

Matsukaze's image of woman is memorable!

Chapter 4

The Arts and "The Floating World" in the Edo Period: 1603-1867

Although women endured as much repression during the Tokugawa Shogunate or Edo period as during the earlier Ashikaga Shogunate, a few skilled ones succeeded, with increasing support from their families, in indulging their creative bent. Some became poets and painters; others *geishas*, courtesans, or prostitutes. The pleasure quarter where congregated the demimonde as well as actors, merchants, samurai, and those seeking entertainment was called the "floating world" (*ukiyo*) because of its instability. The beauties attracted to this area were immortalized by such artists as Utamaro and Haranobu in the great wood-block prints (*ukiyo-e*) for which Japan was known the world over.

Politically, the climate was tightening, as efforts were made to centralize Japan even further. To this end, Oda Nobunaga, a paternalistic feudal lord (*daimyo*) who ruled over three provinces in central Japan, seized Kyoto (1568), the capital, thus strengthening his rule. To insure his power, he reduced the military power of the monasteries and the temple-castle of the True Pure Land Sect in Osaka. After his assassination by one of his vassals (1582), his finest general, Hideyoshi Toyotomi, fearing deceit on the part of rivals, ordered that the remaining members of the Oda family be killed and that those who had rebelled against his power be crushed. Political unity was achieved by the year 1591 and peace reigned in Japan following more than three hundred years of continuous civil war.

On the international scene, however, Hideyoshi sought to conquer China by gaining access to it through Korea. The Koreans resisted, and fierce fighting ensued. Hideyoshi's death in

1598 saw the end of his war plans. One of his vassals, Tokugawa Ieyasu, assumed power after killing the remaining members of Hideyoshi's family and suppressing all sources of rivalry. What was the cost of the ensuing political stability? Isolation, repression, the rule of an autocratic, military, medieval, and feudal dictator, and the growth of a powerful brand of nationalism (Edwin O. Reischauer, *Japan Past and Present*, 80-107).

To maintain a rigid hold on his people even while preventing any possible military coup, Hideyoshi limited *daimyos'* repair of their castles. He also prevented the secretion of arms and soldiers on their estates. Anyone entering the city of Edo (the future Tokyo), moreover, was searched to insure that no arms were being smuggled into the city. When a *daimyo* returned to his country estate, his wife and sons were kept hostage in Edo. Careful counts of women leaving the city were made in order to prevent hostages from fleeing (Reischauer, 83).

* * *

The cloistering of upper class women during the Ashikaga Shogunate continued during the Edo Period. Their education, however, was even more severely curtailed. Moral instruction for the living out of a woman's life was obligatory. One of the main sources from which the Japanese drew their new role model was the *Series of Biographies of Women*, written by a Chinese lady during the Han dynasty (202 B.C.E.-220 C.E.). More than one thousand books on woman's morality were printed in Japan during the eighteenth century, the most important of these being Kaibara Ekken's (1631-1714) *Great Learning for Women*. Indeed, it became the Bible of every household. Unlike the Chinese tracts which were written by women, the Japanese books of morality were authored by men who were generally uninterested in enhancing the welfare of the female sex. Their intent was rather to see that women kept their places; that they remained basically uneducated in order to be able to concentrate on obeying their husbands and tending to household duties. Such dicta were in keeping with the strict Neo-Confucian ethic.

Had the image of woman altered? One may answer both positively and negatively. Due to a renaissance of Neo-Confucianism, girls were taught from their earliest ages that they were inferior to men and, therefore, must limit their pursuits to home, children, and conformity to the man's wishes. Women, generally speaking, had to prove their extreme virtue in the clan-oriented Edo environment. They were kept under strict surveillance with regard to reading material. *The Tale of Genji* and other classical narrative and poetic works were recommended by some educators, while others felt that such works were immoral and, therefore, not favored. Girls and boys were educated in the same manner until the age of seven, after which they were separated, and text choices for girls were then limited to works on manners and comportment. From ten years of age, girls were forbidden to leave their homes, occupying their time learning whatever was necessary for the proper running of a household: sewing, weaving, and arithmetic (Patricia Fister, *Japanese Women Artists. 1600-1900*, 12).

By the end of the eighteenth century, education for the less affluent was extended to instruction in reading, writing, and arithmetic, and certain trades as well. In the private schools for wealthier classes open to women, exposure to the outside world began: women read stories about love and sexual exploits, and learned of forbidden mysteries. Reading became an exciting and enticing pastime for both the school girl and the cloistered young lady—a means of escape into a world of fantasy (Fister, 12).

Although upper class samurai, *daimyo*, and court noblewomen were restricted to the inner quarter of their homes, palaces, or castles, enjoying even less freedom than their sisters from merchant classes, they nevertheless spent considerable time learning various arts. Many wrote poetry and were well-trained in calligraphy. As in Heian times, it was believed that these two arts enhanced a woman's allure. It also facilitated the obtaining of a post as lady-in-waiting in the imperial palace—a position for which samurai women vied. To be attached to the court was not only prestigious, but strengthened the possibilities of better, more economically rewarding marriages.

Because upper class samurai, *daimyo*, and court ladies had a plethora of servants to tend to household problems, they had leisure hours at their disposal, many of which were devoted to enhancing their wardrobes, considered to be a reflection of their husband's affluence and power. The ladies chose the right clothes and color combinations to wear at specific ceremonial functions and studied the fashions of the day. When not occupied in fulfilling official duties, they entertained themselves by playing games such as cards, go, and shogi; identifying incense; and guessing the author of a verse drawn from one hundred classical Japanese poets. Such pastimes sharpened their memory. Women were allowed to attend Noh plays if these were performed in the palace, castle, or court (Fister, 15). Despite strides made in certain professions, women were still barred from performing in Noh.

The more realistic, colorful, and emotional Kabuki—a drama form which appealed to the needs and tastes of the newly powerful merchant class—has remained popular ever since its inception in the mid-seventeenth century. It is far more accessible and appealing than the aristocratic Noh, with its large revolving stage on which so many violent scenes are enacted in a stylized manner around historical and/or domestic dramas. Like Noh, from which many of its elements derived, it is an eclectic art, encompassing song and dance, and banishing women from its domain.

More was expected of the samurai wife than of the court noblewoman. While both owed complete obedience to their husbands, the samurai wife was expected to carry out her husband's ideals and concepts of honor and courage. Women were provided with pocket daggers and were expected to use them in defense of their chastity or to commit suicide if the occasion warranted it. Accordingly, they were taught how to cut their throats after having tied their legs together so that their dead bodies would be found composed and in the proper position. If a woman overheard someone plotting to kill her husband, she frequently took his place, offering to die for him, thereby upholding the *bushido* ("the way of the warrior") code of ethics. Despite the fact that the *daimyo* and samurai looked down upon the merchant class, they nevertheless repleted their fortunes by arranging marriages for their progeny with the daughters of wealthy entrepreneurs (Geoffrey Parrender, *Sex in the World's Religions*, 116).

The rising new scholarly movement of "national learning" (*kokugaku*) sought to revive the ideology and values of a "purer" and more "Japanese" past through the study of ancient historical and literary texts. Kamo no Mabuchi (1697-1769) rescued from the past an anthology of Japanese poetry compiled in the eighth century, the *Manyoshu*, going so far as to insert anti-Confucian sentiments into the work. It was he who encouraged the classical scholar and literary theorist, Motoori Norinaga (1730-1801), to start a philological exegesis of Japan's earliest historical chronicle, the *Kojiki* (*Record of Ancient Things*)—a compilation of myths, legends, songs, clan genealogies, and historical accounts. What was learned and promulgated was the important role played by women in the formation of Japan. Amaterasu had been the progenitrix of the Imperial line, and many rulers prior to and during the Nara period had been women. The *kokugaku* movement encouraged women to study and to indulge their creative bent as painters and as composers of *waka*. It also promoted the function of the shamanesses, helping them reaffirm their dwindling places in Shinto ceremonies.

Shinto Shamanesses

In a land dominated for so many hundreds of years by Buddhism and Neo-Confucianism, Japan's growing nationalism gave rise to an increase in the power of Shinto. It also accounted in part for a concerted isolationism during the Edo Period. Shinto scholars busied themselves looking toward Japan's glorious past, taking pride in the study of their nation's beginnings. The revival and dissemination of the myths and legends narrated in the *Kojiki* and the *Nihongi* (*Chronicles of Japan*), which emphasized the glories of those ancient centuries, convinced the Japanese of their superiority over the Chinese.

With the growing importance of Shinto sects, some of which were founded by women, prominence was given to faith-healing. The Tenrikyo ("Teaching of the Heavenly Truth"), for example, was founded by a peasant woman, Nakayama Miki (1798-1887). After years of suffering, she fell into a trance, experienced moments of possession and developed, so it has been claimed, healing powers. In 1869, she started writing a long poem of 1711 verses, *Ofudesaki*, which, she said, came to her automatically—an example of what twentieth-century Surrealists term "automatic writing." The *Ofudesaki* became part of her sect's scriptures (Parrender, 118).

Ever since ancient times, shamanesses had served at Shinto shrines, ministering sometimes as a medium (*miko*) and interpreting the will of the gods and/or of their ancestors. The *miko* was not only invited to Shinto shrines to perform a service as mediator between heaven and earth, but was summoned to imperial courts, towns, and villages to reveal the wishes of the Deities as well as to promulgate the rules and regulations for certain ceremonies. Nor was sex a deterrent to their powers. On the contrary, it was an enhancing factor. There were, nevertheless, elements in the government and society who sought to temper the activities of the *miko*. But they were unsuccessful.

"The Floating World"

Many of the famous courtesans of the period congregating in the "floating world" (*ukiyo*), were portrayed by artists working in the newly-developed industry of wood-block prints (*ukiyo-e*). The technique allowed many hundreds of copies of one picture to be reproduced, sold, and admired throughout Japan—and the world. Other industries involving women's ware, such as exquisite silks, brocades, and weaving, grew in importance and, because of the quantities sold, their prices became affordable to the masses.

It must be noted that artists of the Edo Period portrayed women's bodies differently than had medieval artists. The ideal body in centuries gone by, generally speaking, was well rounded, strong, full-breasted, and with relatively heavy hips. Women's childbearing activities were most important to the society of the time. By the seventeenth century, standards had altered. In genre wood-block prints, women were delineated as thin, at times wan, with oval rather than well-rounded faces.

Although the Edo period was both politically and socially repressive for women, they did sell their talents at the flourishing amusement centers. Edo enjoyed such economic prosperity and such an outflow of cultural activities that prostitutes (*joro*) were attracted to this city from all over Japan. A petition was circulated asking authorities for the permission—granted in 1618—to establish a regular quarter for prostitution. The section of the city, characterized by its many weeds and rushes, was given the name of *Yoshiwara* (moor of rushes). The quarter's director, Shoji Jinyemen, called the "prince of prostitutes," oversaw the clearing of the land, the building of the brothels, and the smooth functioning of the complex in less than two years.

Regulations for prostitutes and for brothels were as follows:

1. No prostitute could carry on her trade outside of the special area allotted, nor could prostitutes go from one house to another.
2. A guest was not allowed to remain in a brothel for more than twenty-four hours.

3. Prostitutes' clothes must be dyed and not adorned with gold embroidery.
4. Brothels should not look imposing. Their inhabitants must perform whatever municipal duties that are expected of them.
5. People of a suspicious nature frequenting the quarter must be reported to the authorities (Lee Alexander Stone, *The Story of Phallicism*, 598-601).

After the fire of 1656, when Edo was virtually burned to the ground, a larger and different area of the city was awarded to the houses of prostitution. In order to attract clientele, children performed dances outside of some brothels. By 1769, singers, whose functions included more than singing (*geiko*) had replaced the children who were, in turn, succeeded by geishas (*gei*, performing arts) (Stone, 602).

It was common practice to sell women into the *Yoshiwara*, using registry offices (*jogen*) to effect the purchase. Agents from these offices were sent to the country to buy, borrow, or steal women and girls, who were then taken back to Edo. In order to prevent them from running away, their clothes were removed from their rooms at night. If girls were purchased, their indenture papers were signed by the parents, the registry office receiving a ten percent commission for the transaction. They were permitted to practice their trade until the age of twenty-five, although frequently they remained another two years (Stone, 604).

Prostitutes in brothels usually had two rooms at their disposal, while in the luxurious houses, they sometimes had three. They would decorate their living room with utmost care, since it was there that their guests were received. In cheaper brothels, prostitutes lived together in a common room, the private apartments being reserved for the guests. If a prostitute became ill, she was relegated to a small dark room, far from any of the clients. If she were dying, she was returned to her parents. It was not uncommon for the owner or director of a brothel to allow a dead prostitute to be cast into a common pit. Double suicides of the prostitute and her client or patron were recorded in the eighteenth century. As a deterrent to such a practice, some brothel-keepers exposed the dead bodies of the lovers in the streets, like animals. Only later were they buried. Since it was believed that animals had no ghosts, and therefore no spirits which could return to earth or to whom one could pray, those who had taken their own lives were bound hand and foot, their bodies wrapped in matting, and then thrown into a common grave.

Although they bore exquisitely poetical names—Evening Mist, Filmy Cloud, Garden of Flowers, River of Song—prostitutes lived a usually difficult life. Brothels, too, were endowed with poetic names, to enhance their allure: House of the Ten Thousand Plums, House of the Myriad Flowers, House of the Dragon Cape, etc.

Evidently Edo's *Yoshiwara* district filled a need in Japanese males; otherwise it would not have been so popular. The man's relationship with his wife—a mother figure and the dominant factor in the household—was so painfully unsatisfactory that he sought entertainment and release outside the family structure, both with prostitutes and geishas.

The concept of the geisha was an outgrowth of Tokugawa society. It resulted from centuries of traditional courtesans and dancing girls making up the world of the aristocracy and then, increasingly, sought by the growing business class man and warrior-aristocrats. The lot of the geisha, who was trained in the arts of singing, dancing, conversation, story telling, and *samisen* (a three-string, plucked chordophone), was different from that of the licensed prostitute. Parents, to increase their income, frequently arranged to have their little girls taken into geisha houses or adopted by the owners of these establishments, where they would be taught the prescribed arts. Although a client might be deeply attracted to the beauty, charm, and sensual proclivities of these highly trained women, only after serious courting according to prescribed rules could the man hope to have sexual intercourse with them. Nor was it infrequent for the geisha to require a contract to be signed by her lover, which established the period of time she would be his mistress. In some cases, men married their geishas. Whether the geisha sang, danced, gestured, or indulged in clever talk, her demeanor was suggestive and enticing, offering the man everything he could not find at home—everything his suppressed and enslaved wife was forbidden to give him. Moral laxity, the accepted system of concubinage, and the legal recognition of children born out of wedlock, presented no problem in Japanese society, as long as the wife agreed to such double standards (Stone, 606).

Geishas were religiously inclined, praying to their God, Inari. Dressed in colorful kimonos, they went to their temples to worship Him on the first and fifteenth day of every month.

Inari, the God of rice in ancient times, by the eleventh century was identified with the Fox God, perpetrator of both good and evil. Because foxes were believed to have been endowed with supernatural powers, to them were ascribed infinite vision and ability to hear everything that was said or even thought on both human and inhuman levels. They also had the power to transform themselves into beautiful women as well as other beings. The geisha looked upon Inari as a beneficent power, able to comfort her in her sorrow, rejoice with her in joy, heal her in her illnesses, and answer her prayers for a child (F. Hadland Davis, *Myths and Legends of Japan*, 93).

Although rich geishas sometimes married, poor ones, if they had daughters, trained them in their profession, as "art persons," then sold them to geisha houses in other towns, after which they might never see them again.

The Arts

Pictorial, literary, and musical arts were inspired by the "Floating World"—the name used to describe the dazzlingly heady but unstable state enjoyed in the company of the prostitute. Although "Floating World" was an ancient term, applied in Heian times to the Buddhist's "sorrowful world"—that is, the earthly world of illusion—in the late seventeenth century the pun on *sorrowful* (*uki*), and (*uki*) *floating*, altered its meaning. The new meaning for the word *ukiyo* referred henceforth to brothels and licensed amusement areas frequented by the increasing urban society. Although such works as *The Ukiyo Bathhouse* or *The Ukiyo Barbershop* attempted to teach Japanese men a Buddhist and Confucian sense of restraint and control over their sexual desires, they had little effect on their actions (*Sources*, 434). The "Floating World" has been depicted as follows:

> Living only for the moment, turning our full attention to the pleasures of the moon, sun, the cherry blossoms and the maple leaves, singing songs, drinking wine, and diverting ourselves just in floating, floating, caring not a whit for the pauperism staring us in the face, refusing to be disheartened, like a gourd floating alone with the river current: this is what we call *the floating world* (*ukiyo*) (Joan Stanley-Baker, *Japanese Art*, 186. Quoted from Asai Ryo Ryoi, *Tales of the Floating World*).

Prostitutes and geishas were increasingly portrayed by artists such as Hishikawa Moronobu, Suzuki Harunobu, Kitagawa Utamaro, and others. Many wood-block prints were *shunga* ("spring pictures")—another name for describing explicit erotic art. Artists, such as Utamaro, for example, sought out all types of women to paint, not merely for provocative reasons, but also to study them in their daily activities and environment and to arrest the joys and pathos of their lives. Dressed or undressed, in the act of making love, playing shuttlecock, looking at blossoming flowers, sitting by the river, gazing at the moon, drinking sake, going to the temple or to the theater, women were fertile field for Utamaro's genius.

Nor did he neglect to draw the homebody as she cooked, sewed, cleaned, or reared silkworms. Utamaro's *shunga* are well known: his series of twelve color prints, *The Poem-Pillow Picture Book*, are among the most erotic of *ukiyo-e*.

Popular writers emphasized both sex and money in their works. Ihara Saikaku (1642-93), in his novel *The Man who Spent his Life at Love-making* considered by some to be pornographic, created a hero who journeyed around Japan making love to thousands of women and hundreds of boys. The theme of homosexuality is fleshed out in Saikaku's *The Great Mirror of Manly Love*. Buddhist temples and the close relation between master and disciple encouraged homosexuality, as did the comportment of members of the samurai class who gave themselves to the economically and politically well-placed older members in exchange for their protection. In *Five Amorous Women*, Saikaku depicted the goings-on in teahouses, bathhouses, brothels, and theatres. His depiction of the perfect woman runs as follows:

> ... he would like to hold in his arms a living replica made from [the woman in the picture he held in his hands. She was] ... from fifteen to eighteen years of age. Her face, which had an up-to-date look, was roundish and of the color of pale cherry blossoms. Her features were flawless: the eyes, by his wish, were not narrow; the thick brows did not grow too close together; the nose was straight; the mouth was small with regular, white teeth; and the long ears, which had delicate rims, stood away from the head so that one could see through to the roots. Her hair at the forehead grew naturally and with no trace of artificiality. The back hair fell over her downless slender neck. Her fingers were pliant and long with thin nails. Her feet could not have had the breadth of eight copper coins; the big

toes curled upwards and the soles were translucently delicate. Her body was above average in size. The hips were firm and not fleshy, the buttocks full. Elegant in movement and in dress, her bearing possessed both dignity and gentleness. She excelled in the arts required of women, and was ignorant of nothing. There was not a single mole on her entire body. (*Sources*, I, 435).

Pictorial eroticism—scenes of sexual intercourse in various positions—is featured in a thirteenth-century Japanese *Scroll of Initiation*, believed to be a copy of a tenth-century Chinese scroll. One of the most significant differences between the Japanese drawings and their Chinese and Indian predecessors is that the former depict men with grotesquely enlarged genitals—not caricatures, as were the slightly inflated sex organs with which Chinese and Indian artists endowed their men, but as large fantasy images. Was it, perhaps, wishful thinking?

Creative Women in "The Floating World"

Some courtesans and prostitutes revealed unusual skills in the arts as *waka* poets and as designers of woodblock prints. In one of Torii Kiyonobu's (d. 1729) works of art, she depicted a courtesan painting a scene of willows along a river bank while her admiring patron observed her.

Ohashi was one of the best known eighteenth-century courtesan poets. She had been sold to a brothel by her samurai family, which had fallen onto hard times. Beautiful, intelligent, trained in poetry, music, the tea ceremony, and incense identification, she continued her studies in Kyoto while continuing to work in the brothel. There, Ohashi composed *waka*, which she would offer to some of her visitors who received them with great pleasure. In time, the humiliation of having to endure a trade she despised worked on Ohashi's psyche. No medication could cure her illness. To a visitor's question why she was so unhappy, she replied that she hated her life, at which he advised her to follow the Buddhist path and detach herself from the floating world. Ohashi did just that: one day, during a terrifying thunderstorm, rather than hide as she was wont, she faced the flashes of lightning and pounding noises. After a huge thunder clap, she felt she had experienced a state of enlightenment. Leaving the floating world, she devoted herself to the study of

Zen, and married a man who loved to chant music from Noh drama. Gradually her interest in religion grew; after asking her husband for a divorce, to which he agreed, she became a nun (Fister, 69-71).

Ohashi's calligraphed *waka*, written, as was the style, on decorated paper purchased in Kyoto, was placed asymmetrically and diagonally over a delicate, light-blue, almost make-believe background. The contrasting of her heavily and lightly inked characters against such a pale background created both a dramatic and an ethereal effect. The contrasts activated dynamic interaction between the color tones, thereby setting up energetic patternings. Such juxtapositions triggered an emotive mood, as attested to in Ohashi's *Waka on Decorated Paper*, which delineated the pain of lovers upon hearing the chirping of an early morning bird—a metaphor and prelude to their imminent separation (Fister, 69-71).

> On the morning after,
> Let your parting
> Be like a dream
> I cannot forget
> The wretched cry of the bird (Fister, 76).

Compelling, yet disciplined and reserved, Ohashi's simple verse reveals the complex feelings associated with farewells. The metaphors she uses—the "dream" and "cry of the bird"—suggest the involvement of both the earthly and the spiritual realms. The use of the adjective "wretched" reveals the wrenching nature as well as the affliction and dejection of severance of emotional bonds, while the "morning after" suggests the cyclicality of separation, similar to a recurring dream.

In a *haiku* (5-7-5 syllable pattern), Ohashi conveys the Buddhist sense of emptiness by using the most prosaic terms, not to create a mood of negativity, but rather one of nonediscrimination: a state divested of all tension, yielding pure nothingness.

> Whether I sit or lie
> My empty mosquito net
> Is too large (Kenneth Rexroth and Ikuko Atsumi, *The Burning Heart*, 55).

At this stage of the author's life, she has reached beyond the world of sensation into one of *egolessness*. The Taoists refer to this stage as *emptiness*, equivalent to *ch'i*—that is, to an impalpable, unknowable, yet existing sphere in the cosmos. Like *pneuma*, it transcends all feeling; it purges all thought.

Poetry and Paintings

Although many women must have painted and written poetry during the Edo period, few of their works are extant and still fewer names of their authors remain. Only the scantiest biographical information concerning these creative women is available.

Chine-jo, living in the late seventeenth century, was the sister of Kyorai, considered one of the ten finest disciples of the lonely wanderer and explorer, Basho (1644-1694). Looked upon as the greatest of *haiku* poets, as well as the most influential, Basho's faith in the saving power of poetry is implicit in his *Records of a Travel-Worn Satchel* (1687-88). His influence on Chine-jo, whether overt or covert, seems marked, judging by the following poem by her hand.

> The fireflies' light.
> How easily it goes on
> How easily it goes out again (Rexroth and Atsumi, 52).

As fireflies pass through the air, they are cut off from the dross of earthly preoccupations and attachments. Like intuition, the light emanating from a firefly is transient, momentary, vibrating, not as steady as is moonlight. Yet, even their flashing luminosities increase one's perceptions and permit the experience of a certain fleeting reality, as aloof and unsteady as life itself. Although what is born is extinguished, its ephemeral presence is meaningful for the onlooker—who is also a participant in this cosmic process.

Enomoto Seifu-jo (1731-1814), a *haiku* poet, also approaches her work from a mystical point of view. Her appreciation of what others might consider routine and banal is evident in the following *haiku*.

> Everyone is asleep
> There is nothing to come between
> the moon and me (Rexroth and Atsumi, 56).

"Asleep" implies a divestiture of the rational sphere, of consciousness, of the thought world, while at the same time a receptivity to the subliminal spheres—to ancestral images lying inchoate in the collective unconscious. As the moon penetrates the mind of the sleeper during this quiescent period, its tender and mellow rays cast their hazy glow on the vaporous world which the sleeper enjoys. By sharing the sleeper's personal and collective memories—experienced from time immemorial—one glimpses a domain almost always inaccessible to personal awareness.

Teahouse Poets

Teahouses, which became popular in Japan during the Edo period, not only offered their patrons the wonderful brew which had been brought to Japan from China in the twelfth-century, but were highly prized as meeting places for poets. Many teahouses were managed or owned by women. Tea-drinking, initially introduced to China by the Zen teacher, Eisai (1145-1215), was turned into an art by Sen no Rikyu (1521-91). During periods of political or social stress, warriors and merchants of all classes found it particularly appealing and relaxing to withdraw to the tearoom, there to experience the quietism of the moment. For many, the *spirit of the tea* was conducive to feelings of Emptiness sought for and known to Zen philosophers: that instant when the differentiated world is transcended and a domain of infinite possibilities is opened to them (Daisetz T. Suzuki, *Zen and Japanese Culture*, 300).

The construction of the teahouses according to certain regulations assured the creation of the proper mood for the client. They were usually built in an asymmetrical or "one corner" style, typical of Japanese art. The ceilings were relatively low and the walls without decorations, except for a *kakemono* (a hanging scroll painting or calligraphic work) hung in front of a vase which had a single flower bud. The papered windows allowed only a soft light to penetrate the tearoom. The fragrance emitted from the incense, the perfume of the wooden walls, and the sound of the gentle outdoor breezes, blended with the boiling water in the "singing" kettle which had been placed over the brazier. The atmosphere within permitted a tranquil and meditative condition to prevail—the transcendentalism of Zen (Suzuki, 301).

Open-air teahouses were also popular. The Matsuya, for example, managed by the poetess Kaji in Kyoto, was the gathering place of poets and scholars. Little is known of her life except that she was given a fine education and that her *haiku* and *waka* were admired by some of the outstanding poets of her day. Her popularity and fame were such that Utagawa Kuniyoshi included portraits of her in his *Stories of Wise and Strong Women* (1841-42).

Kaji composed her poems in response to her customers' demand for souvenirs. She would brush these onto golden brown sheets of paper on which flowering plants had already been painted in gold. Such was the stunning background of her *waka*, *Waiting for Spring Blossoms*:

> As I wait,
> Even in darkness
> Of my dreams
> There are visions of the
> Cherry blossoms at Katano no mino (Fister, 78).

The tranquility encapsulating Kaji's verbal visualization bespeaks an unconscious yearning for love. As daylight is superseded by the blackness of night, and the incense burner still emits its fragrance, serenity permeates the atmosphere, conjuring up visions and dreams. The image of cherry blossoms, associated with love and with women's lips, is also one of nature's recurring motifs: the festival of rebirth. As if by some sleight of hand, the everyday world seems to vanish during the dream, giving way to a glimpse of eternity.

Yuri (1694-1764), Kaji's adopted daughter, followed in her mother's footsteps. She managed the Matsuya teahouse and authored fine *waka* in her leisure moments upon her customers' request for souvenirs. Unlike her mother, Yuri lived in happiness with the samurai, Tokuyama, bearing him a daughter, Machi. After ten years of life together, Tokuyama was called upon to take over his family's leadership. Although he wished to take Yuri and their daughter to live with him, she declined, aware of their differing social status and the problems that might arise from such a disparity. Yuri spent the rest of her years in Kyoto directing her Matsuya, writing poetry, and providing for her daughter's education (Fister, 73-75).

The following *Waka Dedicated to Reizei Tamemura* was written by Yuri in honor of her poetry teacher, the court-noble Reizei Tamemura. He not only had been her guide and inspiration, but had given her the courage to pursue her creative talents.

> Too humble a gift
> Is this jadelike arrowroot's
> Flower coronet—
> Yet for how many autumns
> Have I made this offering? (Fister, 80).

Unlike other *waka* poets, Yuri spreads her calligraphed verse over an entire page. Because her brushwork is more spatially set out, it seems freer, as if floating about or gently propelled, resulting in a rippling effect. The viewer is awakened to a sense of vastness as well as aloneness. The antithetical nature of the cosmos invites Juri to juxtapose precious "jade" with the "arrowroot"—a common starch-yielding tropical plant. Nevertheless, the arrowroot has its ornamental and regal side; it is a crown celebrating greatness. So, Yuri makes this offering in her *waka* to the great art of the poet Reizei Tamemura.

Forming a veritable dynasty of poets, Machi, like her grandmother and mother, also practiced the verbal art, choosing the name of Ike Gyokuran (1727-1784). Although she inherited the Matsuya after her mother's death, it had perhaps outlived its popularity, for by 1802 it had vanished.

Poet/Painters

Poetry and painting for many women artists during the Edo period was but a single art. The works of Ono Ozu and Ryonen Genso offer examples of just such a fusion.

Ono Ozu (1559-1631)

Brought up by attendants on the domain of General Oda Nobunaga (1534-82), Ono Ozu was later sent to Kyoto to study painting, calligraphy, music (wind and string instruments), chanting (*joruri*), and *waka*. That she also studied the tea ceremony added to her list of accomplishments (Fister, 26-7).

Whether she was the concubine of or attendant to the General Toyotomi Hideyoshi (1536-1598) is not known. That she married Shiokawa Shima no Kami, a retainer of the Toyotomi family, is accepted by most scholars. Because of her husband's alcoholism, Ono Ozu was granted a divorce, after which she earned her living tutoring affluent and highly placed noble ladies (Fister, 26).

Ozu's gifts as poet and calligrapher attracted the attention of the shogun, Tokugawa Ieyasu (1542-1616), who engaged her to teach these arts to both his wife and daughter. Another Tokugawa shogun, Hidetada, asked her to paint his father's portrait. She served other shoguns and their families, becoming the prototype of the high-ranking and cultivated woman.

Her paintings with their calligraphic inscriptions are reminiscent, thematically, of the works of literary men as well as those of Zen monks. One of Ozu's inked hanging scrolls features Hotei, the God of Laughter and Contentment. He is depicted in a traditional manner of whimsicality and playfulness. His large linen bag (*ho-tei*), legend tells us, contains all sorts of Precious Things. The child beside him in the painting gleefully touches the bag with both hands, hoping to peer into it and discover some treasures inside. Humor and tenderness mark Ozu's bold ink lines, while the many gradations from dark to light tints enhance an inherent spirit of banter, drollery and wit. The calligraphed verse above the figures reads as follows:

> Not knowing of
> "Goodness" or "evil,"
> The young child
> Is taken as a companion
> By this pure spirit (Fister, 29).

The "young child" in the poem and painting, living close to nature, has never been exposed to the world's conflictual polarities; he cannot yet distinguish between himself, living in the empirical domain, and Hotei, who as Divinity exists in a transcendent realm. Unaware of the dichotomies between good and evil, he exists in a universal sphere—the *All*. "This pure spirit," referring to the merry-making God, enjoys lighthearted fun and frolic as he looks at the little boy with a twinkle in his eye.

Ozu's calligraphed curved lines above the painting, with their freshly inked internal spirals and elongated strands inscribed with a finely pointed brush, inject a naive dynamism to the poem. It is as if the little boy were growing increasingly excited at the prospect of opening the God's bag of treasures. As Ozu's lines swing and curve in rapid successions a sense of fluidity, openness, and elegance add to the quality of the drawing.

Ozu's other works include calligraphic inscriptions with portraits: one of Daruma, an Indian sage associated with meditative Zen and the Zen tea drinking ceremony; another featuring Kakinomoto Hitomaro, one of Japan's early and greatest poets, who served as poet laureate during the reigns of Empress Jito (686-697) and Emperor Mommu (697-707); still another depicts the great poet Kitano Tenjin, transformed into the God of poetry and art, best known under the name of Sugawara Michizane (845-903), and celebrated at Shinto shrines. So outstanding were Ozu's verbal patternings that her new calligraphed style was given her name: *Ozu ryu* (Fister, 29).

Ryonen Genso (1646-1711).

Known for her beauty and her poetry as well as for her portraits of well-known Zen abbots, Ryonen Genso is also admired for her spiritual idealism. In one of the rare extant examples of her calligraphed works, she tells of her youth, her sensitivity to nature, and her deep commitment to Zen Buddhism.

> When I was young I served Yoshinokimi, the granddaughter of Tofukumon'in, a disciple of the imperial temple Hokyuoji. Recently she passed away; although I know that this is the law of nature, the transience of the world struck me deeply and I became a nun. I cut my hair and dyed my robes black, and went on a pilgrimage to Edo. There I had an audience with the monk Hakuo of the Obaku Zen sect. I recounted to him such things as my deep devotion to Buddhism since childhood, but Hakuo replied that although he could see my sincere intentions, I could not escape my womanly appearance. Therefore I heated up an iron and held it against my face, and then wrote as my brush led me.
>
> Formerly to amuse myself at court I would burn orchid incense;
> Now to enter the Zen life I burn my own face.
> The four seasons pass by naturally like this,
> But I don't know who this is amidst the change (Fister, 30).

Evident in Ryonen's autobiographical statement is her need to love and be loved. Her view of death as a deprivation and painful loss suggests the intensity of her inner struggle to come to grips with her Zen Buddhist training. To attain a state of detachment as Ryonen seems to have experienced permits her to glimpse "the absolute perfection of Reality, from which we all come and to which we all return and in which we all are; a world of multitudes passes away and comes again, but what is at the back of it always retains its perfect beauty unchangingly" (Suzuki, 82).

Because of Ryonen's incredible will and sense of discipline, she attempted to rise above the feeling world to which she felt enslaved. The sacrifice of her most precious feminine attributes was the way she chose to effect a spiritualization of her mundane life: not only did she cut her hair in order to be acceptable as a student of Zen Buddhism, but she uglified her face by holding a hot iron against her skin. Divested of earthly femininity, she was able to begin her religious quest.

The burning of orchid incense, allowing the essence of the flower that symbolizes purity and spirituality to permeate the atmosphere, reveals her identification even at an early age with Zen Buddhist thought. Incense, associated with the element air, is a sublimating force. Confucius, commenting on the orchid's exquisite characteristics, identified it with the perfect or superior man—a spiritual force on which Ryonen projects and which she would like to penetrate.

That she no longer lives in linear time is evident in her reference to the passing of the four seasons, paradigms of the annihilation of her ego and the tranquility that derives from *Cosmic Oneness*.

Ryonen's *waka* exemplifies her technical skill as a calligrapher as well as her philosophical depth as a poet.

> In this living world
> The body I give up and burn
> Would be wretched
> If I thought of myself as
> Anything but firewood (Fister, 30).

Ryonen is able to communicate an entire intuitive universe in her *waka*, divested of artifice but replete with nuances of sentience. Like lightning, she cuts through the fabric of matter, thereby producing increasing consciousness of the infinite power within the finite being. That instantaneous movement, primordial in Zen Buddhist thought, is so rapidly experienced that it sparks, flames, and enlightens. Ryonen realizes that her mind has been released from its shackles; no longer is it imprisoned by the body. In the words of the Zen master, Daisetz Suzuki:

> The thing is not to try to localize the mind anywhere but to let it fill up the whole body, let it flow throughout the totality of your being (Suzuki, 27).

Gone is the intellectual sediment and dross wedding the earthly poet to empirical existence. What remains is perception, intuition, the impalpable *pneuma*—the breath that conflates heaven and earth.

That Ryonen became a Zen abbot—a post few women occupied at this time—was a great and well-deserved honor. As a calligrapher, her lines were charged with energy and firmness, but with cloudlike delicacy as well. As a poet, her trajectory from personal to impersonal, earth to rarified spheres, conveyed in concrete, swift, and powerful images, indicated the vastness of her experience. What psychologists call the collective unconscious, a primordial and undifferentiated ocean in which opposites cohabit—inner light/darkness; emptiness/fullness—had been encountered by Ryonen. She had experienced the inchoate, the self-contained, and the preborn within her being.

Sasaki Shogen (c. seventeenth-eighteenth centuries)

Shogen was trained by her calligrapher father in this ancient art. After her husband's death, Shogen, like Ryonen, became a nun and spent the rest of her life teaching calligraphy to noblemen and women, acquiring a considerable reputation in the field.

Emphasizing outline rather than shading, Shogen's calligraphed works, including poems by the Chinese Tu Fu (712-770) and other writings from *The Book of Songs* (c. 600 B.C.E.), reveal her mastership of both Chinese and Japanese scripts. Her representations encompass a variety of lines—at once smooth and broken, firm and pressured, bold and timorous—pointing up increasing momentum and drama when called for by the text. Her brush tip, in keeping with the mood of the moment, darkens or lightens, thins or broadens, intensifies or slackens, depending upon the energy expended. That Shogen's calligraphy demonstrates a profound sense of confidence and belief in her own talents is unusual for women artists of her era.

Haiku Poets/Painters

The mere mention of the seventeen-syllable *haiku*—the shortest form of poem in literature—evokes a verbalized, nonintellectual scene. In the briefest of images, the artist/poet must convey the profoundest of feelings toward the mysteries of nature.

Kaga no Chiyo (1703-1775)

One of the most distinguished female *haiku* poets, Kaga no Chiyo, accompanied her verse with paintings. A student of Tagami Shiko (1665-1731), one of Basho's ten disciples, she eventually surpassed her teacher in sensitivity and artistry.

Chiyo, the daughter of a scroll mounter, is said to have composed her first *haiku* at seven. Whether she married or not is unknown. What is known is that, after the death of her parents, older brother, and his wife, she carried on the family business alone. After the age of fifty, she decided to adopt a couple, as was a common practice for the childless in Japan. In that manner, husband and wife would not only live with her, but would inherit the business, and carry on the family tradition and name. Although Chiyo, feeling at peace with her conscience, was ordained a Buddhist nun in 1754, she lived in her home and not in the temple, as was traditional. From that time on she devoted herself to writing and travelling. Unlike other upper class merchant and samurai women whose lives were severely restrictive, nuns were allowed to travel and meet with other poets.

Chiyo wrote the following *haiku* to celebrate her ordination:

> Not coiffuring my hair
> Will leave my hands free
> To spend my time at the *kotatsu* (Fister, 56).

To single out hair-cutting in the *haiku* is to indicate a sacrifice implicit in a transformation ritual. For the poet it meant the voluntary renunciation of worldly functions in favor of the free, unbonded, transcendental domain. Hands, which play such an important role in Buddhism—each gesticulation, form, and placement of the finger representing a specific meaning—also suggest continuous grasping for things of this world. For Chiyo, the freeing of her hands suggests a liberation from earthly matters, which had served to fetter mind and body. Now, as she sits at the *kotatsu* (footwarmer), these same hands will serve to write her *haiku*, but also to show her the way to transcendence.

One of Chiyo's most celebrated *haikus* was written on her way to a Buddhist ceremony at Higashi Honganji:

> Ah! Morning-glory!
> The bucket taken captive!
> I begged for water (Suzuki, 224).

The flower is the catalyst that opens her up to the essence of Beauty and Eternity. Such objects as the flower, the water, and the bucket are all interrelated in the story she tells. One summer morning when Chiyo had gone out to draw water from the well, she was struck by the manner in which the morning glory vine had woven itself around the bucket. So profoundly moved was she by the comeliness of the flower before her that she stopped in her tracks, unwilling to disturb this exquisite image, to defile this holy object. So stunned was she by the numinosity of her vision that she momentarily forgot the reason she had come to the well. After returning home she went to her neighbor's well to draw water.

Chiyo's poem conveys that *single* moment when she was so deeply absorbed in the morning glory as to be divested of the material domain. While contemplating its strange beauty, she and the universe became "one absolute morning-glory blooming all by itself" (Suzuki, 246). For the Zen Buddhist, it is during this unique moment, when the poet saw the flower and it saw her, that fusion between subject and object had been accomplished. All had become *one*: the universe, the flower, and the poet—in Eternity. Suzuki writes:

> There is no one seeing it and admiring it. It is the flower seeing itself, absorbed in itself. At this supreme moment, to utter even a word would be altogether out of place. Chiyo, however, is human, she recovers herself from the reverie and murmurs, "Ah! Morning-glory!" She can say nothing more for a while (Suzuki, 246).

A prosaic object, such as the everyday morning glory which grows like a weed in Japan, can generate transcendence in the viewer, thus internalizing while also externalizing a deeply religious experience. Chiyo had succeeded in putting herself outside of herself, so to speak. Only on her return to the worldly plane does she once again become conscious of her surroundings and the object of her trip to the well.

The monk-poet Mugaian Kihaku published 546 of Chiyo's *haikus* in *A Collection of Nun Chiyo's Verses* (*Chiyo-ni kushu*, 1763). Other important commissions may have helped relieve the physical suffering she endured from her severe asthma. The following *haiku* intimates that during her declining years, Chiyo was compelled to spend much of her time in bed.

> Late autumn drizzle—
> In one room, my yesterday
> And Today, too, have passed away (Suzuki, 57).

The autumn of life or seasonal cyclicality invites heavenly waters to bathe the parched land and stir the poet's imagination. For Chiyo, as is generally true of Zen Buddhists, no event, image, or minute is meaningless. Nor is one entity more significant than another in its connection with the primary source of life.

As Chiyo alters her focus from the outside to the inner world, from the multiple to oneness in her room, a microcosm comes into being. While the poet abstracts—or compresses—an entire linear vision, its accompanying feeling textures participate in non-linear Time schemes—that is, Eternalness. Yesterdays and todays, each fold and enfold into the other, one phase of existence transmuted into the following. Oneness permeates All.

Haiku, the ideal poetic form for Chiyo, allowed her to convey her impulses and feelings in concrete objects, which were then explored, both consciously and unconsciously, on a variety of planes. Whether her verbal images depict or allude to drizzle, rain, ponds, or other watery substances, the fluidity and transparency of her continuously/contiguously reflected spheres of existence are intuitively perceived.

Before she died at the age of 75, she conveyed, as is typical of many Japanese poets, her joy at having been privileged to experience so many of nature's attributes, including the viewing of the moon. This celestial body encouraged her to accept the quietude necessary to meet and finally embrace death.

> I've also viewed the moon
> From this world
> Now I too shall wane (Suzuki, 58).

The moon, with all of its rich poetical associations, sheds an inner light which is experienced in the deepest folds of the poet's mind/psyche: the collective unconscious, there where emptiness ("mind of no-mind") exists. Only then may its reflection be experienced inwardly and the rationally bound thought-world be freed from its constraints. Then may the egolessness of Oneness be known. Everything moves throughout the world in response to the intricate shadows cast by the moon's rays. The Invisible Spirit manifests itself in its continuous movement which serves to inspire the poet with moments of tranquility.

Never does Chiyo respond via rational means to this mysterious force as it traverses its immense distances. Bypassing all hindrances or attachments, she glimpses beyond the material domain while observing the waning moon's rays. As increasing darkness enclothes the universe, thereby shutting out the glare of worldly existence, all is enveloped in receding pallor, in increasingly dark-blue colorations, parallelling a human's diminishing life-span. The transformation in terms of moon glow from an individual to a collective sphere suggests that the poet, like the celestial body, is never caught up in worldly limitations.

Chiyo's handscrolls, on which many of her *haikus* were calligraphed, are also effective and harmonious. She uses large and small space and forms—a tiny bird standing on a huge pestle for example. The mundane object was her catalyst, as it had been Basho's. Envisioned under different atmospheric conditions, the concrete world generated in her increased awareness, opening her up to a vast and continuously renewed aesthetic and spiritual dimension.

Tagami Kikusha (nee Tagami Michi) (1753-1826).

Kikusha, whose name means "hut of chrysanthemums," was born into a samurai family. Her father, a poet of Chinese-style verse, allegedly encouraged his daughter to pursue her studies. Following her husband's death after only eight years of marriage, Kikusha began composing *haiku* and then traveled, as Basho had, seeking inspiration from the world around her.

Like other *haiku* poets, Kikusha emphasized flower symbolism, the moon and its shifting illuminations, and various aspects of nature—mountains, falling leaves, pine trees, etc. Like Chiyo, whose poetry she so deeply admired, Kikusha became a fine calligrapher. To add to her accomplishments, she studied the art of the Zen tea ceremony. After visiting the temple at Hagi, Kikusha, like Chiyo, became a nun of the Shin sect of Pure Land Buddhism, giving up her mundane existence to devote herself to poetry.

That she journeyed frequently and intently suggests a need for solitude, a wandering spirit, and a passionate love of nature. Her feelings of wonderment at the spectacular mysteries and uncertainties of life triggered her poetic sense. Like the sun and the moon, also eternal wayfarers, she reacted movingly to nature and its variegated appearances. When, during one of her trips, she became lost in the mountains, Kikusha distilled her understanding of the Infinite in the following *haiku*:

> Amidst the deep mountains
> On my hat
> Only the sounds of falling leaves (Fister, 62).

Impressed by the beauty and grandeur, as well as the isolation of a mountain top rising so powerfully into the cloudy expanse, Kikusha feels removed from mundane life and in touch with Nature. It is from the highest mountain peak that earth meets heaven and that the spirit ascends to celestial spheres via its vertical axis. It is not merely a question of the mountain's height that overcomes the poet, nor solely its immutability; it is its depth as well—that which lies within its and the human's volcanic spirit.

The "hat" in Kikusha's verse refers to both the Taoist and the Buddhist understanding of mountains: the summit corresponds to the head—that part which permits an individual to leave the earthly sphere and penetrate cosmic dimensions. Like the crown, the "hat" is the seat of intuition, the symbol of receptive influences, a mediatrix between this world and the next. It allows the poet to keep in touch with the supernatural.

Autumn, accompanied by falling leaves, arouses in the poet feelings of forlornness, not in the negative sense, but rather in the heightened awareness of archetypal aloneness. Cyclicality alters the appearance and coloration of trees and bushes, as well as the austerity of a mountain under increasingly fading light. At night, when weariness sets in and longing for the eternal sphere beckons the wanderer, the poet is encouraged to reach out beyond the differentiated world.

Kikusha's travels, taking her repeatedly to Kyoto, to Kyushu, and many other areas, to seek out poets, painters, and musicians, also heightened her fame. A highly trained student of *ch'in* (lute), she was permitted to perform at Horyuji temple in Nara (1812) on a treasured instrument of this house of worship. The lute, it must be remembered, was as much a revered instrument in Japan as it was in China. The Chinese endowed it with eight qualities: happiness, sweetness, elegance, subtlety, sadness, softness, resonance, and strength. Everything about the *ch'in* had symbolic value: it was made of the dryandra tree on which the Phoenix bird was said to alight; its lower end conformed to the four seasons; its twelve primary notes were endowed with male and female sexes, and its five strings symbolized the five elements; two more strings were added to the instrument by a later emperor (C.A.S. Williams, *Outlines of Chinese Symbolism and Art Motives*, 258). The *ch'in*, along with other string instruments, is identified additionally with melancholy, purity, fidelity, and determination.

Kikusha played the *ch'in* before the statue of Prince Shotoku (573-621), a devout Buddhist who had served as "regent" during the reign of his aunt, Empress Suiko, the temple's founder (607). She wrote the following *haiku* to commemorate the event.

> A fragrant breeze
> Is blowing from China
> Over these seven strings (Fister, 65).

Fragrance, like perfume and incense, have spiritual value in Kikusha's poem. It also evokes the memory of something experienced and transmitted to others; it is invisible yet present. The breeze corresponds to the element air, a mystical power which spreads its fragrance throughout the universe while also intoning, according to Chuang-tzu, both "earthly music" and "heavenly music" (Suzuki, 259, 225). The wind, blowing from China where musical instruments were invented by the legendary Emperor Fu Hsi (2953 B.C.E.), invites the hearer to perceive some higher force wafting instrumentalists into increasingly refined spheres. The purity of the experience allows the poet to communicate with unlimited domains, thereby enabling her to divest herself of human interference. The utilitarian rational world vanishes and in the process heightened awareness takes over.

Defining her life experience at the age of fifty-seven, Kikusha wrote:

> It is said that a man less than one hundred years old has the worries of one thousand years. In contrast to this saying, I have the enjoyments of one thousand years. In my life, entertainment is my trade and I entertain myself alike with those I know and with those whom I do not know. I enjoy years spent in traveling and I also enjoy returning home. I enjoy both criticism and praise. I have devoted myself to enjoyment and I hardly have time to fold my fingers to count my age (Fister, 65. From *Taorigiku*, 1813).

Painters

Because women were relegated to their homes and could not compete with men in the workaday world, we know the names of only a few distinguished female artists.

Kiyohara Yukinobu (1643-1682)

Because Yukinobu's family had strong ties with the famous Kano school of painting, her participation in the group was greatly facilitated.

Founded by Kano Masanobu (1434-1530), and continued by his son, Kano Motonobu (1476-1559), and another descendent, Kano Tan'yu (1602-74), this family-oriented school functioned until the end of the nineteenth-century. Masanobu's scenic paintings, known for their clear-cut lines as well as their mood of stillness and ethereality, were not strictly Zen-oriented. Yet, a feeling of transcendence permeates them. Motonobu, a more decorative artist, is known for his strong ink tones and unforgettable compositions of birds, gnarled pine branches, hills and multiplaned backgrounds. Kano Tan'yu's precise copies of Chinese paintings and their moral tone were deeply appreciated by his official patrons, the Tokugawas.

Yukinobu, who was married to one of Tan'yu's pupils, was a derivative painter. Her brushwork, deeply influenced by Tan'yu's, inspired her to paint both Chinese and Japanese style landscapes—birds, flowers, and figures on large screens, hanging scrolls, and albums. What distinguishes her work from that of other members of the Kano school are her portraits of women.

Yukinobu's painting of Murasaki Shikibu, the author of *The Tale of Genji*, is arresting. It features the Heian author in the process of writing her narrative or diary and, in front of her, a semi-unrolled text resting on a desk. The overlapping layers of her silk and brocade clothing are colored in bold tones in *yamato-e* style—that is, with formalized decorative bravura. Excellent draftsmanship and confident brushwork mark this striking composition of a woman upon whom all women looked with admiration.

A Palace Scene in a Snowy Landscape depicts an incident described in Sei Shonagon's *Pillow Book*. Shonagon is featured, in Yukinobu's colorful hanging silk scroll, in the process of rolling up a bamboo blind to reveal a snow-filled garden, evoking the *Pillow Book* incident. When the empress asked Shonagon "How is the snow on Hsiang-lu peak?" the talented and perceptive writer, aware of the reference to a Chinese poem by Po Chu-i, answered by having the blinds rolled up as indicated in the ancient verse, impressing everyone in the room with her fine memory and wit (Fister, 41).

Yukinobu's painting of Shonagon, in keeping with the Heian introspective and refined *yamato-e* style, emphasized linear modelling, depth, and texture in her brushwork. Her colors, seemingly applied in flat layers, suggest volume by means of color intensification. The many layers of clothes—frequently twelve—worn by Heian women, are evoked by gradations in hues, and give the impression of depth perception. The simplicity of the depiction adds to its sophistication.

Emotions are intensified by the feeling of spatiality created in Kiyohara Yukinobu's painting, while the interaction of clouds, mist, and sky in the background give the impression of endlessness. Like a Noh stage, inner and outer space seem to be integrated: the two trees standing on a snowcapped hill to the right of the painting, the two stones to the left also daubed in snow, draw attention to the asymmetrically placed house within which the small figure of Sei Shonagon appears. Stillness and tranquility permeate the singularly harmonious and yet moving painting (Fister, 41).

Yukinobu's pastoral, bird, and flower scenes are equally arresting. Her depictions of four asymmetrically-laced chrysanthemums, each flower and petal clearly and incisively delineated in her fine brushwork; or her boat scenes with pines, rushes, and reeds set on the side; or her seasonal works, with moon, sun, shedding golden rays throughout, all produce sensations of delicacy blended with stylization in a world rich in latent possibilities.

Yamazaki Ryu-jo (1716-1735)

Encouraged in her painting endeavors by her father who was a shogun's vassal, Ryu-jo displayed a distinct talent for the popular *ukiyo-e* or "floating world" subjects. Her depictions of courtesans, some of which were drawn when she was but thirteen, were influenced by well known *ukiyo-e* artists, as for example, Hishikawa Moronobu, whose painted prints were hand colored in orange-red. Later on, Suzuki Harunobu, perfecting the woodblock technique in such works as *Viewing Maple Leaves by the Waterfall*, featured an orgy of colors—whites, pinks, greys, oranges, lilacs. Harunobu's color print in *Girls Fording a Stream* reveals not only his creative use of color, but his intuitive sense of harmony (Stanley-Baker, *Japanese Art*, 152; Peter C. Swann, *A Concise History of Japanese Art*, 283-4).

Ryu-jo's depictions of courtesans, alone or accompanied by a man, also offer a feast of color: brilliant reds, blues, and greens. Although her youthful works do not reveal the sophistication or dexterity of the brushwork of a Moronobu, Harunobu, Kiyonaga, or Utamaro, they do convey good taste as well as a subtle sense of drama. Her hanging scroll, *Courtesan Viewing Cherry Blossoms*, attests to her progress as an artist. The mood of joy and of hope aroused by the cherry blossoms, highly appreciated by Japanese poets and artists and identified with the courtesans' brilliant ruby-red lips, are sharply contrasted to the sadness and despondency of the graceful figure looking down at some fallen blossoms, indicating the ephemeral nature of happiness and of life (Fister, 50).

Although from a distance the lives of courtesans seem exciting and thrilling, titillating moments are few as compared with the endless suffering of these docile women—particularly those sold into brothels by their families. Like the petals of the cherry blossoms adorning the branches of the trees in Ryu-jo's hanging scroll, *Courtesan Viewing Cherry Blossoms*, the courtesans' pleasures in the "floating world" are easily carried away by the wind. The undulating river brushed into the background replicates the incessant motility of manifest nature.

Ryu-jo's *waka*, painted in rapid and wiry script to the right of the cherry branches, seems to be floating in the air. It emphasizes a mood of uncertainty and despair, perhaps unknown to the public, yet starkly present for those who see beyond the surfaces.

> To tread on them is bad;
> Yet if she doesn't step, she cannot move,
> And there is nowhere else to go.
> Scattered here for her pleasure—
> The mountain cherry blossoms (Fister, 51).

The antithetical tones implicit in the above *waka* are evident in the care taken by the courtesan to avoid stepping on the dying cherry blossoms scattered on the ground. Like the well known *sakura* cherries, paralleling the spring equinox in duration, happiness is brief. The petals detaching themselves with ease from the branch symbolize an ideal Zen attitude toward the precariousness of life and the inevitability of death.

Not to tread on beauty, not to experience life in all of its manifestations, however, is to opt for stillness, paralysis, and stasis. To imbibe the visual beauty of these scented and divinely colored blossoms even as they die and scatter is to experience elevation and to reach spiritual heights. The gnarled tree trunk in the left foreground, representing the difficulties of worldly existence, and the small figure of the attendant observing the willowy courtesan's torment, underscore an attempt on her part to deal with and finally accept the notion of separation and abandonment.

Like Nishikawa Sukenobu and Toshusai Sharaku, who depicted Kabuki matinee idols celebrating specific performances, or arrested actors in certain roles, so Ryu-jo also painted *Young Actor Holding Narcissus.* Unlike the sharp, brash, and frequently cruel lines of Sharaku's actors, which reveal a whole inner world in brief but expressive strokes, Ryu-jo's simple lines convey a virtually motionless image. Her brushstrokes give the impression of arresting time, thus enabling her to capture the warmth, but also the incipient conflict, in the psyche of a dual personality: the *onnagata*, for example, the man portraying woman in theatre, the man who breathes and emulates the stance and studied refinement of the female.

The colors used by Ryu-jo are aesthetically exciting. The rust and black tones of the clothes, the white plum blossom colorations, and regal gold hues used in her painting actively participate in conveying an atmosphere of artifice as well as a mood of melancholia and intense grief. Her intention was perhaps to reveal the spirit or essence of the role portrayed by the performer, or might it not be the artist's own conception of the actor's world?

Artists and Literature

The new Japanese school of painting, the *bunjinga* ("literary men's painting"), was established in China under the name of *wen-jen-hua*, during the Ming dynasty. According to its Confucian credo, every scholar-official was obliged to be a musician, poet, philosopher, literateur or painter. The repressive Tokugawa Shogunate encouraged the burgeoning of such training, thereby accounting for the growing importance of this intellectual group or class. Not only did the *bunjinga* see to the furthering of tradition, but it kept the thinking individual focused on the arts rather than on politics. Many of its members, gathering in Kyoto, Osaka, and Edo, occupied official positions under the shogun or *daimyos*; others taught Chinese classics in schools; and still others were Confucian scholars. Wherever they gathered, they formed Chinese language study groups, wrote poetry, and painted.

The use of chiaroscuro, deep and light tones along with wet and dry touches, add a personal note to the landscape paintings of the *bunjinga*. Although its members did not copy nature in detail, they usually traveled to the sites they wished to depict, opting for a subjective approach. The addition of calligraphed poems to the visualization added the literary note, thus incorporating, for many, another dimension. It opened up the viewer of the image and the reader of the written language to the desired feelings of transcendence (Noritake Tsuda, *Handbook of Japanese Art*, 240).

Although *bunjinga* was known as the "literary men's painting" group, women—usually wives, sisters, or daughters of participants—were also active as painters and poets and were for the most part accepted by the male poets. Among the best known were Ike Gyokuran, already mentioned, Ko Raikin, and Tani Kankan. Intellectually inclined, their liberated behavior patterns contrasted sharply with the restricted lives of other women.

Ike Gyokuran (1727[8?]-1784)

Ike Gyokuran conceived powerful paintings of chrysanthemums, peonies, and bamboo, as attested to in her *Spring Landscape* in which she adds a dreamlike subjective note to her Chinese-style coastal village scene. The peach blossoms, hills, houses, and people, although detailed and textured, take on dynamic and rhythmic qualities. They seem to emanate from the various planes of their inhabitations. The fluid undulations distorting Gyokuran's grandiose scape balance it out by lending it a strange compositional value.

Ko Raikin (eighteenth-century)

Two Birds by Ko Raikin, also in the Chinese bird and flower tradition, stand out by the boldness of their brilliantly toned plumage, the pastel hues of the large and inviting peonies, and the variety of shadings of the leaves. A fluid and dynamic note is added to the peony stalk depicted on the diagonal, to the right of which are calligraphed Ko Raikin's descriptive lines (Fister, 91).

By emphasizing pure form in *Two Birds*, as well as in *Landscape with Fisherman* and *Landscape*, Ko Raikin adds a lofty feeling to her visionary works. Unlike Ike Gyokuran's panoramic scapes, however, Raikin's are small, highly detailed, and almost glazelike in their poetic rendition of mountainous clouds in the background and trees and an immobile body of water in the foreground. The tiny and lonely figure of a fisherman casting his line from a boat, pursuing his individual path in an infinite universe, is reminiscent of Chinese painting (Fister, 92-3).

Tani Kankan (1770-1799)

Tani Kankan's *Fishing in the Moonlight* seems to absorb nature in its entirety. In contrast to Raikin's tiny fisherman sitting in his barely visible boat, her fisherwoman is significantly larger. The river and hills in the background fade into one of those remarkably mystical mountain cloudscapes, with peaks emerging from and disappearing into evanescent hazy mists of greys and whites—the entire vision utterly imposing in its depth (Fister, 94).

What singled out the *bunjinga* group from other artistic circles was the extraordinarily progressive nature of their relationship with women. Not only did many of them encourage their wives, sisters, or daughters to enhance their skills, but they also taught them how to achieve their goals. Quite unlike most of the married Japanese couples, husbands and wives associated or influenced by the *bunjinga* not only related to each other but also enjoyed each other's company. Artistic wives did tend to the home and children, and fulfilled other obligations expected of them, but the considerable freedom accorded them during their leisure hours to develop their minds and their art, in addition to the intellectual and emotional bond they experienced with their husbands, augured well for future generations of women.

Chapter 5

Ladies Make Waves in the Meiji Period: 1868-1912

The two-and-a-half centuries of Tokugawa supremacy came to an end in 1867, when the new shogun surrendered his rule of Japan to Emperor Meiji ("Enlightened" or "Illustrious rule"). Although supporters of the Tokugawas did fight in the hope of continuing the shogunate, the "Restoration" of the emperor, whose motto was "Revere the Emperor, Repel the Barbarian," took place at the cost of very few lives. The imperial capital was moved to Edo, the administrative center of Japan during the Tokugawa shogunates, and renamed Tokyo in 1868.

Because Emperor Meiji was only fifteen years old and too inexperienced to rule a state, first Prince Saionji and then Prince Konoye, descendents of the Fujiwara family, were appointed Premiers. They were instrumental in dismantling the feudal structure, at least nominally, and paving the way for the emergence of modern Japan.

When Emperor Meiji came of age, the "aura of sanctity" surrounding his person was so great that he became a "cult" figure—a God-emperor. As the emperor's prestige grew, the spirit of ultranationalism, the Confucian ethic of order and discipline, and the religio-political wing of Neo-Shintoism also increased in popularity and power (*Sources of Japanese Tradition*, II, 135).

Westerners, however, were intent upon penetrating Japan. Russian ships had attempted to open its door in 1739, 1764, and 1768; an English ship entered the port of Nagasaki in 1808, and Commodore Perry arrived at Uraga Bay in 1853. No match for the superior Western armaments, the Tokugawas reversed their traditional policy of expelling the foreigner and began a new and more amenable one. Some of Japan's finest students, including even a scattering of young women, were sent abroad. Studies enlarged in focus to include commerce, economics, industry, reform, new warfare, and modernization. Cultural changes were also evident in literature, art, and music. Religious toleration was accepted; linguistic reforms were advanced. The Chinese (*kanbuncho*) style was given up in favor of a prose approximating the spoken language. Although the Japanese continued to adhere to the Chinese system of counting years by "year periods," that is, according to the emperors' reigns, they adopted the Western calendar.

Education for girls, so restrictive during the previous centuries, began to expand. Not only were girls accepted in a variety of schools; they were also allowed to study multiple disciplines, including music. Indeed, the first graduate of the national music school was the sister of the well-known writer, Koda Rohan (1867-1947). Although there were few women writers and painters, there were, nevertheless, some outstanding ones during the Meiji era, such as Higuchi Ichiyo, Yosano Akiko, Yamakawa Tomiko, Okuhara Seiko, and Noguchi Shonin (Donald Keene, *Dawn to the West*, 165).

Higuchi Ichiyo (1872-1896)

Ichiyo's father, a farmer who bought samurai status, moved his family to Edo prior to the Meiji Restoration. Although his dream of fortune never materialized during his lifetime, the Higuchis lived in relative comfort. Ichiyo had always felt a sense of pride in her so-called ancestry as well as in her father, whom she adored. He, in turn, was aware of his daughter's gifts, and paid particular attention to her education. But the death in 1887 of Ichiyo's brother, employed by the Ministry of Finance and upon whom the family's hope rested, left her father weak and despondent. A group of unscrupulous businessmen involved him in what he thought would be a remarkably lucrative venture, which decimated his funds. His death in 1889 left the family penniless.

Despite the fact that Ichiyo had been the best student in her class, she was obliged, at her mother's insistence, to withdraw from formal education at the age of eleven. Old-fashioned in her thinking, Mrs. Higuchi preferred that her daughter tend to household matters rather than improve her mind. Ichiyo continued, however, to study *tanka*, the classical thirty-one syllable form of Japanese poetry (five lines of five, seven, five, seven, and seven syllables), considered appropriate for a young lady. She enrolled in 1886 in a private school, Hagino-ya (House of the Bush Clover), directed by Nakajima Utako (1841-1903), a highly considered *tanka* poet.

Although *tanka* was innovative and still was a popular art form in Japan from 700 to 1500, by the time of the Meiji era it had grown dull, arid, and repetitious. Its thematics, primarily revolving around nature and love, were limited and static. Few writers sought to experiment and refine its technique. Ichiyo's *tanka*, prior to her enrollment in the Hagino-ya, followed the well-worn traditional and unexciting path. But her point of view and approach to writing broadened, both stylistically and topically, as she began reading such classical works as the *Kokinshu* (*Anthology of Japanese Poetry, Ancient and Modern*, 905), *The Tale of Genji*, and *Essays in Idleness*.

Socially, Ichiyo was also enriched by meeting a group of girls from different backgrounds from her own at the Hagino-ya. She became friendly with Tanabe Kaho (1861-1943), daughter of a well known statesman, who was interested in *gesaku* ("literature of jestful writing") and in Heian classical works; and with Ihara Saikaku (1642-1693), whose realistic writings brought him fame, and others, thereby paving the way for her intellectual and artistic growth. That Kaho's "Nightingale in the Grove" (1888), considered by the critics to be the first impressive story written by a woman of the Meiji era, had earned its author thirty-three yen in royalties whetted Ichiyo's appetite. Her dream was to be able to support her family through her writings. Fiction would be her medium.

So poor had the Higuchi family become after the father's death, that the mother, Ichiyo, and her sister took in sewing and laundry, and went out to do housecleaning. Despite her miserable situation, Ichiyo was not one to yield to despair. She had her heart set on studying the art of writing, and hoped to do so with the successful writer and journalist, Nakarai Tosui (1860-1926). Having been summoned as a laundress by the Nakarai family, her dream seemed to grow increasingly realizable. When she became friendly at the Hagino-ya with a girl who knew Nakarai's sister, the meeting with her idol became possible. Ichiyo describes her first meeting with Nakarai (April, 1891) in what was to become her extraordinary diary, consisting, by the time of her death, of sixty volumes.

> Mr. Nakarai would be around thirty, I suppose. I know it's rude of me to write about his appearance, but I'm going to go ahead and set down my impressions. He has a beautiful complexion and gentle features—the kind of smiling face that children take to immediately. He's a tall, strapping man. He really is someone to look up to.
> During the afternoon, he talked discursively about the novels that are popular now: how the kind of fiction he admires isn't appreciated, how infantile the audience for newspaper serializations has become, how you can't sell anything that isn't already a twice-told tale of traitorous samurai or oversexed women.
> "None of my stories now are the things I really want to write," he confided. "It embarrasses me to think what a critic or a scholar would make of them. But what can I do? I'm not writing these things to further my reputation. I have a mother and father and sister and brothers to feed. I have no choice but to ignore the critics. If I had the freedom to write what I wanted," he laughed loudly, "it would put an end to the bad reviews" (Robert Lyons Danly, *In the Shade of Spring Leaves*, 31).

Nakarai agreed to read the first part of a story Ichiyo had written, but commented rather negatively on her flowery and overly-refined Heian-type prose, urging her to write in a more realistic style. Although downcast at first, Ichiyo was determined to succeed, no matter how much physical and mental strain would be required. Her visits to Nakarai continued and although she had sought an intellectual relationship with her teacher she fell in love with him. Because his reputation as a womanizer frightened Ichiyo, their relationship was apparently limited strictly to friendship. Her deep feelings for him were imparted in poetic and sensitive terms in her diary. In the following sequence, she writes of her excitement preceding each of her visits to her mentor's home.

> The next morning I woke up early, and, when I looked outside, the sky was completely covered with black clouds. Today of all days it was surely going to rain, I pouted. "In that case, maybe you'd better not go," suggested Mother. "No. I can't break the appointment, when it was for my sake that the whole thing

had been arranged," I protested. "Unless it rains hard, I *must* go."

As I was getting ready, the bank of clouds began to disperse. I set out delighted at this change in the weather. But near Tamachi, dark clusters reappeared everywhere. And all of a sudden it started to rain, as if a bowl of water had been overturned. What was the point of going back now? Either way, I was in for a soaking. I might as well go on then, I reasoned, and found myself a rickshaw.

The lodgings were in a newly cleared area in Ogawamachi, to the south of the Kokushkan market. This was the first time in my life I had ever been to visit anyone at a rooming house. For a second I lost my nerve. But hovering about the door wouldn't accomplish anything, I told myself. So I took a deep breath and went in, asking for Mr. Nakarai (Danly, 35).

Ichiyo had much to learn about life and writing. A moat lay between her and Nakarai. His style, for example, was more colloquial, whereas hers was refined. They did have similar goals: both wanted to sell their works in order to support their families. In that Ichiyo also wanted to make her mark on literature, she began questioning herself as to how much help Nakarai could give her in this regard. Would she really be able to learn the art of story-telling from him?

Nakarai was a writer of *gesaku bungaku* ("jestful writing")—that is, a type of prose fiction popular in Japan during the eighteenth and nineteenth centuries. Written in glib vernacular, *gesaku* revolve for the most part around actors, courtesans, and the hardships endured by members of the "Floating World." In time, the *gesaku* lost its novelty. Looked upon as superficial, frivolous entertainment, it no longer answered the needs of the new generation, which sought to probe psychological depths and down-to-earth reality. The respect intellectuals held for the *gesaku*'s advocates and practitioners began to wane. Nor did the strict neo-Confucians consider subject matter revolving around geishas, courtesans, the demi-monde, and the world of the theatre, appropriate for the people's reading (Irene Powell, *Writers and Society in Modern Japan*, 3).

If Nakarai could not help her achieve her goal, the independent minded Ichiyo decided she would chart her own course. She set out a rigorous plan of study for herself, going to the Ueno Library whenever time permitted. The reading of well-known Edo fiction, such as the historical romances of Takizawa Bakin (1767-1848), enlarged her horizons. An inveterate reader since childhood, Ichiyo loved those peaceful and instructive hours spent in the library, her respite and escape from the boredom of housework, sewing, and washing. Her reading allowed her to enter into another world—that of the mind—as she notes so poetically in her diary.

> Not a cloud was in the sky. The sunlight baked everything within its reach, and the dust from the gravel in the road rose like smoke. I cut through the university and came out into Ikenohata, where the scent of lotuses carried over from kayacho. It was such a fresh smell that I felt invigorated, and I pursued it. Willow branches rustled at the side of the pond. Sei Shonagon had no use for them in full leaf, as I remember, but what a cool shade they give on a summer's day. The pond itself was a great respite from the heat. Water lilies all but covered the surface. A breeze played across the flowers, lifting now a pink petal, now a white, and revealing the underside of the lily pads. I could have done without the rowboats moored in a corner of the pond, however. No doubt they are for gathering lotus roots. What's more, at the edge of the garden was the back wall of the riding track that was crumbling and pathetic-looking, which did make it a little better, or is that just my own taste? As I climbed the steps to the Toshogu, the breeze and the dew beneath the cedars felt wonderful; here it didn't even seem like summer.
>
> Crowded as it always is, the library I had expected would be unbearably hot today. But the ceilings were so high and the windows so wide that a pleasant breeze blew through the room. It was almost too cool, a welcome surprise. Whenever I come to the library, there are always lots of men but never any women. It was quite odd, I thought, going about my business as I always did, copying down the titles of books I wanted, putting down their call numbers, bringing them up to the counter along with all the men. "This one's not right. Please redo it," said the man behind the desk. I felt my face flush, and I was on the verge of trembling. I thought that if anyone looked at me, or spoke to me, I would disintegrate. I was bathed in sweat. For a moment I lost all desire to take the book (Danly, 40).

Nakarai launched his own magazine, *Musashino*, in February 1892, whose goal was to bring to public view the works of new writers. Although he offered no remuneration, he solicited a short story from Ichiyo, who accepted to write "Flowers at Dusk" just for the pleasure of seeing her name in print. The narration related the tragic story of a girl whose unrequited love for her childhood friend leads to such unhappiness that she wastes away and dies. "Flowers at Dusk" was unoriginal and immature. Nevertheless, it was a step in the right direction. Her second story, "The Last Frost of Spring," about a merchant who drives his benefactor to bankruptcy, and is based on her own father's unfortunate experience, was overly complicated and lacked style. Because the *Musashino* was not financially viable, it ceased publication after only three issues (Keene, *Dawn to the West*, 170).

Still, Ichiyo pursued her goal. Characteristically, she notes in her diary:

> In this world, perseverance is more precious than treasure.... It is not that my mind is unaware of the fact. Why, then, do I have trouble persevering? In the winter it is bad enough, but in summer it is even worse: as I study by the lamp, I struggle to fight off drowsiness. I pour ice water over my face, and for a while this revives me. But in no time I am warm again, my arms and legs are overcome with the same old lethargy, and before I realize it I have put my head down on my books. I am always embarrassed when Mother finds me like this and wakes me up with her "What have we here?" just as I am starting to dream. I open my eyes and resolve to work harder. I take up my book and can remember reading two or three pages when the same thing happens again. No matter how many times I go through my resolutions, they don't seem to do any good. The sages said our bodies are gifts from our parents; in China when they felt drowsy they would prick their legs with an awl, and the pain, hard as it was to bear, would make them alert again. But when my mind isn't on my work, then even when my eyes are open, nothing from any book sinks in. This weakness of the flesh is certainly lamentable (Danly, 46).

Financially, however, matters reached an impasse. Ichiyo's mother, who had overborrowed, was again obliged to ask friends for more money despite the endless work of sewing, cleaning, and washing she and her two daughters endured. When Nakarai offered to introduce Ichiyo to the poet and writer, Ozaki Koyo, also an important publisher of fiction and the literary editor of the newspaper, *Yomiuri Shimbun*, she was thrilled at the prospect.

Meanwhile, severe problems had arisen between her and Nakarai. Her mentor seemingly had spread false rumors that she was his wife. Shocked and humiliated, she took the first steps leading to her break with Nakarai: she declined his offer to introduce her to Ozaki Koyo and subsequently refused to visit Nakarai. Emotionally, however, the severing of such a close bond was devastating, as is evident from the following entry in her diary:

> We sat down across from each other by the brazier and talked solemnly. I am a great one for getting sentimental. To think that this was the last time I would see him filled me with an unutterable wave of despondency....
> We chatted for a while. There were many things to say, but finally I thought that I should go.
> "No, no—give me a parting gift and stay a little longer. Who knows when we'll have another chance to have tea together like this? Don't go yet."
> It was not that I didn't know by now what his feelings were. But as I thought of the reason we were forced to part I was filled with a profound hatred for the man. What kind of friend was it who would spread the rumors that he must have? I didn't know what to believe. What I did know was I was not going to let him overwhelm me with more lies. And yet, face to face with him, I felt my heart being pulled back again. His sad words made me cry. I was appalled at my own spinelessness (Danly, 74).

Friends now suggested that Ichiyo send a manuscript to *Miyako no Hana* (*The Flowers of the Capital*), a literary magazine which had published the works of the novelist, Futabatei Shimei, as well as the works of Ozaki Koyo and other well-known writers. Ichiyo's "In Obscurity," a *gesaku*-like story centering on a potter and his devotion to his art, was accepted and published in 1892. Despite its overabundant descriptions, its melodramatic events, and its lamentations on the dying art of Satsuma porcelain—previously works of unique beauty but mass-produced during Ichiyo's day—her fiction tale was well received by critics. It brought her the attention for which she craved.

Other stories followed and Ichiyo's reputation began to grow, as she began publishing in other reviews such as the *Bungakkai* (*Literary World*), founded by a group of young men influenced by Western ideas regarding emancipation, individualism, and romanticism. *Bungakkai* published Ichiyo's very fine short story, "A Snowy Day" (1893), based on her visit to Nakarai on a cold February day. Although she was never officially a member of the western-oriented group of writers, Ichiyo gained knowledge of the latest literary works and theories by her contacts with the young authors whose works were published in *Bungakkai*.

Ichiyo learned another lesson: to become a really fine writer she would have to branch out and no longer write the same sentimental *gesaku*-style stories. She must find inspiration elsewhere. By immersing herself in the writings of the popular Ihara Saikaku, whose complete works were published in 1894, Ichiyo not only expanded her turf but revitalized her creative bent. Saikaku was considered the originator of Japanese realism by some of the finest intellectuals of the day, including Koda Rohan, Ozaki Koyo, and Mori Ogai. Saikaku's depictions of lowly life, his humor and pathos, would slowly and incisively wean Ichiyo away from her overly refined and precious style towards a more plebeian and colloquial impress.

Also influential in her change of literary style was the fact that she and her family had opened a small store in the Yoshiwara (Floating World.) Exposed for the first time to the *realities* of the lives of courtesans, geishas, and actors, Ichiyo listened to their stories and their cant, closely, passionately, and empathetically. Hadn't she herself known the depths of despair? Her unrequited love for Nakarai, her extreme poverty, the humiliations she had had to endure doing laundry, sewing, and housework for others, the shame she felt during visits to her former schoolfriends from wealthy families—all had impacted on her. Her clothing was old, shabby, even threadbare; while that of her friends was stylish and fashioned from gorgeous fabrics. Now, for the first time, Ichiyo, identifying with the downtrodden, would be writing from her own guts. No longer was it a question of setting down intellectual frames of reference or structuring artificial sequences of events. What she would now write would be *real*.

The first tale upon which Ichiyo was to build her reputation was "On the Last Day of the Year" ("Otsugomori," 1894). There was an authenticity about her new writing that her prior works lacked. Grim in outlook, "On the Last Day of the Year" tells the story of an orphan, Omine, who earns her keep as a servant in the wealthy Yamamura household. Her ailing uncle, the one person whom she loves, asks her to borrow some money from her employer so that he can pay the usurer and feel at peace with himself. Because Mrs. Yamamura refuses to advance her the money, Omine resorts to stealing two yen from the drawer. But Mrs. Yamamura's dissolute son has observed her in the act. Compassionate for the first time in his life, he decides to take even more money from the till and leaves a note for his mother, informing her that he needed some funds. Omine's theft is never discovered. Although saccharin to our modern taste, the genuineness of the feelings depicted, the truth of the details included, the contrast in the characters, and the natural and even colloquial dialogue, indicate the Ichiyo was now on her way to becoming an innovative writer.

"Growing Up" ("Takekurabe," 1895), considered her masterpiece, not only earned her the admiration of literary critics, but also served to attract readers and admirers around her person. Influenced to a certain extent by Saikaku's thematics, "Growing Up" takes place in the Yoshiwara quarter and describes the distressing conditions under which children were being reared in that neighborhood. Shorn of any childhood joy, these young people had been thrust, unbeknown to them, into a sordid and grim environment. Divested of sentimentality, Ichiyo's detailed scenes are not only effective, but artistic; her verbal images are reminiscent of some of the wood-block prints by Harunobu, Moronobu, Kyonaga, Utamaro, and Sharaku.

Having learned the technique of creating mood and of detailing a background scene, Ichiyo no longer produced just sketches, that is, stories revolving around melodramatic moments and contrived scenes with stilted dialogue or monologues. "Separate Ways" (1896) reveals a growing confidence in herself as a writer. For the first time, perhaps, she relied on her own resources and feelings to draw her characters, rather than having recourse to artificial devices intended to frame events or marshall suspense. Ichiyo had finally reached down to her *feeling* world, there to deal simply and straightforwardly with such matters as loneliness, the meaning of friendship, and society's indifference to the traumas of others.

In her plotless story, "Separate Ways," Ichiyo proves to be a master in sounding out living human relationships. Her characters, a rambunctious sixteen-year old orphan (Kichizo) and a seamstress (Okyo), are unforgettable. Almost like a stage play, "Separate Ways" opens as the "stylish" and attractive Okyo rises from her sewing to answer a knock at the door. Kichizo, the apprentice in the umbrella shop, asks to be admitted. Although far from attractive—"He had spindly shoulders and a small face" and was so short they called him "Dwarf"—he knew he could always count on Okyo's kindness. Indeed, her home was his refuge, his warmth, his world. On this visit, he brings some rice cakes to be warmed on Okyo's brazier. He takes the occasion to remind her of her promise that she would one day sew a nice kimono for him. "It's a dream, that promise," she answers, smiling. Excuses, rationalizations on his part; he needs her kindness and her love. She is like a sister to him, he confesses dreamily, even believing his fantasy. Okyo, perhaps with tongue in cheek, attempts to bring him back to reality by telling him that they are not related since he had neither brothers nor sisters. Devastated, he bursts out:

> So there is really no connection between us. Boy, I'd sure be glad if someone like you would come and tell me she was my sister. I'd hug her so tight. After that, I wouldn't care if I died.

Kichizo had often wondered, as orphans frequently do, whether it would not have been better for him had he died at birth. But then, he adds, perhaps those very people who have been kind to him during his life, were really members of his family. This feeling of hope or wishful thinking has kept him buoyed up during moments of utter despair and solitude, as he carries out his daily and uninteresting job: that of oiling umbrellas. Although he had a reputation of working well and rapidly—he could repair and oil as many umbrellas as three grownups—his employers not only did not appreciate his talents, but were even unpleasant to him. Because he had neither home nor relatives, he had gotten into the habit of taunting young people. "Dwarf! Dwarf!" they screamed to him. Kichizo's violent temper would then erupt. How best to avenge himself? By frightening his enemies. Kindness alone could stop his rampages. Perhaps he reacted overtly to kindness, clinging desperately to those who showed him the slightest affection. When Okyo moved into the neighborhood and sought customers whose clothes she could mend, she befriended Kichizo, suggesting at the time that he take out his anger by pounding on the fulling block. Only with Okyo did Kichizo feel at home. He enjoyed responding to her gentleness and was moved by her understanding.

A change in their relationship occurs one cold December evening. Dreaming in his own private world as he walks along the road, he kicks a little stone into the ditch to mark time. "The moon above shone brightly on the white winter roads," he notices, just as Okyo, now elegantly outfitted, happens to appear behind him. Without mincing words, she informs him that she is leaving the neighborhood and the tenement in which she lives. Aghast at the thought of her departure and his utter loneliness, he questions her. Okyo has accepted to become some rich man's mistress.

> "It's not that I want to. I don't have much choice. I suppose I won't be able to see you any more, Kichizo, will I?"
> With these few words, Kichizo withered. "I don't know, maybe it's a step up for you, but don't do it. It's not as if you can't make a living with your sewing. The only one you have to feed is yourself. When you're good at your work, why give it up for something so stupid?"

Kichizo's moralizing serves no purpose; Okyo is tired of her world and seeks escape from boredom, drudgery, hard work, loneliness, and ugliness. Rather than think of Okyo's welfare, Kichizo focuses on himself, as is natural. Although feelings of betrayal well up in his heart, he finally comes to accept the hard brutal fact that *loneliness* is one's only reality. He vows that "From now on, I won't have anything to do with anyone. It's not worth it." No matter how long and hard Okyo tries to explain that her departure is not an abandonment, he only "stare[s] at her with tears in his eyes."

Because Ichiyo's study of loneliness and lovelessness emerged from her life experience, she no longer had to rely on sparkling events, complex plot lines, lengthy descriptions of the outer world, or an effete classical style to interest her reading public. Inwardness, linguistic austerity, precision, and restraint would serve to accentuate the drama of the boy's unforgettable and poignant hurt.

Ichiyo had learned how to focus on a single theme, or a single feeling, in depth. "Growing Up" received favorable reviews; publishers offered her advances, asking for more of her works. Admirers and well-known writers as well as novices visited her, but her increasingly debilitating state of health prevented her from further writing. Ichiyo died of tuberculosis, the disease which had taken her father and her brother, on November 23, 1896, at the age of twenty-four.

Yosano Akiko (1878-1942)

Akiko (Shoko Ho), of different ilk from Ichiyo, perhaps unwittingly became one of the finest *tanka* poets of modern Japan. Her first book, *Tangled Hair* (1901) made waves in artistic circles, for never before had a woman poet dared to broach the subject of sensual passion, nor mention various parts of the female anatomy in poetry. Courageous and defiant, as well as gifted, Akiko was a feminist intolerant to men's negativity towards women and their domineeringness over her sex. Assertive and bold, she had confidence in her talent and in her physical beauty, and sustained vigorously her strong belief in the emancipation of women. Emotionally and physically independent, she conveyed her feelings authentically in her writings, unperturbed by the many feudal-minded and indignant critics who tried to downplay her originality.

Perhaps Akiko's seriousness of purpose was partially due to her restrictive upbringing. One of eight children, she had been humiliated by her father, the owner of a confectionery shop in Osaka, who begrudged her existence as a girl unable to replace the boy he had accidentally lost two months prior to Akiko's birth. So angered was he at the thought of having a girl baby that he left home for several days. On his return, to placate her husband, Akiko's mother sent her to the home of an aunt for three years, where she received her mother's visits at night. Only after the birth of another boy was Akiko brought home. When her autocratic father realized how gifted she was, he began to take an interest in her and her education, sending her to an all-girls' high school. But upon graduation in 1892, the running of the family's store fell on her shoulders, and she was unable to follow her own bent.

Although her father had seen to her early education, Akiko harbored resentment toward him all her life. Disregarding his restrictions, the strong-willed Akiko began reading the books in his excellent library: Heian literature, Edo novels, as well as contemporary works. Poetry attracted her most powerfully. Unbeknown to her father, she began frequenting young would-be poets—revolutionaries in the writing world. She and her new friends wanted to rid the literary world of the standards set by the Imperial Poetry Bureau (1871) or the Old School, as it was called. They rejected the conventional and formalized rules set down for *tanka* writers. Unaware of the transformations impacting on the literary community since Japan had been opened up to the West, the Old School seemed to plod along in dull and routine imitations of what their ancestors had accomplished so brilliantly (Yosano Akiko, *Tangled Hair*, 1-23).

A move was under way to modernize the effeminate language of the *tanka*. Akiko and her group believed that *tanka* style should now be simple and strong or, as they phrased it, "masculinized," and its themes liberated. Perhaps one of the most active instigators of this new movement was Tekkan Yosano (Yosano Hiroshi, 1873-1935), who founded "The New Poetry Brotherhood of Tokyo" in 1899 and launched the *Myojo* (*Morning Star*), a journal intent upon reinvigorating what had grown arid and stale. Akiko, Tekkan's future wife, and Tomiko Yamakawa (1879-1909), his girl friend, both became members of the group.

Tekkan, the twice-wedded womanizer, caused Akiko untold grief before and after their marriage in 1901. Despite the eleven children born to them, jealousy and rancor marked their relationship. Not only was he unfaithful to her; he was not even a good provider. Publishing her writings steadily, Akiko's reputation mounted as Tekkan's waned. It was she who raised the money to send her husband to Europe, hoping such a journey would inspire him to produce some great works. She joined him six months later in 1911, but both returned to Japan the following year.

Although Tekkan was the group's founder, it was Akiko who was instrumental in creating its new style. Energetic and fearless, she expressed her political, social, and aesthetic beliefs openly and boldly. Her humanitarianism—compassion for the prostitute, the poor, and the sick—was well known. A pacifist as well as a socialist sympathizer, she wrote poems against the Russo-Japanese War, and was among the first, it is believed, to have criticized the system in print other than political tracts. Akiko's defense of the socialist and anarchist martyrs who had been executed in 1912—an act that sent shock waves throughout the world—motivated her to articulate her ideas in a memorial dedicated to them. A feminist and individualist, she militated for the improvement of women's place in society. An intellectual as well, she taught many women how to write *tanka*, authored novels, essays, stories for children, and also translated *The Tale of Genji* into modern Japanese.

Akiko's essays, *How to Compose Tanka* and *Talks on Tanka*, invoked new themes and fresh rhythms and images for *tanka*:

> Some poets seem to think there is a specific type of tanka to be categorized under "shasei" or "description of nature" as distinct from "expression of feelings." I do not agree. In my opinion, all tanka are lyrics expressing feelings. Some may refer to fruits or flowers or may sing of mountains or forests, but that does not necessarily make them sketches of natural objects or landscapes. Like love poems, they too express the poet's *jikkan* ("actual feelings"). Jikkan are made to emerge by various stimuli, such as an event in life or the sight of natural objects or a landscape, yet in all cases they form the core of the subject matter to be treated in the poem. Hence every tanka ends up becoming a lyric (Ueda Makoto, *Modern Japanese Poets*, 55).

Poetry, for Akiko, was not designed to reproduce reality, as in a photo; nor was it a cerebral exercise or intellectual disquisition; nor a strictly objective art. Rather, it was the articulation of an affect, an instinctual reaction to some object, scene, person, idea, or sensation. A poem, for Akiko, was intended to convey *actual feelings*, which should be authentic but not ordinary or common, and go beyond strictly routine, everyday reality. Fantasies revealing fresh sense impressions or thinking states would be different—even unique.

Although Akiko was not the originator of the classical "emotional" approach to *tanka*, she was instrumental in reinjecting traditional fervor into both *tanka* and *haiku*. The art of poetry, which had become jejune and ossified during the course of centuries, was to become, thanks to Akiko, something unique. Neither a narrative, nor a discussion, nor a journalistic account of an event, the new art of poetry was an *immediate experience*.

> Art lies deep in the painter's soul. It does not lie in the subject to be painted.
> The artist does not live in nature. Rather, nature lives in the artist.
> A work of art is an image of the self. It needs: first, the self; second, the self; third, the self; absolutely, the self (Ueda, 56).

The importance of replicating the immediacy of the physical experience in the word is expounded in Akiko's essays and revealed in her poetry. Spontaneous and ebullient rhythms, in consort with earthy and sparse imagery, flash forward in the following *tanka* in which the reader experiences a sweetheart's sensations as her lover journeys to her home under pouring rain.

> My lover has come
> To this poor house of mine . . .
> The tree of pink blossoms
> Wet with spring rain,
> How like a woman in love!

The "poor house" does not necessarily refer to the girl's economic situation, but rather is typical of the Japanese way of deprecating whatever one possesses, be it on a material or a personal level. The "tree," a living force which serves to bond heaven, air, and earth in a single unity, is further enhanced by its pink "blossoms" which will, upon the lover's arrival, burst into bloom. But flowers, symbols of beauty, are seasonal, as is love and life.

Poetry was a paradox for Akiko: a disciplined outpouring designed to invoke the essence of an impulse, crystallized in the word. Thus does the *jikkan* ("actual feeling") individualize what is universal.

> In actual human life each individual forms a new class all his or her own, like a new plant that has emerged through mutation. Among individuals there are a great many differences, since all lead their lives with different aims and in different styles. The human psyche differs from one person to another, just as fingerprints do. Different persons use the same word "love," but each person's love differs in density, intensity, and color, far more so than plumes of wisteria differ in length. That is the "truth" in human life (Ueda, 61).

Akiko neither masks nor dissimulates her passions. They are revealed in striking physical images and bold psychological, but also palpable, insights in the following *tanka*:

> You have yet to touch
> This soft flesh,
> This throbbing blood—
> Are you not lonely,
> Expounder of the Way? (Akiko, *Tangled Hair*, 7).

Visceral and explicit, her joy in sex is conveyed undiluted, uninhibited. Written, perhaps, prior to her marriage, when Tekkan was still her lover, it openly advocates the pleasures of tactile sensations and bodily contact. Brazen in her lustful song, she views the beauty of love in all of its ramifications, not to be taken lightly, but as part of a religious *Way*—a call to live life in all of its plenitude.

Is it any wonder that Japanese traditionalists and moralists were shocked by Akiko's outbursts? They decried her immodesty, her defiance and, in their opinion, shameless sexual approach. Akiko was intent upon ridding society of the double standard and overturning the outworn traditional ideas of Japanese men who regarded women not only as inferior to them, but as objects, playthings whose sole function on earth was to procreate and see to man's pleasures.

The next *tanka*, more visual than the preceding, resembles a painting. Here, the poet depicts a woman in her bath, viewing her own body with feelings of ecstasy and delighting in its mystery, its voluptuousness, and its fertility:

> In my bath—
> Submerged like some graceful lily
> At the bottom of a spring,
> How beautiful
> This body of twenty summers.

Symbol of whiteness and purity, the lily is identified with the phallus because of its pistil or seed-bearing organ. The lily's erotically enticing aroma—an aphrodisiac of sorts—spells intimacy. When submerged in deep or shallow water, the kinetic image becomes a metonymy for lovemaking and the outpouring of sexual passion. Unlike so many of her contemporaries, who viewed the body as an unfit subject for poetry, Akiko's unabashed revelations were considered by many critics to be doubly contemptible: because of the immodesty of the images and because a woman had authored them.

Even more explicit is the following poem, where the sexual act is depicted both tactically and representationally.

> Softly I pushed open
> That door
> We call a mystery,
> These full breasts
> Held in both my hands.

Tender and cushionlike sensations are aroused in the woman as her hands fondle her "full breasts." The act is the prelude to entry into the very heart of what had once been a forbidden and secret area through the door leading to a world of mystery. The newly opened orifice allows the rite of passage to be enacted, by which two worlds become one. Access toward revelation is unlidded and unsealed; love, in the sexual or creative realm of the artist, is natural and beautiful.

The poet, preoccupied and melancholy, in her next *tanka* is featured leaning on a railing for the support, strength, and solidity her thoughts cannot give her. Like wind, ideas are living entities, paradigms of eternal change. For the Japanese, sensitive to the various kinds of wind—summer breezes, winter squalls, or those tussling and propelling drifting rains—each is endowed with its own characteristics, fragrances, meanings, and colorations.

> Leaning against the railing
> And lost in endless thought,
> I look at the autumn wind
> Passing over
> The purple flowers.

Autumnal wind, sensed as white and sad, preludes winter's divestiture. Similar associations may be made with lespedeza flowers, which are either white, for purity, or purple, for regality.

Tense, perhaps jealous, and certainly anguished, the woman in the following poem cannot sleep; nor does she have even the peace of mind to rest:

> Restless night,
> My tangled hair
> Sounds against my koto!
> Is it three months of spring
> And not one note struck?

Her "tangled hair" reveals not only her physical discomfiture expressed by tossing and turning throughout the night, but her anguished state of mind as well. The image of "tangled hair," for the Japanese, also has an erotic flavor. Before a woman (or a man) was permitted to be seen by a man (or woman), everything about her/his face, body, and dress had to be fully composed. Disheveled hair was considered indecent. That Akiko's hair, a symbol of beauty, is in disarray, refers both to the past, when she was at the height of sexual passion, and to the present, in the loneliness of abandonment. Three months have elapsed since she saw her lover; three months since she played the *koto* (a thirteen-stringed Japanese harp). Her instrument, as her heart and body, lie fallow.

Dreams, fantasies, excitement, memories, flame or passion in the raw, are the catalysts that enable Akiko to convey her sensations directly. Each experience, providing it is authentic, is fertile field for poetry and yields a delicately felt, invisible, yet complex feeling. Akiko's method of instructing budding poets in the art of *tanka* is through example, as did the Zen monks. The following is a paraphrase from Buddha's sermon on Vulture Peak: when Buddha was asked to teach the law, rather than articulate his principles, he showed a flower to his disciples, which he turned around in his fingers. Poetry, likewise, is suggestive and not didactic. It is intuitive and not rational. It is *feeling* and not cerebral. It is mystery.

Yamakawa Tomiko (1879-1909)

Although Akiko was the finest Japanese woman poet of her day, and according to some, of all time, mention must also be made of Yamakawa Tomiko's works. Lesser in stature than Akiko, nevertheless, she too, perhaps, had something different to offer the reading public.

After graduation from the Girl's High School in Osaka, Tomiko enrolled at the Women's University in Tokyo; she married at the age of twenty-one, and remained a widow two years later. Although she authored only one volume of poetry, *The Garment of Lovemaking*, in collaboration with Akiko and Chino Masako, she delved deeply into the woman's world and its secret passions.

Intellectual though her relationship was with Akiko, it perhaps reached its greatest intensity in their sexual love for each other and in their love for Tekkan. Although acutely jealous of Tomiko's relationship with her husband, Akiko's passion for her rival was, to say the least, complex in nature. The intimacy of these three creative spirits was of such a nature as to cause them to code their writings, each endowing the other with special names, at times even interchanging them, thereby adding to the poem's willed ambiguity. Familiarity with the flower world is necessary to understand some of the subtle ramifications embedded in their *tankas*. For example, Akiko and Tekkan frequently refer to Tomiko as "lily"; Akiko is the "white lespedeza"; and Tekkan is the "white hibiscus."

The happy and productive relationship between the three poets, however, was to come to an untimely end. After diagnosis and treatment for tuberculosis at Kyoto University Hospital, Tomiko was informed that her father was dying of the same disease. Despite the winter snows, she insisted on making the trip to her native village, Kohama, in Fukui Prefecture. A servant allegedly carried Tomiko on his back part of the way to her father's home. After her father's death, she took to her bed and died in the spring of 1909, at the early age of twenty-nine.

It has been suggested that the following self-explanatory poem conveyed her feelings of love and grief in a farewell to a brief and poignant life.

> I leave all the scarlet flowers
> For the woman I love
> And hiding my tears from her
> I pick
> The flower of forgetfulness (Rexroth and Atsumi, 67).

Okuhara Seiko (1837-1913)

The daughter of a samurai, Seiko had since her earliest days been interested in literature, philosophy, Chinese, poetry, calligraphy, painting, and the martial arts. An extant photograph of Seiko reveals features that were strong and determined. That she wore men's clothing and cut her hair added to her masculine appearance.

Seiko excelled in whatever discipline she undertook, including the tea ceremony. After moving to Edo from her home town of Koga, she began to entertain artists at a restaurant in Ueno. These get-togethers or celebrations, as they might be called, lead to great conviviality on the part of the participants, as well as to animated discussions of the arts, in which Seiko revealed herself to be a skilled conversationalist.

Accepted by the *bunjin* (literati), Seiko was admired as artist and teacher. In 1872, she had a boarding house constructed to house her female students, while the males were obliged to commute, and she is reputed to have had as many as three hundred students at one point. Seiko's fame gained her the honor of being the first woman in the later centuries to be granted an audience with the Empress.

Her enviable reputation brought her financial gain, which she channelled to the rebuilding and enlarging of her home, and to traveling. Seiko's art works were displayed in teahouses, restaurants, and stores, but gradually tastes began to change. Western art influences resulted in outright imitations of European painters and poets and the creation of *nihonga*—a modified traditional Japanese painting with European motifs, as distinguished from Western-style oils (*yoga*). The dull and lifeless *nihonga* revealed the Japanese taste for "modern styles," even while diminishing the popularity of *bunjinga*.

When Seiko moved out of Edo to Kamikawakami (in Kumagaya), her style also changed. Although continuing to paint landscapes, birds, and flowers, the freedom of her former brushwork now yielded to more disciplined, form-oriented, and detailed images. Considered the quintessence of her art, these later works remained in demand throughout Seiko's life, and are still sought today (Fister, 163-5).

In *Summer Mountains* (1883), one of her outstanding paintings, Seiko follows the Chinese scholarly tradition of Mi Fu (1051-1107). The various layerings in her scape are distinguished both via the verticality of the lines and the gradations of its hues and contours, thereby embedding her vision in a contrasting, even oppositional atmosphere of mysticism and realism. The separation by deep and heavy mists of the two off-center mountain ranges in her panorama, the top one rounded and the lower one peaked, imparts a mood of mystery and secrecy, but also a touch of the empirical in the heavy dampness following the rains of the early summer months. The two barely visible scholars seated in one of two tiny pavillions are featured gazing at the lake before them as they listen to the gentle, mesmerizing sound of the water. The vacant areas juxtaposed to the trees add a mystical quality to the composition.

Cranes, a pair of scrolls which bear the inscription, "Great and boundless joy to your descendants," are more realistic than *Summer Mountains*. The boldness of its forms and compositional design, in addition to the variety of its hues, add to the potency and vigor of the painting. The greens, ranging from brilliant to duller tones, the thin gold lines tracing the veined leaves, and the whites fading into the empty areas, add to the painting's symbolism and drama.

Each scroll features a group of six white cranes. As habitual mounts of the Taoist Immortals, cranes were endowed with sacrality. Because flying cranes were able to reach the Islands of the Immortals, they symbolized longevity as well. Cranes, the Japanese believed, could live for thousands of years since they possessed the secret art of breath control, which humans attempted to imitate. It was customary, when wishing young and old a long life, to offer them images of cranes. Moreover, a crane's whiteness represented purity and cleanliness; their heads, painted cinnabar red, indicated vitality—that is, a concentration of *yang*. Their beauty and dancelike walking enraptured the bird's beholder.

The peach tree under which the cranes are standing on the right scroll of Seiko's painting guards individuals from evil. Symbolizing fecundity, virginity, marriage, and fidelity, peach trees also protect those sheltered by their branches from thunder storms and harsh winds.

In the left scroll the cranes are protected by a gnarled pine tree. In that the Taoist Immortals ate the seeds, needles, and resin of pine trees, these, too, were identified with longevity. Religious factors are also involved: in Japan, the *hinoki* cypress tree is used for the building of Shinto temples and for the making of their ritual instruments. Shintoists place pine branches on both sides of the entrance to their homes, a sign welcoming the kami living in its branches. In that it recalls the famous pines (male and female) of Takasago, this tree is a paradigm of love and conjugal fidelity (F. Hadland Davis, *Myths and Legends of Japan*, 159).

Seiko's paintings combine general traditional symbols and colorations with her own personal stamp, through which she turns a memorable occasion into an eternal work of art.

Noguchi Shonin (1847-1917)

The daughter of an Osaka physician, Shonin was considered highly precocious by her parents and teachers, having learned to read and write at the age of five by copying the Chinese characters on her father's medicine labels. As gifted at *waka* as in *koto*, Shonin also showed talent for painting, which she began studying at the age of eight. After her father's death in 1862, she sold some of her pictures to support her mother and herself, even responding to a dare to complete one thousand paintings in twenty-four hours (Fister, 174-6).

After studying with several masters, Shonin concentrated on landscapes, flowers, plants, as was typical of women painters. So rapidly did her reputation grow that she was obliged to travel in Japan to fill her commissions and was even asked to paint the sliding door panels around the Empress's sleeping area. Married in 1877 to Noguchi Masaakira, the son of a well-to-do sake brewer who at first took a dim view of her activities but later helped her to find patrons, Shonin supported her husband after dismissal from his father's business. She resumed the life of an itinerant painter and became a teacher as well, gaining appointment as professor of painting at the Peers' Girls School in 1889. Four years later, she submitted a prize-winning painting at the Chicago World Exposition. Illness compelled her to resign her teaching post in 1899, but left her time and strength to pursue her painting, which continued to earn praise and prizes. Finally, she was named instructor to the Higashi Fushimi princess, and, later, to other members of the imperial family. Her appointment as official painter to the Imperial Household in 1904 was the culmination of a brilliant career (Fister, 165-7).

Shonin was determined to succeed in the art world:

> Once deciding to pursue something, one must have strong determination to the death. No matter what art is pursued, the path will not be easy. One must fight against difficulties. An old proverb says that when grief comes, it doubles courage. If one gives up halfway, one should never have started. Unless one is superhuman or has outstanding character, it is not good to be too wealthy, nor to be too poor. Worrying about food and clothing, one cannot devote oneself to being a good painter. On the other hand, acquiring too much wealth can make one too relaxed, and this obstructs mastery of an art (Fister, 167).

One of her fan paintings depicts a lady in the process of preparing the objects necessary for the complicated ritual of a Zen tea ceremony: cups, a banana leaf, etc. The only objects she chose to include—books, scrolls, pine branches—attest to a scholarly approach to both art and life. That she portrayed a woman conducting the tea ceremony rather than a man, as was the custom, is indicative of a feminist point of view. Shonin not only took every opportunity to speak out for women's education; she was inspired to paint women in multiple occupations, such as lute and flute playing, listening to music, and reading, as may be seen in her *Women Practicing Arts in the Garden* (1872) (Fister, 174).

Shonin did not omit depictions of courtesans involved in intellectual pursuits, as, for example, in *Two Bijin*. No matter the class or the profession, she stressed education. In the *Two Bijin* painting, a graceful courtesan is seated on the floor reading a book. In front of her are decorated sheets of paper upon which she will transcribe a poem. Other objects belonging to the scholar are also implicit and explicit in the painting: books, a table, and three plants (orchid, bamboo, and plum).

Shonin's landscapes and floral paintings are equally arresting for their compositional design, expert brushwork, and variety of textures which lend greater authenticity to trees, leaves, floral designs, and rocks. At times, she combines the ancient Chinese "boneless" painting style (omitting the ink outlines) with a Japanese technique that gives the impression of dropping ink or color pigments on a wet area of the paper or silk. Such an approach endows flowers and other objects in the painting with the glow of multiple intensities and the mystery of a variety of dimensionalities. When brushing gold wash on an empty space in her painting, Shonin not only created a kind of abstraction, but enhanced the underlying excitement and drama of the scene itself.

* * *

Much was done during the Meiji era to liberalize and enhance the lot of women. The period saw the demise of the feudal system, at least legally, if not always in practice; it witnessed the official end of the samurai class and the beginnings of a legal code based on equality. That Western influence also grew, due to improved communications, was not always a positive factor, at least in the domain of the arts. Nevertheless, many Japanese were fascinated and excited by the foreign technology and culture entering their land.

What was also of import was the fact that women's rights were coming to the forefront. An interest in women's educational opportunities, for example, was fostered by the minister of education, Mori Arinori, and by the educator, Fukuzawa Yukichi. The passing of a law in 1872 requiring the compulsory education for men was far from being momentous; but that it included *women* was nearly revolutionary. At the conclusion of the Meiji era, ninety-percent of Japanese girls were attending elementary school as compared to ninety-nine percent of Japanese boys (Dorothy Robins-Mowry, *The Hidden Sun: Women of Modern Japan*, 40-42).

A new approach to woman's education was now in sight—a factor that would go a long way in enhancing the welfare of both the family and the nation. According to Mori, the new industrial age in Japan warranted a fresh focus that would encourage *all* nationals to participate in the betterment of their land. This advanced point of view led to the opening of the Tokyo Normal School for Women in 1874, whose goal was to train Japanese girls for the teaching profession. A woman doctor, Yoshioka Yayoi, founded the first Japanese medical school for women in 1900; and a year later, Japan's first college for women was established (Fister, 161).

Chapter 6

Modernism: The Circle Completed

With the death of Emperor Meiji in 1912, the Japanese throne became a mere symbol. The new emperor, Yoshihito Taisho, Meiji's mentally backward son, ruled in name only until his son, Hirohito, became Prince Regent in 1921.

The younger generation of generals, admirals, bureaucrats, businessmen, and intellectuals assumed new importance in the Japanese political system. They not only enjoyed leading their "docile" people, accustomed to centuries of feudal and oligarchical rule, but they also delighted in their newly acquired position of power in the early decades of the twentieth century. Japan's industry and technological output were strengthening; commerce and industry expanded as an aftermath of World War I. Business empires, such as Mitsui and Mitsubishi, became more influential in post-war Japan than even the military, the bureaucrats, and the rural landowners.

Democratic and liberal legislation led to the 1921 universal manhood suffrage bill which gave voting power to the entire male population—upper classes as well as peasants and city dwellers. Intellectuals, supported by white-collar workers and some laborers, founded left-wing and liberal parties, such as the Farmer Labor Party, the Social Democratic Party, and the Communist Party. By 1925, however, the threat of a dictatorship by the proletariat served to encourage the passage of a law designed to stamp out "dangerous thoughts"—an excuse to crush the Communist Party by sending its members to prison until they recanted.

Extreme nationalism, conservatism, and fanaticism were on the rise, as was the power of the military. A system of indoctrination, as well as rigid concepts of paternalism, were fed to the population, becoming the basis for fierce and fanatic devotion to the might and authority of the Emperor and the army clique. Freedom of expression was curtailed; liberal educators and statesmen were obliged to resign; political parties were dissolved. Silence was the rule of the day. Business was also compromised, armaments and munitions becoming the most important commodity. The Rape of Manchuria became a reality in 1932—the prelude to Japan's aggression in World War II (Edwin O. Reischauer, *Japan Past and Present*, 142-192).

* * *

The role of women during the Meiji era had improved on the whole. Not only had they become better educated, but many had been permitted to work. Emperor Taisho's attitude toward women proved to be more liberal than that of his ancestors. When he was crowned Emperor, the Empress was given, for the first time, a throne of her own. When still a Crown Prince, Taisho not only gave his wife permission to enter a carriage before him, but he took his meals with her—an incredible step forward in a Japan where women were traditionally accorded so little status. Statistics show that couples married later during Emperor Taisho's reign, at twenty-three rather than at sixteen, than they did during the early Meiji era. The decline in divorce figures was attributed to the increase in the age as well as the status of women who married (Joy Hendry, *Marriage in Changing Japan*, 22-25).

That women were permitted to divorce at all indicated another forward leap. Whereas, at the outset of the Meiji Period, a man was permitted to divorce his wife on the grounds of sterility, adultery, jealousy, disease, or even for disobeying her parents-in-law, by 1873, a wife had the right to appeal for divorce on the grounds of her husband's desertion, imprisonment, profligacy, or illness. The Meiji Civil Code (Art. 808) of 1898 stated that mutual consent was sufficient grounds for divorce, although abuses of all types could still be found (Hendry, 22).

Despite these and other steps forward, a basic antagonism between the new democratic ideals and the traditional social structure and family system persevered during and after World War I. Confucianist and samurai credos, the belief in the divine ancestry of the Emperor, and arranged marriages, were antipodal to the growing practice of free unions. Indeed, the samurai viewed personal choice in marriage and love as "barbaric," "backward," "disruptive," and a negative act toward family and nation. Yasu Iwasaki wrote in 1930 that it was deemed a sign of mental and moral weakness to "fall in love." Love was considered "effeminate and unmanly." Courtship simply did not exist. The practice of arranged marriages, even at this late date, led to many suicides by young lovers forced to live apart (Hendry, 24).

Nevertheless, changes for the better did take place in the field of education. More women were reading books, magazines, newspapers, and attending plays and films than before. Alongside the prototypes of the traditional good mother and wife, there arose a new image: the wife as her husband's companion and friend, rather than simply his housekeeper. In defiance of tradition, couples sought to live alone rather than with their mothers after World War II, when the very thought of a happy marriage was still considered innovative.

The new Japanese Constitution of 1947 codified what had heretofore been considered shocking and disruptive concepts of marriage:

> Marriage shall be based only on the mutual consent of both sexes and it shall be maintained through mutual cooperation with the equal rights of husband and wife as a basis. With regard to choice of spouse, property rights, inheritance, choice of domicile, divorce and other matters pertaining to marriage and the family, laws shall be enacted from the standpoint of individual dignity and the essential quality of the sexes (Article 24) (Hendry, 26).

Primogeniture was abolished and marriage regulations changed. If a girl was over twenty, she no longer needed parental consent to marry. Women were given the vote in 1946. The emperor disclaimed his divinity on January 1, 1946, thereby effecting the separation of state and religion. Textbooks were changed, and history and mythology became separate disciplines.

Although a milestone had been officially reached and the abolition of patriarchal authority had become law, in practice conservatism still prevailed. Even in the 1960s, the consensus was that wives and mothers should not work; women were exploited in the workplace, receiving less salary for the same work as the man; and marriages continued to be arranged.

* * *

Was it because women were beginning to come into their own that an astounding body of poetry and prose was being published following the Meiji era? Or was it simply that women's writings were no longer dismissed and discarded, and therefore remained extant?

Poetry

The 31 syllable *tanka*, a popular form since the early eighth century, was still popular in the twentieth century. Refined and experimented upon by the creatively inclined throughout the centuries, by such poets as Yosano Akiko, the *tanka* was revivified in the 1920's. With the introduction and translations of Western poetry, beginning with *A Collection of New Style Poems* (1882), English, American, and French Romantic, Parnassian, Symbolist, Naturalist, and Surrealist schools of verse had taken root in Japan. Exposure to new literary forms and theories had enriched and perhaps to a certain extent revitalized the poetic establishment. A case in point was the introduction of free verse into Japan.

That imitation of Western poetry, fiction, and art was at first servile is understandable. In time, however, poets, nourished from the outside, began assimilating new elements, melding the foreign with the subjective. They reactivated their inner groundbed, which in turn enabled them better to respond to the rhythms and images of their own inner voice.

Tanka Poets

Twentieth century women *tanka* poets, although frequently writing in the traditional style, conveyed their emotions in fresh patterns and in compellingly new approaches to the word/object. Only a handful of the plethora of women authors of *tanka* can be discussed in these pages: Saito Fumi, Baba Akiko, and Nakagawa Mikiko.

Saito Fumi (b. 1909)

Saito Fumi's father, a right-wing army general who also authored *tanka*, must have had a strong influence on his daughter, who started writing *tanka* at an early age and became one of the most noted of modern *tanka* poets. Her verses, as attested to in the following poem, reach beyond the dainty and fragile images and sensitively imaginative structures typical of traditional feminine poetry:

> The palm of the hand
> is not aware of dying as
> without compulsion
> it becomes cold and hardened
> and only slightly shrunken (*Anthology of Modern Japanese Poetry.* Trans. Edith Marcombe Shiffert and Yuri Sawa, 151).

In that the hand is identified with the aggressive act of taking things for oneself when given the order to do so by the brain, it conveys the notion of activity, power, and domination. The poet, however, is referring only to the palm, or the inner or more secretive side of the hand, which allows those knowledgeable in the art of palm-reading to prognosticate a life span. As object, the hand is no more aware of what the palm predicts than the person's brain is cognizant of the fact that it is the storehouse of past, present, and future. Although mystery surrounds the exact nature of what will be, time—the aging process—is ceaselessly at work, transforming what had once been soft, warm, and nimble, into the cold, hard, and shrunken hand of the dead body.

Powerful and incisive in her realistic but also compassionate awareness of the meaning of life, the palm of the hand for Saito Fumi is a metonymy for the human being. In that it is part of the process that causes growth and decay, it, too, alters its being, evolving, constructing, and creating. When young, then, the palm/body is instrumental in enriching and helping to fulfill life's essence. But it also engages in the whittling away process, in the slowing down, the diminishing, the rigidifying, and contracting of a once healthy and dynamic individual. Awareness of the activity taking place occurs when the palm/body shrivels before the observer's eye.

What is haunting in Saito Fumi's poem is her ability to use the image of the palm of a hand as a metonymy to convey the quintessence of her philosophy. Equally incisive is her following *tanka*:

> In my inner self
> where it stands up piercing me
> the hollow cavern

> has in times without a wind
> the ultimate of darkness (Shiffert and Sawa, 150).

Interiorizing her probings, Saito Fumi now refers to "the hollow cavern," that is, the head—that part of her being that houses brain and psyche—as an inner cosmos endowed with its own climate and topography. Once deprived of activity and divested of thought, stasis prevails in the individual. For the Buddhist such an outward condition is positive, for it is during this time/space span that the Void or Emptiness is experienced and that primigenal darkness, or what alchemists call *nigredo*, comes into being. Outward immobility catalyzes inward activity and with it a potential world from which everything emerges—including the life of the poem.

Baba Akiko (b. 1928)

Born in Tokyo and a graduate of Showa Women's University, Baba Akiko is a scholar, a *tanka* poet, and the author of critical studies on *yokyoku* (lyrics for Noh drama). In the following *tanka*, Akiko discloses her vision of nature as experienced in verbal tonalities and reverberations:

> In the autumn when words sound
> like the echo of a stone ax,
> some demon in me
> wants to rise up and walk away (*The Burning Heart*.
> Trans. by Kenneth Rexroth and Ikuko Atsumi, 74).

Baba Akiko's seasonal identification is, of course, a commonplace in *tanka* poetry. What distinguishes her verse from that of past poets is her personal understanding of autumn. For many, it spells unhappiness—a period of diminishing warmth when the sun's increasingly curved rays are less powerful. The autumn skeletonizes trees and divests the land of growth, preluding the most desolate time of all—winter. For Baba Akiko, however, the cyclical process of birth, formation, maturity, and decline, like a human life, is not a negative condition. On the contrary, autumn brings new tonality and luster to her world represented in her poem. Singly or in *tanka* formation, the word reverberates in the emptiness of a leafless forest; cutting and jarring, it resonates like a stone ax, pounding, pulverizing, and crushing. Its explosive cacaphonies echo over and over again. That life force—that demonic will within the poet—

transcends whatever would destroy it. Alone it lives on, having the power to reject whatever the hurt. Rising up, it ambulates on its own within the poem.

Nakagawa Mikiko (1895-1980)

Born on the island of Shikoku, Nakagawa Mikiko made her home in Tokyo where, as an author of essays on poetry and literature and professor at Kyoritsu Women's College, she also became editor of a *tanka* magazine called *Columbine*. Although her *tanka* images are for the most part traditional, she infuses new life into them:

> How far
> will that wild duck still go
> through evening waves
> swollen in the open sea
> where it struggles on alone? (Shiffert and Sawa, 149).

Because ducks usually swim in couples, they symbolize for the Japanese conjugal felicity as well as vital power. In Nakagawa Mikiko's *tanka*, however, the duck swims alone in the vast ocean of life. No longer young and energetic, it nevertheless braves the "evening waves" as it makes its way into the rough and smouldering "open sea." Because of its unlimited expanse, this body of water becomes a metaphor for primordial existence—the collective unconscious associated with the feminine. Life in all of its forms gestates within these informal and tenebrous waters.

Because the water element includes both superior and inferior realms, it has also been associated with *Tao*, the all-inclusive sphere into and out of which everything streams, without ever overflowing or drying up. For the Buddhist, the "open sea" refers to the Buddha Mind—that Intelligence which gives birth to the pearl, or, in Nakagawa Mikiko's case, to the word.

Haiku Poets

Haiku (7 syllables) poets also disclose a modern consciousness in their approach to this traditional verse form. Their reshapings are evident in the verses of Sugita Hisajo, Hoshino Tatsuko, Yagi Mikajo, Kiyoko Tsuda, Hashimoto Takako, and others.

Sugita Hisajo (1890-1946)

Born in Kagoshima, the well-educated Sugita Hisajo married a painter and wrote irefully about the years spent with her husband. She "gave up diamonds," she wrote, "gave up a carriage, all to marry an artist, and then he didn't paint one picture! Instead, he stooped to becoming a country schoolteacher!" (Donald Keene, *Dawn to the West*, 135).

Early in her career, Sugita Hisajo wrote *haiku* for the magazine *Hototogisu* (*The Cuckoo*), then founded her own magazine, *Hanagoromo* (*The Flowered Kimono*). Passionate and at the same time reserved, Sugita Hisajo's *haikus* are distillations of pulsations ejaculating from her powerful sexual drives and her many love affairs. The overt sensuality of her verses have been compared to the covert sensations recorded by such classical women poets as Komachi and Izumi.

Although she was able to inject new vigor into her *haiku*, Sugita Hisajo was at a loss to adapt to her empirical situation: the wife of a country schoolteacher. She suffered a nervous breakdown, lost her sanity, and spent her last days in a mental institution.

Some of Sugita Hisajo's *haiku*, influenced by the *The Tale of Genji*, may be viewed as virtual transplantations of Lady Murasaki's images. Unlike the Heian writer's controlled style and accepting views on life and love, Hisajo's intensely powerful feeling world flared. Her verbal ejaculations were her means of liberating herself from an ingrown negative and repressive view on life imposed upon her—and other women—by society. Abrasiveness pervaded her psyche; struggle and fire rather than harmony ingrained its very fibre.

> O flower garment!
> When I take it off,
> various strings coil around me (Rexroth and Atsumi, 79).

Using the well-worn image of the flower, representing beauty, ephemerality, and sensuality, the poet revels in the stunningness of her world. When *depetaling* the flower or, continuing the metaphor, removing her outer core—clothing or mask—she reveals herself plain before the world. But instead of feeling liberated, she paradoxically experiences constriction. Unadorned, she feels the critical and severe views of the outside world, impacting upon her body/poem, constraining, binding, concatenating, and crippling it. Society's tendrils, encoiling themselves about her in an ever tightening grip and grasp, have fixed and stratified her once fluid feelings. Only when dissimulating her inner chaos by concretizing such images as a "flower" does she feel free to reveal the tremulous nature of the passions inhabiting her inner world.

Hoshino Tatsuko (b. 1903)

Hoshino Tatsuko was the daughter of a leading *haiku* poet, Takahama Kyoshi. Identified with a relatively superficial world, Hoshino Tatsuko never varied her thematics; never did she veer from descriptions of domestic happiness. Derivative rather than innovator, she not only followed the style and thematics of her predecessors, but succumbed as well to Western influence—especially surrealism—as the following *haiku* demonstrates:

> O brightness
> of peony's buds
> softly splitting open! (Rexroth and Atsumi, 83).

The double flowers and innumerable petals of the peony symbolize richness and honor in the Orient. Red peonies are identified with cinnabar, from which the drug of immortality is derived; the white ones, with purity. Hoshino Tatsuko's reference to a bud represents an immature element that has not yet reached full development. Incompletely opened, the bud, an organism to be distinguished from the parent, will in time divide, split, and open. In so doing, it releases an inner energy, an instinctual force, allowing freshness to emerge—and the poem to be born.

Yagi Mikajo (b. 1924)

Born in Osaka, Yagi Mikajo first studied with Hirahata Seito, a *haiku* poet and psychiatrist, and then struck out on her own. Although her approach to poetry was surrealistic, she did not merely incorporate its image-making procedures into her verse, but created her own distinctive visceral and powerful visions.

> The genitals of woods
> in full bloom;
> its gills are breathing (Rexroth and Atsumi, 84).

Yagi Mikajo's *haiku* is self-explanatory. Erotic in its figuration, as was Akiko's whose work she admired, she focuses in her fervent verse on the genitals, a pleasure-giving as well as a reproductive agent.

Free Verse Poets

The influence of Western meter and rhythm patterns on Japanese poets found expression in their choice of free verse, which was appealing despite its direct contradiction to traditional Japanese compositional values. Hagiwara Sakutaro (1885-1942), one of the most important proponents of modern verse, wrote:

> The true, artistic free verse is based on the spirit of regular meter; it is created by making and breaking metered verse. The man who starts off writing Chinese characters abbreviated in whatever manner his own whims dictate, without a proper foundation in the "bones" of orthodox penmanship, will never succeed in writing characters correctly. Poets who have not been trained from childhood in the orthodox poetics certainly will not be able to compose even free verse (Keene, *Dawn to the West*, 256).

Free verse attracted young poets, tired of the restrictive nature of *tanka* and *haiku*. For many it became a passion, a virtual religion. Although the list of poets writing in free verse is long, for reasons of space only some of the works of Tada Chimako and Shiraishi Kazuko will be treated here.

Tada Chimako (b. 1930)

Her male contemporaries who labeled Tada Chimako an "intellectual poet" were paying her no compliment by Japanese standards. Men believed females incapable of treating any other themes but those revolving around affairs of the heart, nature, or household items. During Heian times, however, intellect and poetry were partners and not antagonists.

Chimako, a highly cultivated woman and modernist as well, having translated some of the works of Marguerite Yourcenar, Claude Lévi-Strauss, Saint-John Perse, injects ideational value into her writings, as in classical times. Her words are drawn from her thinking and feeling worlds: phonemes vibrate with provocative rhythms and unheard-of tonalities and sensations. Tada Chimako's verses frequently reveal a melding of Western extroversion and the Buddhist meditative introversion. In her essay, "The Mirror of Velasquez," she states clearly that the marriage of mind, feeling, and senses are for her the ultimate joy in the poetic creation.

> In poetry all the elements work functionally, each word having a numerical value that changes constantly along with the changes of syntax. When dealing with even a short poem the reader must engage his intellectual energy to follow an equation of almost infinite complexity. How does such difficult work come to be experienced as pleasure? Because the concrete images and situations and structures presented by the poem satisfy not only the senses and the emotions but also the brain's capacity for performing intellectually delicate work. And when to the satisfaction with decoding is added the poetic impact of glimpses of the utterly unexpected, of some other world, the resulting pleasure can approach that bliss which is among the most sublime experiences available to humans (*A Play of Mirrors*, Edited by Ooka Makoto and Thomas Fitzsimmons, 140).

In her poem, "Me," Tada Chimako conveys the ecstatic feelings provoked during the act of composition.

Me

> Happy as a cabbage
> I am planted in the earth.
> When I carefully strip away the words
> I'm wearing
> my absence is revealed—
> and the existence of my roots (*A Play of Mirrors*, 140).

The collective or universal "Me" injects a mood of childlike spontaneity and unabashed energy into the very affirmation of the subject/poet. The earth seems flooded with sunshine, as the subject concretizes her vision of the poetic principle. The allusion to the common "cabbage," to the "earth," and to herself "planted" within its depths, lend a succulent quality to Tada Chimako's verse. Soil, rock, vegetation, and the mineral world are sources of food for her.

Although nothing appears to be esoteric in her lines, the seemingly prosaic analogies and images are symptomatic of a solid and powerful inner core. Not from delicate and evanescent hues or textured fabrics does Tada Chimako's inspiration burgeon, but rather from her own *black earth*: that darkness which lives inchoate within her collective unconscious, activating and sustaining the growing process. To write takes time and effort, as does the planting of a seed which then burgeons and ripens into the "cabbage"; each leaf, like the word, is plucked for food by the hungry.

The poet, giving birth from within her own earth/blackness, "strips away the words," as though she were decorticating the cabbage of its leaves. The cleansing process ensues: the poet removes the residue and unpalatable parts from each of the leaves in preparation for the eating process. Similarly, the poet shears away, sometimes ruthlessly, the grime of tradition fastened to each word. What remains? The most profound of elements—the roots of the poem: its song, its essence, the object/word in all of its glazed purity.

To remove, take off, shed, is to uncover and expose what lies bare within the poet's most secret realm. No longer hiding behind any garb, just as the cabbage is shorn of its outer leaves, the poet's "absence" and her "existence" are exposed unto her roots. The word "absence" in Zen Buddhism refers to Emptiness—that is, the Void, where eyes can hear and ears can see true reality. The phenomenological domain surrounding the poet—the cabbage and the earth images—represents the world of differentiation, accessible to others. Because the poet can leap from one sphere of being to another and is no longer confined to her sense-world, she can plunge directly into her roots, her Emptiness, the ungraspable inner creative life force, the *Tao* which transcends daily experience. As Mencius wrote: "The Tao is near and people seek it far away" (Daisetz Suzuki, *Zen and Japanese Culture*, 11).

Kineticism in terms of abstract time is emphasized in Tada Chimako's "Dead Sun." Movements into a past and a future are locked in an eternal present.

> shedding beads of light
> the child crawls up
> into a world not yet wrinkled
>
> turns a somersault
> the hourglass flips
> a new time begins

> the child picks up stars to skip like stones
> ancient fish laugh and flip their fins
> splashing the feet of god
>
> soon the child grows
> heavy with memories
> the world is filled with footprints
>
> yawning
> the child leaves
> dead sun stuck in his pocket (*A Play of Mirrors*, 145).

The child at birth, living in an as yet undifferentiated world, responds spontaneously to light and to the growing process as it crawls out of its sheltered existence, attempting in its own way to examine everything within its grasp. For the young, the world is "not yet wrinkled." Everything is tantalizing excitement. Hours, days, weeks, and months are naught in the child's "hour-glass," for days are always beginning anew. Vital and vigorous, life and all of its wonderment seems within the child's reach—"stars" that "skip like stones," "ancient fish" that "flip their fins" as they splash "the feet of god." No demarcations exist in the unlimited fantasy world of the young, imagination takes precedence, making everything and anything possible—god and human, mineral and vegetal, all is in all and is all.

When the child grows up, however, it is burdened with its personal past as well as with that of its ancestors. Fatigue and boredom take over in an alien world. Conscious of boundaries and barriers, the child becomes an adult, the rational sphere imposes itself, discernment and objectivity are now required to function. Thus glee is transformed into sadness; the excitement of an ever-expanding universe into tiresome chores. Gone is the child. The non-functioning sun, shoved into the pocket of the adult, is dead.

Tada Chimako is at her best when she digs deep within herself and her tradition instead of depending upon foreign heroes, especially Odysseus, to feed her poetry. Whenever she focuses on what really moves her, viscerally and intellectually, she cuts through her tendency toward prolixity, aims straight for her target in powerful and even aggressive images and sonorities.

Shiraishi Kazuko (b. 1931)

Born in Vancouver (British Columbia), Shiraishi Kazuko went to Japan when she was seven years old. Her first poems appeared in the experimental journal *VOU* (the title has no meaning) founded in 1935 by Kitazono Katsue, a poet wedded to abstractions and sequences of seemingly unrelated or unlinked images reminiscent of Surrealist writings. In time, Shiraishi Kazuko created her own very distinct poetic style, frequently identifying with the Angry Young Men movement in England and the Beats in America.

Shiraishi Kazuko's verbal asceticism, implicit in her first volume, *The Town Where Eggs Fall* (1951), was the result of her concerted effort to sheer off all adornment so that the remaining words were bone hard. Her habit of reading her poetry to audiences with jazz background music brought her visceral, life-and-sex-work great popularity. Concerned with world events, she openly cried out her fear of catastrophe—a real possibility in today's cataclysm-prone world.

Although she is ultramodern, in no way does Shiraishi Kazuko reject her past. Her poems frequently reflect traditional thematics: the geisha and the prostitute who yearn for love but instead are brutalized by their customers.

Wild, savage, and even ferocious, Shiraishi's free verse is unforgettable for the power with which she ejects her words onto the page in stridulent but ecstatic eruptions. The rhythms and power of her phonemes may burn and bruise the listener as they spew forth in her songs of alienation. One has the impression at times that a typhoon which has been swirling about within her heart/psyche/mind has now been liberated—hurled out into the open, pushing and heaving aside whatever layers impede its march.

Tense and pressured, Shiraishi Kazuko's poems are explosive in their fire and shocking in their alliance of spirit and phallicism. Never are such sensations so well sensed as in "The Man Root."

> God if he exists
> Or if he doesn't
> Still has a sense of humor
> Like a certain type of man
>
> So this time
> He brings a gigantic man root
> To join the picnic

Above the end of the sky of my dreams
Meanwhile

I'm sorry
I didn't give Sumiko anything for her birthday
But now I wish I could at least
Set the seeds of that god given penis
In the thin, small, and very charming voice of Sumiko
On the end of the line

Sumiko, I'm so sorry
But the penis shooting up day by day
Flourishes in the heart of the cosmos
As rigid as a wrecked bus
So that if You'd like to see
The beautiful sky with all its stars
Or just another man instead of this God given cock
A man speeding along a highway. . . . (*Seasons of Sacred Lust: Selected Poems of Kazuko Shiraishi*, Kenneth Rexroth and Ibuko Atsumi, 16-18).

In Japan the phallus is not necessarily considered erotic inasmuch as it symbolizes generative power. Indeed, the phallus is venerated as the universe's creative principle: the origin of life, heat, and light.

The Shinto Homan Matsuri (March 15th) is a fertility ceremony celebrated each spring by the priests of the complex of buildings making up the Tagata Shrine in Komaki City near Nagoya. Its origins date back approximately 1,200 years, when prayers in this rice-farming area were offered for a good rice crop at the outset of the planting season. While the Tagata Jinja section of the Shrine, identified with the male, is dedicated to fertility, the Ogata Jinja, another part of the Shrine, celebrates female fertility. On the morning of the Tagata festival, a labial-shaped tree trunk, enshrined in a sacred palanquin, is paraded through the streets near the sanctuary and its environs. In the afternoon procession, the giant phallus, borne by eight men dressed in the white robes of Shinto priests, is carried through rice fields behind the shrine. The senior priest leading the procession throws handfuls of rice, like holy water, to purify the way. Each of the several Shinto maidens following the procession hugs a two-foot long wooden phallus. After walking about twenty yards, the priests put the phallus down, then it is blessed by the owner of the field, who in turn pours sake for the members of the group. Once the procession is over, the sacred phallus is brought to rest inside the shrine until it is bought by a bidder acceptable to the

Shinto clergy. The new owner must treat this sacred object with proper care, continuously purifying and paying it homage. Never again must it be put on public display (*The Week Ender*, February 15, 1974, i).

By using the phallic image in "The Man Root" Shiraishi Kazuko is combining religion and sexuality in an authentic and powerful unity. Like the phallus carried during the Shinto Homan Matsuri ceremony, so the poet is a true inseminator of words, a continuously self-regenerating, creative power.

Fiction: Short Story and Novel

Twentieth century Japanese short story writers and novelists were increasingly outspoken in the variety of topics they broached ranging from sexual oppression, feminist consciousness, and free love, to political, aesthetic, and spiritual ideals. Avant-garde women writers showed deep understanding and consciousness of themselves as well as of their psychological and empirical situations. Movements were being formed and their goals met.

One of the earliest organizations created by women for the purpose of teaching them about themselves was the Bluestocking society founded in 1911 by Hiratsuka Raicho (1886-1971). The organization's literary magazine, *Bluestocking*, focused on the significant issues of marriage, abortion, and prostitution. Due to coercion by both governmental and educational institutions, the magazine was forced to cease publication in 1916. Nevertheless it remained in the minds of many as a symbol of the woman of the future, who would learn to think and function independently, and would rebel against restrictive social conditions and family autocracy.

Feminine militancy, however, was not to be stopped. It continued its activities for six more years, until women succeeded in bringing about the revision of the Peace Preservation Act, giving them permission to join and participate in political groups and parties. The vote was granted to them, however, only in 1945 (Yukiko Tanaka, *To Live and to Write*, 8).

Although women had been denied permission to function politically during the 1920's and 1930's, many joined unions and became important powers in the labor movement. A woman factory worker, Toyo Muslin, organized an important strike in 1927. A medical school for women funded by the public opened in 1925; the first woman passed the bar examinations in 1938. Growing militarism, resulting in increasing intimidation by the government, obliged women to backtrack. They were urged to work for the good of their country—that is, to bring more children into the world (Yukiko Tanaka, *To Live and to Write*, ix).

Increasingly repressive measures by the military led to greater unemployment, economic distress, and dissatisfaction on the part of women. Despite the fact that women were being silenced in every area by the government, leftists were nevertheless making inroads. Some women, like Hirabayashi Taiko and Miyamoto Yuriko, participated in leftist groups in the same capacity as men, encouraging the adoption of a new platform: to fight the rigid patriarchal system and its belittling of women in the home and marketplace.

Whatever popularity women writers achieved at this time was due not exclusively to their literary innovations, but to their militant feminism and to their flagrantly promiscuous sexual activities as well. Because their worlds had been so restricted, educationally speaking, and because of their arranged marriages which had, with few exceptions, been loveless, women in general knew little about life. Never, for example, were they admitted to men's literary circles, such as the one headed by the much-adulated anti-Naturalist writer, Soseki Natsume (1867-1916), which met on Thursday afternoons. Nevertheless, women authors such as Tamura Toshiko, Nogami Yaeko, Okamoto Kanoko, Uno Chiyo, Hayashi Fumiko, Setouchi Harumi, Tsushima Yuko, and perhaps the greatest of them all, Enchi Fumiko, forged ahead.

Tamura Toshiko (1884-1945)

Little is known about Tamura Toshiko's early years except that she was born in Tokyo, and that her mother, after her father's desertion, was left with two small girls to care for, one of whom died at an early age. She completed high school, but because of lack of funds, Tamura Toshiko had to withdraw from Japan's Women's College a year after entering. Having become a student of Koda Rohan (1867-1947), a writer whose ideological outlook was Buddhist and whose works were filled with heroic characters, she started to imitate her mentor's classical style. Although some of her stories were published, she must have realized that if she did not change course, she would remain a derivative writer. Where to go? What to do? It was at this juncture that she abandoned writing and opted for an acting career. Since Noh and Kabuki theatre were restricted to men, she naturally met with difficulties in her choice of a new career. Disappointed in both the quality of the modern plays produced and in the poor remuneration performers received, she decided to give up her career in the theatre.

When Tamura Toshiko's friend, the promising writer Tamura Shogyo, returned from the United States in 1909, she decided to marry him. Since her husband did not achieve the fame and fortune he expected and barely earned a living, the onus of support fell upon Tamura Toshiko. The couple separated in 1916 for multiple reasons, including emotional and sexual incompatibility. Her suffering, meanwhile, had become a catalyst for her writing which, after a period of growing popularity, suffered a decline. Added to her financial distress was a psychological problem: she had become a compulsive spender, buying all types of useless objects and borrowing money to pay for her squanderings.

Although Tamura Toshiko did not participate actively in Raicho's Bluestocking Society, her short stories followed the group's opposition to the prevailing patriarchal system and its downgrading of women. In such works as "Resignation" and "Vow" (1912), Tamura Toshiko's intent was to probe the inner world of woman and to compare the oppressed and enslaved female of olden times to the modern, independent individual with a goal in life. "My attitude is mine, and my personality, whether or not people are disgusted or repulsed by it, is also mine," her protagonist states in "Vow." Nevertheless, her view of women as revealed in her stories is ambivalent and conflictual, leading frequently to an impasse.

Although Tamura Toshiko longed to be independent, she also sought the security of the home. Floundering and unable to settle matters in her own mind, she was severely criticized by feminists for not presenting more positive characterizations and thematics. Because her heroines rose full blown from her own experience, her own dissatisfactions and her own frustrations prevailed; and she could not endow them with either a strong sense of self-identity or a will to succeed.

Until she met Suzuki Etsu in 1917, Tamura Toshiko's personal life went from bad to worse. After leaving with him for Vancouver (British Columbia), where he worked as a journalist for a Japanese newspaper, her life was happy during the eighteen years they spent there. She wrote *tanka* and essays, but no fiction. After Etsu's death in 1932, however, her life became meaningless. She finally returned to Japan in 1936. Her writings in her native land had already lost their appeal. In 1938, she went to China, invited by the Japanese military, to become editor of the magazine, *Women's Voice*, published by the Japanese occupation government in Shanghai. It was there that she died of a heart attack in 1945.

The opening lines of "A Women Writer" (1913) dramatizes the creative person's dilemma in a poignant as well as a poetic way. She focuses on the agony of a woman writer attempting to come to grips with her deep-seated sense of intellectual sterility and of physical ugliness.

> The head of this woman writer was filled with refuse. She had squeezed all the wits out of her brain, and no matter how hard she wrung it, her bag of wits offered not so much as a single word that was alive nor half a phrase that smelled of warm blood. She had been trying to write a story commissioned by a magazine ever since the end of last year; she pushed an idea around but found it unmanageable. All day long she sat behind her desk, yet produced nothing but a pattern of flax leaves and vertical lines to fit the squares where letters ought to be written (*To Live and to Write*, 11).

Tamura Toshiko's would-be writer, unwilling to shoulder the responsibility for her own deficiencies as artist and woman, blames the tight quarters in which she lives for her literary and emotional failures. Never does her protagonist look within herself in order to discover the reasons for what she considers to be her deep sense of inadequacy. A confrontation might, she probably senses unconsciously, further turmoil by increasing her already deep-seated sense of humiliation. Rather than deal with the inner domain, she looks outside herself: the sun, the sky, trees, anything and everything that might distract her from those burning, corrosive, jarring, and cutting feelings which continue to fester within her being.

Tamura Toshiko's artistry comes into play by her use of a panoply of colorful hues to generate her protagonist's mood-reactions. When, for example, the would-be writer muses on her husband, his face suddenly fills the protagonist's mind's eye and the reader's as well. Indeed, by the wizardry of Tamura Toshiko's colorations and images, and the expertise with which they are continuously interwoven, the reader actually feels the two presences conjured up by the author.

Tamura Toshiko's writing techniques are many and varied. For example, to increase the reality of a situation or an event, she melds sensual and erotic similes and metaphors into her prose in a very personal way: "her lover came to her like the gentle stimulus of a face brush on her skin"; "like the glimpse of the soft glow of celadon green peeking out from under the sleeve of a white silk garment."

To reveal her protagonist's lack of self-confidence, Tamura Toshiko has recourse to a fascinating device: the *persona*, or mask (psychologically, a social face). Her would-be writer, for example, must wear make-up at all times, whether she is alone or with her husband, or anyone else. Indeed, she obsesses about it. She is convinced that were she not to wear this mask, her ugliness would be blatant, overpowering, and destroy every aspect of her existence. After applying powder and rouge her despair dissipates; her faltering ego strengthens. No longer uncomely, she is suddenly transformed into a coquette—which she is not: "She adored herself."

Although Tamura Toshiko emphasizes her protagonist's despair, her writing is neither macabre nor depressing. She relieves her proclivity for tragedy by injecting spurts of humor into her story, as in the following episode, when her would-be writer equates powder with her art.

> Most of her writing, therefore, had been born out of face powder, and so it had the smell of powder.
>
> Recently, however, no idea had come to her, even with face powder. Just as her skin underneath the powder felt dry and cracked, she no longer felt that particular yearning, that sensation of warm blood swirling up within her flesh.

Violence is also implicit in Tamura Toshiko's technique. Feelings of suffocation and strangulation that dominate the scene are conveyed concretely in her negative self-images: "spidery finger nails wrapping around her neck, choking her." Or, when the would-be writer's husband refuses to help her out of her depressed state, she feels as if "the flesh on her face were being stripped away, exposing the bare bones." Unable to sort out her tangled emotions, she flies into a rage, pushing, hitting, and bruising her husband, thereby disclosing the unabashed turmoil of the woman who seeks to make her way alone in life while still dependent on a man for his love and admiration.

Nogami Yaeko (1885-1985)

Unlike Tamura Toshiko, Nogami Yaeko, the daughter of a well-to-do saké manufacturer, received a fine education. Her mother was a kind and loving woman; her father, unusually broad-minded in his educational concept, given the prevailing ultra-nationalistic sentiment in the early decades of the twentieth-century. After completing her four-year higher elementary schooling at home (the small port town of Kyushu) and receiving private tutoring in Chinese and Japanese classics, her parents sent her to Tokyo in 1900 to pursue her studies. After enrolling in the Meiji School for Girls, directed by a Christian who believed in equal education for men and women, she learned to think for herself and not to accept tradition or authority without preliminary evaluation.

Upon graduation, Nogami Yaeko married Nogami Toyoichiro, a young man from her home town, who was also studying in Tokyo, and who proved to be an ideal match for her. His kindness and thoughtfulness were instrumental in furthering her career, and it was he who in in 1907, read one of her stories at Soseki Natsume's Thursday literary sessions. While the master appreciated Nogami Yaeko's talents, he also pointed out her defects: she should write more realistically, include daily occurrences, and read Jane Austen, Emily and Charlotte Brontë, and George Eliot. Thanks to her intervention, Nogami Yaeko's next short story was published in *The Cuckoo* in 1909 (Keene, *Dawn to the West*, 1115).

Unlike Tamura Toshiko, Nogami Yaeko never suffered from extreme self-doubt, either as a writer or a woman. Her writing, of course, did not come easily, but her parents' and husband's supportive ways gave her the self-confidence she needed. Extremely well read in such disciplines as literature, philosophy, and history, she had also become an adept of the Zen tea ceremony and had made her own repertoire of songs accompanying Noh play.

Nogami Yaeko's wealth caused her some problems from a literary point of view. Because she had not experienced the poverty of some of her characters, they seemed to lack authenticity. Although her works are masterfully conceived and structured, Nogami Yaeko is at her best when exploring the dramas of her own middle class and not those of the less fortunate, with whom she was familiar only intellectually.

Despite some negative criticism, she was sufficiently motivated by the feminist ideals of the Bluestocking Society to undertake a translation of sections of the autobiography of Sonya Kovalevskaya—a brilliant Russian mathematician whom she considered a perfect role model for the Japanese woman struggling for equality and respect. Kovalevskaya, a "womanly woman," combined motherhood, wifehood, and career most successfully.

Nogami Yaeko also wrote plays: some were based on Noh drama, such as *Kantan* (1920); others—*Arsonist* (1916), for example—broached social problems. She authored novels dealing with political activism and the struggles of revolutionaries, such as *Machiko* (1928-30) and *Maze* (1948-56). Indefatigable, she wrote not only novels, short stories, plays, and poems, but essays, reviews, travelogues, and biographies as well. She translated works from English to Japanese and was the first Japanese woman author to write about mothers and their children (*A New Life*, 1916). Throughout her long career, she kept evolving as a writer. Even during the war years, when she and her family lived far from Tokyo, she took philosophy lessons from a well-known teacher who had also moved into the area. Although she won many prizes, for some reason she did not enjoy the popularity of other women authors of her generation.

"Full Moon" (1942), a highly sophisticated, tightly-knit tale, is restrained in its conception, but profound in its intensity and arresting in its creation of a "new" type Japanese mother (Noriko Mizuta Lippit and Kyoko Iriye Selden, *Japanese Women Writers*, 24). It opens in a seemingly flippant manner as the narrator, a middle-aged woman from an affluent family, is having her hair coiffed. Although she seems unconcerned about her age, she has her hairdresser pull out any gray hairs she finds. As they chat, they hear coming from outdoors the ominous sound of cawing crows, associated with death. The narrator feels a pang of anxiety.

Smoothly and unobtrusively, Nogami Yaeko begins interweaving the theme of death into her tale. Not surprisingly, when the protagonist reaches home, a telegram from her brother awaits her: "Mother's heart contraction returned." She anticipated this news, she tells her husband, ever since she heard the crows cawing. Despite the fact that she is a happily married mother of three sons, she has never been able to face the possibility of her own mother's death. Now, unconsciously, she listens to her inner voice saying with intensity: "Mother, I'll come home right away."

During the narrator's journey home, her inner and outer worlds blend; elliptical conversations with others fill in background material, explaining the love relationship which binds this tightly knit family. The reader learns that the narrator's mother is an independent and courageous woman, the antithesis of the prototypal matriarch who rules her family with an iron hand, demanding complete obedience from each of its members. The narrator's mother, on the contrary, fosters love and generosity in her children and grandchildren. Hers "was simply a kind of religious persistence toward the family, a mode of life which could not be changed. It pleased her to be alone without interference."

The scientific accuracy with which the aged lady's heart attack is narrated cuts through whatever sentimentality might intrude during the time of crisis.

> We surrounded her, stroking her back, patting her legs and back as mother groaned, clenching her teeth, a cold sweat breaking out in drops on her forehead, her outlandishly high nose swelling . . . With the attack coming on, she held mother's back as she pushed away the hot feeling covers, and kept pressing the hump that rose along the back. It seemed that this helped her somewhat, but I could not easily find the hump. Even the nurse could not press enough, and mother scolded her frantically, "Press harder." She didn't normally raise her voice like this; all the more for this I could sadly imagine what great pain she must be in.

The pain subsided. The mother slept. Unwilling to take pain killers, this stoic woman sought to endure her suffering as long as possible. Visitors arrived. Conversations were lively, rarely focusing on the mother's condition, but rather on the past, her childhood and that of her family. Nostalgic, but never maudlin.

As the narrator kneels to say goodbye to her mother, informing her that she must return to Tokyo to help prepare her niece for marriage, she is shaken by the thought that she might never see this beloved figure alive again. The inevitable telegram arrives in Tokyo: the mother is in critical condition. Once again she leaves to go to her mother's bedside.

> "Mother, I'm home."
> I greeted her with the words I expected to say to a person still alive; my lips trembled, warm tears fell. ... I lifted the cloth: her face was no different from when I had said goodbye; she looked as if she might open her eyes at any moment and say in her usual local accent, "You're back."

An arresting scene features the priests reading the sutras at the mother's bedside and the helpers wearing new *yukatas* over their clothes. Virtually the entire village participated in the funeral and its accompanying electrifying ritual. Burning candles and incense were spaced around the corpse dressed in white and lying peacefully in her coffin. The play of luminosities and the pungent aroma lent the scene feelings of sacrality. The shining trays, to be used for the cleansing meal, the flowers arranged in a shiny brass vase, the white rice powder dumplings and the meal offered the Buddha, added to the aura of this awe-inspiring ceremony.

Nature was working in consort on this occasion: rain fell on the beautiful carriage bearing the mother's body up the mountain to the crematorium, but "neither the pink petals [were] knocked down . . nor [was] the deep red camelia whirling around the gushing water [stained]."

> Mother had turned into white, light, clean bones. As I gathered them with the chopsticks, they made dry sounds like seashells. Although the glasses that had gone in together with her were not found, the silver mouthpiece of her pipe came out as a blackish lump which resembled it . . . after putting as much as could fit in the urn, I wrapped them in the newspaper I happened to find there. The faint warmth felt through the paper was like mother's skin not yet all cool. At the same time, I had the very odd illusion that I was holding my own bones after I was cremated.

The narrator took the ashes to Tokyo, then to the summer home her mother had so much loved. A few days later, at night, under a brilliant moon, the narrator's husband and son dug a hole next to a young Japanese oak. As she placed the urn into the ground, she verbalized a *haiku*, the words coming to her automatically, as if sent by some unknown power:

> Under
> the round moon
> pray you sleep.

In her realistic and restrained mother figure, Nogami Yaeko brought a profound sensitivity to all forms of the life/death experience.

Okamoto Kanoko (1889-1939)

Unlike Nogami Yaeko, Kanoko was not an intellectual nor was she politically or socially involved. Self-oriented and spoiled, her family doted on her, perhaps because she had been a sickly child. Like Nogami Yaeko, she was brought up in wealth. In keeping with family tradition, Okamoto Kanoko was encouraged to write, and was tutored in *tanka*, Japanese and Chinese classics, calligraphy, and music. Later, she became interested in esoteric Buddhism, about which she lectured and wrote extensively.

So debilitated had Okamoto Kanoko become by her family's excessive pampering that her parents advised her not to marry Ippei, a poor art student. Indeed, unable to care for herself, after six years of marriage to him and the death of two of their three children, she was hospitalized for several months in a mental institution. Her husband, a successful cartoonist, finally deserted her and their son. Meanwhile, her father had suffered financial reverses, and her mother and brother had died. Not infrequently, Okamoto Kanoko and her son went hungry. Nevertheless, she composed some *tanka* for the *Bluestocking*. Finally, her husband returned home, became a good provider, and encouraged his wife to pursue her career (*To Live and to Write*, 11).

"The Crane Falls Sick" (1936), admired by Kawabata Yasunari, was based on an actual incident: her meeting with the writer Akutagawa Ryunosuke (1892-1927) at a resort hotel in Kamakura in 1923. She noted their conversations and her reactions to a man whom she so esteemed. When she again met him four years later, she was taken aback by his appearance: he looked like a sick crane. After learning of his suicide, and of his written praise of her in his diary, she regretted not having conversed longer with him, particularly on the subject of Buddhism, which had played such an important role in both their lives.

Many of Okamoto Kanoko's writings revolve around beautiful, charming, superior, and strong women with self-pitying personalities. It is with these women that she identified. So powerful were some of her female protagonists that they dominated—virtually castrated—their men. In her short story, "Mother's Love" (1937), she narrates a mother's passionate and psychologically oedipal relationship with her son.

The narcissistic, self-indulgent, yet psychologically fascinating Okamoto Kanoko admired the writings of such novelists as Soseki Natsume and Tayama Katai—referred to as "I" writers. So obsessive were the "I" authors in depicting the negative and destructive proclivities of their protagonists that they were said to experience masochistic joy in doing so. Equally important were the "I" novelists' explorations of the deeper and symbolic meanings of the minutest actions, gestures, thoughts, and sensations of their heroes and heroines. Generally speaking—and this is true of Okamoto Kanoko's confessional works as well—they concentrated on autobiographical incidents. Her incisive style, replete with glaring details and written without reticence, is partially in the "I" tradition.

"The Tale of an Old Geisha" (1938), considered one of her finest works, is of the "I" type. It is an uncompromising exploration of female sexual drive and the manner in which it manifests itself physically and psychologically. So deft is her exploration, so objective is her study of the various characters, that one senses that the mind dominates, that one cannot but conclude that the mind dominates, and that feeling, although implicit, has been severed, arrested. What remains? A gaping wound.

Reminiscent at times of the *ukiyo-e* woodblock prints, "The Tale of an Old Geisha" gives a minute account of a woman's need to define and structure her life. She can do so, however, only through others. Manipulative, although outwardly kind, she attempts in every way to feed her ever-expanding vacant inner space. Self-possessed and in complete control of her acts, her facial muscles, and her bodily movements, the woman's exquisite form, endowed with multiple strategies, ambulates through the pages with grace and sensuality.

The prototypal geisha, having been trained since childhood to stifle her feelings, remains forever masked. Her true sentiments may be gleaned from the veiled glances or furtive looks of her "beautiful bluish oval eyes" wearing a "melancholy expression," a "blank look," or one of "solitude." A fine musician and conversationalist, the old geisha begins taking *tanka* lessons in order to appear more intellectual at parties. The complexities of the geisha personality is defined as follows: "A geisha was like a multi-purpose knife. It did not have to be particularly sharp to cut any one way but it definitely had to be able to serve many purposes."

When the old geisha decides to remodel her living quarters in semi-Western style, a young electrician, Yuki, is called in to effect the installations. Cheerful and carefree at first, he goes about his job with passion and a sense of fulfillment. The geisha is intrigued when Yuki refers to his work as a "passion." The analogy brings to mind the many times she had accomplished the sexual act without any feeling. Admiring Yuki's ambition, she decides to finance his studies and his various other projects. Rather than working arduously, however, now that he has leisure, Yuki's incipient narcissism emerges. Each time he looks at himself in a mirror he is filled with a sense of pride in his strong and appealing masculine body. To be an inventor, he concludes with pleasure, would suit his image of himself. Yet, when it comes to the discipline needed to bring his ideas to fruition, he seems incapable of self-control.

The old geisha visits Yuki together with her adopted daughter, Michiko—a "capricious girl" who hopes to attract him to her orbit. A product of the geisha environment "where love is treated like a commodity," Michiko approaches him—or any man—from a commercial point of view. Her heart, "had hardened while it was still that of a child." Was she *really* attracted to Yuki or not? He, on the other hand, expresses not the slightest interest in her. He noted that she was well developed on the outside, but "was hopelessly unripened" inwardly.

The old geisha finally understands the change which has taken place in Yuki. As long as he had a goal, as long as he dreamed about something happening at some vague future time, he felt excited. Now that everything material was available to him, he lacked incentive. All seemed a bore. The old geisha, hoping to bring excitement to his life once again, hoping he would pursue his experiments, plans an outing with some young girls. He was taken by one.

> [He] smelled scented hair oil, and he saw, at his chest height, the plump white nape where the borders of the nape hair were receding into a misty white skin exposed beyond the red lining of her color. On her thickly made up profile with a cheek that shone like white enamel, a high nose cut a fine line with statue-like clarity.

Nothing, however, came of the meeting.

In time, Yuki feels "trapped" by the old geisha. He leaves for an inn by the sea, where he seems to find temporary calm. But he also becomes aware of his own powerlessness, his inability to escape the geisha's subtle but domineering ways. Like a caged animal, he knows he cannot "go beyond an enclosing line drawn on the ground." Oppressed at the thought of his dependence upon her and his "loneliness" when away from his benefactress, he makes his way back to her, only to depart at some future date, and again return. When deprived of Yuki's company, the old geisha is filled with a "sense of tremendous loss—something irreplaceable, lost forever." Although a gnawing maw envelops her, the cyclicality of the departures and returns is proof of her power over him: the male, too weak to fend for himself, and the female, nourished by this very impotence.

> Sadness deepens in me,
> And my life flourishes
> Ever more.

The female characters so frequently depicted by Okamoto Kanoko, obsessed by their self-indulgent needs and desires, feed on frail and emotionally feeble youth. Subtle in their devious and manipulative ways, perhaps even unconscious of them, they, like the *vagina dentata* type, become castrating demonic forces.

The expertise with which Kanoko relates the old geisha's need for power and her autoerotic psychology is accomplished with sensitivity and with depth. Only by depotentiating the male does she experience some semblance of release and satisfaction. Only through her aggressive behavior could her pathologically immature ego draw sustenance from those around her: her daughter, a younger image of herself; and the equally unformed narcissistic Yuki, also reflecting some of her dreams of accomplishing great things.

Okamoto Kanoko's "The Tale of an Old Geisha," a many-layered story, bears comparison with some of the work of Tanizaki Junichiro. Both idealized women's bodies for their sensuality—he, more from a metaphysical point of view; she, by underscoring the flesh and blood qualities of creatures she looked upon as strong and independent. In their writings both authors revealed their own emotional frailty in unique verbal sculptures.

Uno Chiyo (1897)

Shortly after her birth in Iwakuni, in southwestern Japan, Uno Chiyo was left without a mother; her tyrannical, despotic father remarried and fathered five more children. She completed high school, then taught elementary school for a year. A nonconformist, she wore heavy makeup and flamboyantly colored kimonos, which the school administration frowned upon. Flaunting the school's regulations, she entered into a relationship with one of her colleagues, which led to her dismissal. Two years after her father's death in 1915 she went to Korea, then moved to Tokyo where, after enjoying a bohemian existence, she married her cousin Fujimura Tadashi, an insurance company employee. The couple moved to Sapporo, where Uno Chiyo worked as a seamstress and invested in a boarding house. In an effort to increase her income, she tried her hand at writing short stories, submitting one to a Tokyo newspaper that was sponsoring a contest. Her story, "The Powdered Face," won first prize. Next she submitted "To Open a Grave" (1922) to the magazine *Chuo Koron* (*Central Forum*), but receiving no reply, she went to Tokyo to discover the reason for the editor's silence: perhaps her anti-establishment piece—an incisive attack on the hypocrisy of the teachers and administrators of the village school in which she taught—was unprintable? To the contrary: not only had "To Open a Grave" been accepted, but the day she went to Tokyo was the day it saw publication (Lippit and Selden, *Japanese Women Writers*, 208).

Uno Chiyo remained in Tokyo, where her sexual and intellectual life took on rhythm. After divorcing her cousin, she lived first with the novelist Ozaki Shiro, and then, from 1930 to 1935, with the painter, Togo Seiji, who inspired one of her outstanding works, "Confessions of Love." With Kitahara Takeo, whom she married in 1939 and divorced in 1964, she founded *Style*, the first fashion magazine in Japan, which proved to be successful. After the war, Uno Chiyo began designing kimonos, then founded a design institute in 1949, which failed ten years later, but she never allowed herself to be discouraged by adversity. Her next step was to found the magazine *The Literary Style*, for which she wrote a highly prized novella, *Ohan* (1961). The story relates the plight of a man dominated by two women: his undemonstrative and rather bland wife, Ohan; and the domineering former geisha, Okayo.

Uno Chiyo's extraordinarily incisive and artistically fashioned short stories did not focus on social matters but on actual happenings in her own life. *The Puppet-Maker* (1943), for example, was based on her souvenirs of the eighty-year old puppet carver whom she had interviewed on the island of Shikoku. Although many of her short stories have been identified with the "I" novel, Uno Chiyo, unlike Okamoto Kanoko, is not self-indulgent nor narcissistic. On the contrary, her eye is vigilant, objective, and analytical as it dredges up her characters' least impressive traits, but never in order to solicit pity for them. Nor does she feel any shame for their acts—or for her own forthright behavior. In "To Sting" (1966), Uno Chiyo uses a parable to state her point of view.

> Once upon a time a scorpion, noticing that a turtle was preparing to swim out to sea, asked to be taken on his back, explaining that he himself could not swim. The turtle was not willing. He said, "Once we're out at sea, you'll want to sting me." To this the scorpion replied, "What nonsense is this? If I sting you, we'll both sink, won't we? If I sting you, I'll drown!" So, in the end, the turtle agreed and, taking the scorpion on his back, set out to sea. But the scorpion did not keep his promise. No sooner were they out at sea than the scorpion stung the turtle so hard that his pincers seemed to go all the way through the turtle's shell to his belly. "So, you've stung me, after all, have you? Well, you're going to drown with me," said the turtle, to which the scorpion replied in a sad voice, "I know it. But stinging is in my nature. I can't help stinging. Don't hold it against me" (Keene, *Dawn to the West*, 1130).

Such was Chiyo's approach to herself and to life in general.

To know herself *plain* was not, however, an easy task, judging by her identification with her protagonist in "A Genius of Imitation" (1936) (Tanaka, *To Live and to Write*, 190). Confessional in nature, the work focuses on the author's struggle to find her inner core as woman and writer—those factors that make her unique, that motivate her alone, and not merely the woman who seeks to win fame at the expense of her own creative integrity. "A Genius of Imitation" is a forthright, objective, and detailed inquiry into the writer's depths. Narrating the events in her life, the protagonist recalls her early fantasies of wanting to be "like" others, "imitating" others; in her imagination she was "like" the hero fighting for her country, or the healer, Florence Nightingale.

The virtually scientific self-interrogation increases in intensity as the narrator passes from childhood to adolescence. Fascinated by the "adult" world, she reads surreptitiously those very magazines and newspapers forbidden to her by her dictatorial father. She had made up her mind to accomplish great literary feats "like" other writers, always keeping the popular motto in mind: "In antiquity, woman was the sun." And *she* would certainly shine "like" the sun. As an adult, she craves for fame—to be "like other celebrated women writers. "Like" is still her motto; but "like" whom?

To write "like" someone else would be a travesty of the meaning of creation, an injustice to her *feeling* world—to her talent. While probing, she questions her motivations. Why does she always want to be "like" someone else? She draws analogies between herself and women's behavioral patterns in general: females were always wearing new clothes, buying or borrowing different outfits. Would she, too, change her writing style with the same ease?

Meanwhile, the narrator's first marriage having been dissolved, she marries a writer who, she decides, will also be her teacher. She will write "like" him.

> When I wrote a line, I'd turn to my new husband and ask how he would have written it, for I had now decided that he—and only he—was my teacher. I saw life through the glasses of this teacher; I thought his glasses were marvelous. . . . My life became indistinguishable from my work, and I became a mere wife in fact and fiction. The pieces I wrote sat still, hunching their shoulders and contemplating me like a demon in the darkness.

Relentlessly she tries to be "like" her other husbands or lovers, "like" other writers, "like" their characters as well. Who was she? What is she? Her need to discover herself had not yet been realized: "I'd certainly like to be a woman whose sense of purpose comes from within."

Uno Chiyo's ideals as a writer were crucially important to her, as they still are to most Japanese women writers who have lived under the aegis of the *mask*. Her continuous and unabated objective probings into her formerly closed inner world allowed her to find her groundbed as author—and as woman artist as well.

Hayashi Fumiko (1903-1951)

Hayashi Fumiko's childhood in Kyushu was both poor and itinerant. Her stepfather, a peddler, was a good-natured man. Her unconventional and kindly mother was married four times and had as many children. Moving continuously from one town to the next, Hayashi Fumiko attended a variety of primary schools. An inveterate reader, she loved to write and made up her mind early in life to do well in school.

Hayashi Fumiko moved to Tokyo in 1922, where she lived with a former lover, who was now a university student. To support herself, she took various jobs as a clerk, a waitress, and a salesperson. Upon his graduation, however, he complied with his parents' wishes, leaving Hayashi Fumiko to marry the girl chosen for him. The catalytic impact of her suffering is revealed in the diary she kept at this time (*Record of Wandering*, 1928-30) and in her poetry (*I Saw a Blue Horse*, 1929). So extreme was her poverty that on certain nights she was obliged to sleep in public toilets or abandoned houses on an empty stomach. Nor did she fare any better with the next man with whom she lived—an egotistical actor who not only spent her money while saving his own, but abused her, and carried on an affair with another woman even while proclaiming his passion for her. The poet with whom she next chose to live beat her, kicked her, and stuffed her into a burlap bag which he then placed under the kitchen floor boards (Keene, *Dawn to the West*, 1139).

Fortunately, Hayashi Fumiko's thirst for masochism subsided; she chose as her next lover a poor art student who was the antithesis of the men she had known. Kind, thoughtful, and stable, he offered her the emotional security and support she needed to pursue her writing during their long life together.

Unable to find a commercial publisher for her autobiographical novel, *Vagabond's Song* (1930), which later sold 600,000 copies, she agreed to its serialization in 1928 in *Women and the Arts*, a literary magazine published and edited by women. Royalties allowed her to undertake a trip to Europe in 1931, where she spent most of her time in Paris. Although she wrote travel accounts and impressions of the places she visited, her resources were limited, life was expensive for a Japanese in Paris, and by the time she returned to Tokyo in 1932 she was suffering from malnutrition.

More short stories followed in swift succession: "The Poor" (1931), depicting society's victims; "Cry Baby" (1934), about a widowed mother who prefers frolicking with her lovers to caring for her little boy; "The Crested Ibis" (1935), focusing on a young woman who feels her possibilities for marriage are nil because of a birth mark that mars her face.

Although never engaged in politics despite her friendships with anarchists, socialists, and proletarian writers, Hayashi Fumiko, accused in 1933 of harboring Communist sympathies, was detained in a cell for nine days. A correspondent, she did all she could to help Japan's war effort, going to China in 1937 (she was the first woman to enter Nanking and Hankow after the two cities were taken); to Southeast Asia, where she wrote about the Japanese victories, thus boosting morale; and to French Indo-China, Java, and Borneo. She worked closely with the Japanese military establishment throughout World War II.

Her postwar fictional writings include *Drifting Clouds* (1951), based on her trip to Vietnam; "Swirling Currents" (1947), centering on war widows; "Late Chrysanthemum" (1948), about a geisha turned restaurateur. Rarely has an acrimonious relationship between a mother and a son been so caustically and incisively recounted as in her short story, "Narcissus," which was published in 1949 (Noriko Mizuta Lippit and Kyoko Iriye Selden, *Japanese Women Writers*, 49-61).

The antithesis of the conventional narrative in which a son leaves a heartbroken mother behind as he makes his way in life, "Narcissus" is a tale that fleshes out a mother's hostility toward her twenty-year old son. Burdened with the support of her clinging progeny who feeds on her strength, this weakly structured and psychologically bruised being floats about without any *raison d'être*. Having suffered some irremediable hurt as a child, his every action and reaction is pathetic and garnished with antagonism.

The story opens as the mother chides her unaspiring son: not only has he failed to find work, but he takes advantage of and lacks respect for his mother. Sitting complacently in their home, he blows circles of cigarette smoke in the air and calls her "honey."

Hayashi Fumiko's underplaying of the mother's turmoil and the son's antagonism toward her sharpens the tension between the two. Controlling both the tone of her voice, her actions, and her language, the mother confesses her longing for a humble, hardworking, "ideal son." Hayashi Fumiko chooses just the right word, image, and stance to heighten that undercurrent of anger raging within the mother as she spars with her "hateful" son. He grins, puffs away at his cigarette, and then, with measured gestures, crushes it in a dirty ashtray. Only later, when she sees him rifling her handbag does the mother utter her irretrievable words: he will now have to fend for himself.

Unprejudiced in her nuanced depictions, Hayashi Fumiko sees the mother as narcissistic and self-indulgent. At forty-three years of age she suddenly becomes aware of the telltale signs of old age, which the author details in the manner of a portrait painter.

> Taking a comb to her rough, lusterless hair, she stroked it down. Her hairline had become markedly thin. Reflecting that it might be because of her intemperate conduct when young, Tamae applied hair oil and tried to get her bangs to hang fully over her forehead. Her lean face with pointy cheek bones seemed somewhat younger. Then she tried to boldly comb the bangs back, pretending that it was an operation. Strangely she suddenly aged.

The mother is shown applying makeup to cover her wrinkles. Is she going out? her son asks. Her affirmative answer is an attempt to elicit pity from her son: someone has to go out to earn money.

> Mama's no longer so strong, though you may think, I'm dependable. Wouldn't you rather leave me and rent a room . . . ? Mama's really tired. You and mama were born to meet as enemies; it was fated from a former life. Don't you want to liberate me now that you're a grown man? No matter what you do, I won't complain, as for me, I too don't want you to complain no matter what I do. . . . Listen, won't you somehow live independently?

Trying as gently as she can, or so she believes, the mother explains that at his age he should be on his own. Finally, she blurts out: "I'm tired of you." To underscore the son's hurt, the author resorts to descriptions of his gestures: he "closes his eyes, while knocking his head against the wall," as if trying to keep his mother's words out of sight, away from his bleeding ego. Never would his wound heal; nor would he ever be whole again. He asks: "You've never even once thought of me with affection, have you, Mama?" But she had, she maintains.

> Of course, mama has at times loved you . . . Of course, since you're the child who hurt my tummy, I think

Modernism: The Circle Competed 213

> deeply of you, Saku, after all. But the time has come when we have to part. Mama thinks so—You were mama's Saku only when you were a small boy. You too now have a grown-up's eyes, so you look at me as though you were a stranger—Mama and Saku, don't you see, were this kind of parent and son. I have no desire to bury myself as I am; I have plenty of desire to work. When I face your maliciousness, I come to no good. Besides, you're a burden to me, Saku—

Hayashi Fumiko resorts to a flashback technique in order to fit the missing pieces into the puzzle. As the daughter of a Taiwan official, the mother had been the product of his rigorous upbringing. When nineteen, she met Ibe, a student at a theological school, eloped with him, and went to live in Tokyo. Money was scarce, particularly after the birth of a son; her husband's extramarital affair ended in his mistress's suicide, after which he left Japan never to return again. Unable to earn a living, the mother was forced to walk the streets.

Hayashi Fumiko once again delves into the mother's painful world, but ever so slightly, deftly, and rapidly, with incisive strokes, like the *sumi-e* paintings of the Zen monks. As a child, his mother's behavior had been a mystery to the son. Although obviously a puritan at heart, her brazen ways with men made him uncomfortable. Most subtly, and unconsciously, he began a campaign to hurt her by frequenting only those women who would support him financially. How better could he take revenge on a mother who kept prodding him to get a job?

Concluding her tale in poignant terms, the mother is seen setting out from home one January night in search of a man who had once helped her. A few days later, her son, who has found a job in the north, informs her that he is leaving home immediately. Only then, when faced with a separation, does her buried tenderness emerge: "Say, if anything happens to mama, you needn't come back—You know me, there may be a moment when I feel like dying in a fit of passion. But you don't have to come, Saku." Gently bidding her good-bye he walks out into the night fog. Alone, for the first time, the mother heaves a deep breath. Is it relief? Sorrow? She goes out into the crowded and brilliantly lit street; sensations of joy tingle within her; it seems pleasant to be alive.

Hayashi Fumiko, a verbal engraver, captures those fleeting, intangible, and utterly complex feelings which grew, festered, and interacted between mother and son. Her contemporary themes, her candid depictions of human relationships, her sensitivity toward the unfortunate, and her unflagging determination to succeed made her one of the most popular female writers of postwar Japan. Courageous and indefatigable, she had authored two-hundred and seventy books at the time of her premature death at forty-eight.

Setouchi Harumi (b. 1922)

The daughter of a merchant, Setouchi Harumi spent her childhood on the island of Shikoku. Because she was frequently ill she had the time to develop her knowledge of the classics. Her imagination and sensitivity were well developed by the time she went to Tokyo Women's College, where she earned her degree in 1943. Her marriage to a teacher ended in 1948, when Setouchi Harumi fell in love with one of her husband's former students. Thrust on her own, she struggled to become an author, writing first children's books, then biographies of notorious sexually active women who strove for equality with men as well as the independence that would give them time to devote to their art. Setouchi Harumi identified with these women as she searched for ways to find fulfillment in writing. She succeeded in her goal.

Confessional in style, a form popular with women writers, "Lingering Affection" narrates the author's affairs with two men: an unsuccessful writer who is older than she and who has been her lover for eight years (Shingo) and the younger man for whom she had left her husband (Ryota). It is a disarmingly simple tale with complex ramifications (Yukiko Tanaka and Elizabeth Hanson, *This Kind of Woman*, 20ff). The story opens as the narrator is gathering up Shingo's clothes which she intends to return to his home in the hope that he will resume his life with his wife. The description of the clothing—the new indigo ikat kimono still bearing the tailor's white basting stitches and the worn and stained garments—represent their life together.

Shingo's clothes, once exciting to her and symbolic of their spiritual and emotional love, are now dead items. As she prepares them for packing, they stir not a single emotion. Indeed, they represent not love but a "habit." Once an enriching experience, the couple's passion has now disintegrated, like the threadbare and dirty garments she is packing with the intent of returning them to his home. She must sever relations with him, she is convinced, in order to survive as an individual and reenter the mainstream of life. Her existence with Shingo has taken on the quality of the clothes she holds in her hand: empty, vacuous—form without substance. The breaking of a "habit" is, however, difficult; it is easier to settle for the comfortable state of inner dependency and the security of continuity. To yield to this facile answer would be to abdicate the very meaning of life: activity, struggle, and change. Moreover, such a stance would arouse resentment with herself, anger over her own weakness.

> It was so much easier and more comfortable to go with the habits entwined with those years than to make an effort to break them. With tears gathering in her eyes as if her strength had failed her, she was shocked to notice that she too was already half-filled with the relief of ennui.

That Harumi focuses on the outer garment is significant in terms of Buddhist ritual. The vestments of Buddhist priests evoke detachment from the empirical world—the condition for which the protagonist was struggling. The robe is crucial to the ceremony of investiture of a Zen patriarch: it is transmitted to the next man of cloth and symbolizes the values he must uphold. The robe, then, exteriorizes both a state and a function.

For Setouchi Harumi's protagonist, Shingo was identified with negative values. The order and "cleanliness" she was attempting to achieve by sorting out his garments replicates her need to tidy or unclutter her own frayed and unsteady emotions. In an inner monologue, she questions her feelings concerning Shingo's clothes: "Was there a shallow feminine concern for appearances?" No, she thought. These objects evoked past sensations and events—"the grimy evidence of his life with her . . . ". Unconsciously, she realized that their relationship had died over a year ago. Yet, detachment was still not hers since the act of folding and unfolding "those garments saturated with the odor of their life together" still had the power to fill her heart with "bitterness."

Whatever was left of their relationship was now based on "compromise" with Shingo's wife. To underscore the importance of this word, the author has recourse to another analogy: "the dust of eight years had settled so thickly upon it that now it was impossible to detect whose endurance and sacrifice had enabled the triangle to be formed in the first place."

Only by confronting Shingo's wife, she thought, would she be able to detach herself from him. Until now, she had considered her to be "faceless and formless," a woman who was neither given to violent temperament, nor to "moral fastidiousness," nor to jealousy. Shingo's marriage had become a wasteland, a sequence of withered desolation, a composite of "dreadful years of loneliness."

Setouchi Harumi dramatizes the slow initiation process the narrator must go through in order to shed her increasingly burdensome relationship. Involuted inner dialogue exchanged with Shingo, his wife, and her young lover weighs heavily upon the protagonist. To help her change her way of life, at least psychologically, she decides to bury herself in her metier (a successful dyer of textiles and an equally successful writer of articles on her art).

Although rage at Shingo's careless behavior with her firms her resolve to be rid of him, there are moments when the narrator regresses, harking back to the times when she and Shingo sipped tea together—a ceremony so significant to Zen Buddhists in the purity of its decor, its music, and its gestures. An esthetic ritual designed to alleviate the troubles of the empirical realm, to discipline passions, and to establish a climate of peace through meditation, the tea ceremony, the narrator believed, would help her transcend daily antagonisms. Tea, symbolizing the Essence, divests the individual of the ego, allowing participation in the *Self*, that transpersonal cosmic factor identified with the intensely active state of silent contemplation.

Setouchi Harumi's narrator, however, rather than truly experiencing the Zen tea ritual, merely participates in its outward movements. Like the gathering together of Shingo's garments, the narrator remains on the surface of this profound religious transformation ritual. As her thoughts wander into her past, she desires to draw closer to him. After allowing herself the luxury of lapsing back into her "habit," she realizes she must no longer linger over a dead past. The very thought of such self-indulgence, symptomatic of a return to "passive complicity and inertia," sickens her. To detach herself from the "habit" would be tantamount to demolishing an old house and constructing a new one.

External reality—the reappearance of her young lover, Ryota—firms her conviction that she must cut her relationship with Shingo. Yet, "while she was giving her lips to Ryota, her eyes were drawn in by the light, and her heart trembled in the presence of Shingo in the shadows beyond that light."

Habit prevails. A condition of stasis sets in. Once again, in ritualistic fashion, the narrator sorts out Shingo's winter clothes, hoping for his imminent departure from her world, but not yet ready to reorder her own life and give it a new direction. As she works at her desk, unable to create a new design, she bursts into tears at the realization that her indecisiveness has sapped all her energy; "all she could do was wail hysterically at the top of her voice." Only then, however, had she allowed her emotions to cut through the incrustations of habit and veneer of manners and prudence. Shouting directly at him, she gives vent to her indignation: "There isn't enough air! It's too hard to breath in here! You breathe all the air, even my share. I'm suffocating!" Still, Shingo did not understand, suggesting that she exercise more, or that it might be a question of digestion.

Stymied in her efforts to change her situation, the narrator one morning boards a train for Nikko—the celebrated Toshogu Shrine—not to visit it, but rather from there to take a bus to a lodge located "among white birch trees in inner Nikko."

> Each time the bus turned a corner of the winding road, twisting so often that Tomoko felt dizzy, a different view opened before them, and the woven design of autumn leaves that adorned the mountains was kaleidoscopically transformed, as if magnificent Persian carpets were being displayed one after another.

The richness and beauty of the landscape replicated a future inner world shorn of "habit," a world in which she would be free to grow wildly, unstunted by the constricting presence of plants and clinging vines. She gets off the bus and absorbs the sight of wind blowing across the field and flowers sparkling in their autumnal garb, as the cold and hardness of winter sets in more bitingly. She is alone.

> In the stillness of deep silence, the chirping of birds echoed now and then as if they had suddenly remembered to sing. Standing all alone in the middle of the paved road that went on endlessly, white and bare in the sea of pampas grass, Tomoko was suddenly captured by the illusion that she had come here seeking a place to die. It was, unexpectedly, a sweet sentiment that eased her heart.

Four days of immersion into nature gave the protagonist the courage to write to Shingo and his wife, informing them of her intent to end her relationship. Back in Tokyo, Shingo angers: he will leave her, he assures the protagonist, and go away as far as possible. To encourage his departure, she helps him on with one of his suits and accompanies him to the station. There, however, she succumbs to an attack of panic. She fears he might commit suicide. She begs him to stay with her in the hotel one more night. He agrees. In the room, he kneeled at her "feet and buried his face in her lap." And she, "Bending her face over Shingo's head . . . felt a dam inside her give way and she burst into passionate crying."

Shingo leaves. Her fear of his possible suicide is alleviated upon receiving a postal card from the beach area where he has gone to stay. While conjuring up a wind-swept sand-duned landscape before her—"the somber Japan Sea, already colored by winter, stretched without end"—she realizes she is now prepared to look for an apartment of her own—to begin life anew.

Setouchi Harumi trenchantly uses metaphor, simile, and image to depict the difficulties involved in detaching oneself from a love relationship which can lead only to stagnation and further deterioration, and finally to self-hatred. Her psychological insight is a true marvel, the result of her own sensitivity as well as her artistry and profound feeling for life's continuous vicissitudes. That she became a Buddhist priestess, spending her days in Kyoto writing and increasing her understanding of religious matters is not surprising, for now she is focused on "an endless stretch of time."

Tsushima Yuko (b. 1947)

Tsushima Yuko, who has a heavy psychological burden to bear, does so with strength, courage, and great talent. Her father, the celebrated novelist Dazai Osamu (Shuji Tsushima), committed suicide at the age of thirty-eight (1948) after several unsuccessful attempts to end his life. The author of such unforgettable novels as *The Setting Sun* and *No Longer Human*, Dazai Osamu explored the changing climate between pre- and post-war Japan, including the breaking up of the tightly structured family unit and the liberation of women. It was he who coined the phrase, "the people of the setting sun," referring to the decline of the Japanese aristocracy.

Although other renowned writers had also committed suicide—Mishima Yukio in 1970 and Kawabata Yasunari in 1972—and the notion of *seppuku* had been ingrained in the Japanese psyche since samurai times, nonetheless, living with the thought of death in the insecure climate of postwar Japan was arduous for the young Tsushima Yuko. Understandably, the motifs of her short stories are death, aloneness, the couple, and desertion of the child by the parent. Abandonment, the subject of many of Tsushima Yuko's poignant tales, compels one to face life's vagaries alone and in an open and objective manner; it is a problematic and humiliating experience for anyone and especially for the Japanese.

Particularly moving, perhaps, because of the biographical element, is her short story, "An Embrace" (Tsushima Yuko, *The Shooting Gallery*, 122-138). It relates the painful emotions of a young divorcee and mother, whose father had committed suicide when she was a child, and whose former classmate, Megumi, had done likewise many years later. Why should Megumi's husband want to see her, she wondered. It had been so many years since she had seen her friend. While meditating upon the question, she probes her own life: she had opted for divorce, raised her child herself, and held a full time job. Why had she gotten married? "I was determined to get away from home. As long as I stayed there I would always be treated like a child. It was to get away." Life with her mother—the father being dead—was untenable, "claustrophobic." Feelings she had not experienced since school days burst forth.

> . . . the sense that however though I tried to act the strength drained through the soles of my feet while my body's surface seemed to desiccate and go rigid. Though I never let myself take that sensation too seriously, of course, for if I did I'd be finished. Instead I would even tell my classmates the truth about my father's death, recklessly, defiantly, as if it weren't important.

The very act of meeting Megumi's husband soon thereafter triggers clusters of associations in her mind. Segments of her past imbricate themselves into her present: the suicide of the mother of one of her classmates; the English teacher who went up to the sixteen-year old student and "without a word, put her arms around her shoulders and hugged her to her breast." The narrator feels pangs of jealousy for such a show of *feeling*. Had the sympathy been verbally conveyed, it would not have impacted upon her with the same violence as the physical embrace.

> Yet part of me wanted to protest to the English teacher: if she hugged Sumiko, why not me? It was years since my father had died, but I was still a child in the same circumstances as Sumiko, and just as entitled to a hug. I hung back in timid anticipation: wouldn't she at least think to look my way, saying, 'Oh, dear, did it happen to you, too?'

The narrator, perhaps even more strongly than Hirota, the husband of her dead friend who had come to see her, was trying to assuage her still-festering wounds.

> I was urgently searching the dim reaches of my childhood self: if I must say something to Hirota, then at least it mustn't be far from what I felt. 'As a child I accepted the fact calmly. You see, there was no other way to think of it but as a fact . . . It was only later, when I was old enough to understand other people's reactions, that I couldn't take it so calmly. People embellished the story in ways that did not agree with the facts, and I became very upset . . . I thought I could count on my mother since she knew the facts, but it wasn't a pleasant feeling to learn that she was actually sorry for me. Because personally I couldn't have cared less. . . . or rather, I don't suppose I could afford to feel sorry for myself . . . '

Time passes. When the narrator again sees Hirota, their conversation takes a confessional turn.

> Since my father chose to approach death himself, I seem to have made up my mind that death was an intimate of mine. "Death" and "parent" may have taken on the same meaning for me, even though my father was only my father as long as he was alive . . . It's a silly illusion I've always had.

As the two part, Hirota takes her into his arms in the darkness of the narrator's doorway: "my body was caught in a strong force. I stared wide-eyed. Hirota was holding me tight. He was pressing his cheek against mine. Before my eyes was his ear lobe, reddened slightly. His cheek and body were soft and warm. I relaxed and wrapped my arms around him. The sound of our hearts reverberated." For the first time since childhood, she had been shown the compassion and warmth for which she had longed her whole life—by one who understood through his own experience the meaning of despair and solitude. And she felt *whole* again.

Tsushima Yuko's sensitivity and the starkness of her heroic prose when confronting her still bleeding wounds are also apparent in some of her other tales, as, for example, "Missing." Here, a mother, rather than face the reality of her daughter's departure, cloisters herself in her home, cleaning its rooms over and over again, tidying up, monologuing with herself. The emptiness of her life and the vacuity of her endless gestures do nothing to diminish her misfortune. After waiting in vain for her daughter's return, she finally walks into the street— into the world—and begins to face the possibility of a life doomed to loneliness—without her daughter.

Indelibly marked by her father's suicide, Tsushima Yuko's hurt, revealed in one way or another in her tales, lends them a rare brand of authenticity.

* * *

The plethora of twentieth-century female Japanese writers allows only brief mention to be made of the following authors.

Miyamoto Yuriko (1899-1951)

The daughter of well-to-do intellectuals, Miyamoto Yuriko received a fine education and authored her first novel, *A Flock of Poor People* (1916), when she was only seventeen. Set on her grandfather's estate in Fukushima Prefecture, the novel revolves around poverty-stricken peasants and the hypocrisy of the do-gooder, wealthy landowners. The success of *A Flock of Poor People* as well as of other writings encouraged her to develop her talent.

Yuriko's autobiographical novel, *Nobuko* (1926), relates her struggle for liberation from her middle-class, conventional family, her unhappy marriage, and her love affair with Yuasa Yoshiko (1896-1982), a translator of Russian literature and a lesbian. Aspects of their seven-year relationship, three of which were spent in the Soviet Union (1927-30), are depicted in her novella, *One Flower* (1927). Her feminist and politically-oriented writings include "The Breast," dramatizing the entry of a day-care worker into politics.

In time, feminist and political issues became Miyamoto Yuriko's *raison d'être*. A year after joining the Communist Party in 1931, she married a literary critic, Myamoto Kenji, who later became secretary-general of the Party. Her writings, subject to control by the increasingly militaristic Japanese government, led to her many arrests. She was sentenced to three years in prison in 1942, but was released the same year when they found her unconscious from heat suffocation, which subsequently caused her severe heart problems and temporary blindness. After World War II, she completed her autobiographical novels, *Two Gardens* and *Signpost*. Her most significant works—*The Banshu Plain* and *The Weathervane Plant* (1946)—are realistic, but of philosophical import as well. The latter depicts her joy at her husband's liberation from prison, but also exposes the problems of resuming married life after years of separation. Unlike other writers who pleasured with each Japanese victory, Miyamoto Yuriko looked upon her people as victims of a ruthless imperialistic military establishment. Relentless in her account of the brutality of the army establishment, she fleshes out its policies which were to blame for her nation's agony. Miyamoto Yuriko was one of the few Japanese writers to set the historical record straight by blaming Japan's militarism for her nation's suffering, rather than the American's use of the atomic bomb. Had the Japanese not declared war, the bombs would not have been dropped.

That Miyamoto Yuriko lived her ideals is a truism. Rather than succumbing to the pressures of the Japanese government during World War II, she participated in the establishment of the anti-imperialist *The New Japanese Literature Association*, worked in the Women's Democratic Club, and, among many other activities, became the editor-in-chief of *Working Women*, a Communist publication (Keene, *Dawn to the West*, 1146-50). That she never looked back with nostalgia to pre-war Japan, idealized by so many contemporary authors, and that she struggled for the liberation of women through her writings, discloses the admirable character traits of an admirable novelist.

Sata Ineko (b. 1904)

Sata Ineko differed markedly from the idealistic Miyamoto Yuriko. Her formal education ended when she was eleven, after which she was sent to work in a caramel factory.

Still, she continued to read despite the little free time she enjoyed. At sixteen, while employed as a waitress in Tokyo, she was able to meet well-known writers. Among them was Akutagawa Ryunosuke, who was impressed by Sata Ineko's intelligence. Her marriage to an abusive, although cultured man, was disastrous, and ended in divorce after one year. While working at a cafe, she met the Marxist, Kubokawa Tsurujiro (1903-74) and married him. After joining the Communist Writer's Federation in 1929 and the Communist Party in 1932, she became deeply involved in helping the proletariat, not only by publishing works describing their terrible living conditions, but also by becoming editor of *Working Women*.

Her proletarian-oriented narrative, *From the Caramel Factory* (1928), based on actual experience, not only castigated the government that permitted child labor, but also the father who had removed his daughter from school at an early age to send her to work in a factory.

Because of the repressive political climate in Japan during the 1930's, and because of her husband's imprisonment in 1932, Sata Ineko found herself obliged to support herself, her children, and her husband after his release. Continuing to write fiction, she altered the story-lines of her tales to make them acceptable to Japan's military establishment. In *A Grey Afternoon* (1939), she treats the difficult roles of working women who also have household commitments. Her husband, although a forward-looking Communist, held traditional attitudes toward women. Not only had he been unfaithful to his wife many times, but as a tubercular he made increasing demands upon her time and her meager funds. The couple divorced in 1945.

Sata Ineko's war activities were neither impressive nor admirable. How she was able to betray her own politico-economic beliefs in favor of those of the military during World War II is difficult to fathom. She had not only surrendered her Communist ideals by writing works acceptable to Japan's leaders, but she actually accepted to travel at their invitation to the war fronts (China, Singapore, Malaysia, Indonesia) to proclaim and foster the military government's point of view. Sata Ineko was expelled from the Communist Party in 1951, but unconditionally reinstated in 1955. To be a member of the Communist Party was for her "an article of faith in her life," and she could not "imagine what her life would be like if she left the party" (Keene, *Dawn to the West*, 1157).

Mountain Torrent (1964), in which Sata Ineko analyzes the errors of her wartime collaboration, denounces (as do others with integrity) the American Peace Treaty signed with Japan in 1952 as a travesty, since the Soviet Union had not been invited to participate. Her anti-Americanism, always flagrant, reached new paroxysms in *Mountain Torrent*, for she needed a scapegoat on which to shift the blame for her own moral failures. What more could be expected of one who chose the road of expediency at the cost of betraying her own ideals?

Hirabayashi Taiko (1905-1972)

Another proletarian writer, Hirabayashi Taiko shared the ideals of socialists and radicals for the betterment of humankind. Upon completion of high school, she moved to Tokyo in 1922 where she frequented anarchists. Fears that political activists would take advantage of the chaos following the Great Earthquake in 1923 led to Hirabayashi Taiko's arrest and subsequent release on the condition that she leave Tokyo. She and her lover, the anarchist leader, Saikai Toshihiko, visited Korea and Manchuria. Hirabayashi Taiko's writings during this period were based on authentic experiences: "In the Charity World" (1927) tells of her child who had died in infancy.

Involved not only in anarchist activities, Hirabayashi Taiko worked in addition for such Dadaist magazines as *GE.GIMIGAM.PRRR.GIMGEM*. Gradually she grew tired of these activities, of her poverty, and her highly promiscuous life. She and Hayashi Fumiko, who were living together in dire straits, attempted to make ends meet by selling their short stories. Indeed, their poverty was such that in order to call on publishers, they took turns wearing the one presentable dress they shared between them. After marrying the leftist critic and activist, Kobori Jinji (1901-1959) Hirabayashi Taiko was able to devote more time to writing, producing such works as "Battle Front" and "Beating."

Antagonistic to militarism and fearful of fascism, both she and her husband were arrested in 1937, together with other leftists who refused to submit to the military clique. Despite tuberculosis contracted during her incarceration, and unlike some of her contemporaries such as Sata Ineko, she refused to yield to political pressure, remaining silent during the war years. Only after the conclusion of hostilities were her works published: "This Kind of Woman" (1946), "I Go Alone" (1946), "I Mean to

Live" (1947), and "Song from the Depths of the Earth" (1948), an exploration of the gangster world (Keene, *Dawn to the West*, 1157).

Because Hirabayashi Taiko did not believe literature to be the handmaid of ideology, she withdrew from left-wing groups. Her fascinating autobiographical *Desert Flowers* (1955-57) tells of her struggle for independence as a young girl, her many unfortunate and destructive relationships with men, and the joys of creative writing and political activism. She worked hard in women's causes after her divorce in 1955, dedicating herself particularly to the abolition of legal prostitution. But she also tried to implement the spirit of these unfortunate women by steering them into positive life styles. Hirabayashi Taiko's characters are hard-working, realistic, strong, optimistic women, who have faith in themselves and in the future.

* * *

The list of twentieth-century women writers is long: Nakamoto Takako (b. 1903), Kono Taeko (b. 1926), Tomioka Taeko (b. 1935), Oba Minako (b. 1930), Hayashi Kyoko (b. 1930), Kurahashi Yumiko (b. 1935), Tsumura Setsuko (b. 1928), Yamamoto Michiko (b. 1936), Takahashi Takako (b. 1932), Harada Yasuko (b. 1928), Tsuboi Sakae (1900-67), Mori Yoko (b. 1940), Ariyoshi Sawako (1931-84), Hiraiwa Yumie (b. 1932), and others.

Because, subjectively speaking, I consider Enchi Fumiko to be the outstanding contemporary Japanese woman writer, the following pages will be devoted to her greatest work, *Masks*.

Enchi Fumiko (1905-1986)

The writings of Enchi Fumiko encompass the most significant elements of Japan's cultural past as well as its present. She was a poet, a mystic, an empiricist, and, above all, she was an artist.

The daughter of a professor of literature at the University of Tokyo, Enchi Fumiko was brought up in an environment where the intellect played a considerable role. Nevertheless she gave up her high school studies to devote herself to drama— mainly Kabuki. Her first play, *Native Land*, was performed at the Tsukiji Little Theatre in 1926. She also committed herself to the proletarian literary movement and joined a Communist organization, from which she withdrew in order to avoid any undue problems for her father. Rather than carry through her original intention of leaving her family, she took a less rebellious path, marrying in 1927 a young journalist, Enchi Yoshimatsu, whom she did not love. She remained with him until his death in 1974.

Enchi Fumiko subsequently turned her attention to novels since they afforded her, she believed, greater freedom of expression than did plays. Her trilogy, *The Thing Which Removes Red* (1955-56) explored the dark realms of the woman's psyche. Her novel, *The Waiting Years* (1957), dramatizes the plight of three women victims caught up in the stress syndrome of the paternalistic Meiji family system. One of her short stories, "Boxcar of Chrysanthemums," focuses on one woman who accepts the fateful and tragic course of marriage to a mentally retarded man. One of Enchi Fumiko's major contributions was her translation of *The Tale of Genji* into modern Japanese (1967-72). She was also the recipient of many of Japan's most coveted literary prizes.

Her masterpiece, *Masks* (1958), unique not only in Japanese literature but in world literature as well, takes readers into the heart of the feminine world: its mysteries, its sacred and profane rituals, its exorcisms, and its initiatory rites. In Enchi Fumiko's matriarchate, the unexpressed is more important than the expressed: silence rather than the spoken word, emptiness rather than fulness, formlessness rather than form. Behind each word, image, line, color, object, gesture, and protagonist, there lies a hidden realm that tingles with excitement and inspires awe.

Masks is a modern reworking of ceremonies that might have taken place during the Heian period. It deals with the secret world of priestesses and shamanesses and the protagonist, Mieko Togano, is a contemporary incarnation of this type of elusive and mysterious woman. Absolutely essential to her is the continuation of her family, and, by implication, of her own eternality through reproduction. Mieko's daughter-in-law, Yasuko, is the medium through which she will bring her ideas to fruition. Both Mieko and Yasuko are widows; both view the man as a stud, excluding him from any personal or feeling relationship. In such a matriarchal context, sex becomes sinless and impersonal (Esther Harding, *Psychic Energy*, 163).

Masks is divided into three parts, each bearing the name of a specific feminine Noh mask. Since women were denied roles in Noh theatre, the mask worn by the male impersonators incarnates an unclear and undefined sex as well as a personality. Once the male actor dons his feminine mask, he vanishes, and *it* takes over. The mask itself may be said to be archetypal: it exists in a universal and timeless domain; it also represents a pattern of behavior, and forms the structural dominant of the psyche. Unmodifiable, immutable, and unaffected by the world of contingencies, masks are used as accessories in ceremonies and rituals in Japan, and are also considered to be instruments of possession, capable of capturing and vitalizing—or destroying—what is human and inhuman in life (Kazuko Sugisaki, "Staging the Dream—Japanese Noh Theater and the fiction of Anais Nin," *Anais. An International Journal.* Vol. 6, 1988, 77-85).

The first section of Enchi Fumiko's novel is entitled *Ryo no onna*, referring to a mask representing the vengeful, transhuman spirit of a woman tormented beyond the grave because of an unrequited love. The mask from which the second section takes its title, *Masugami*, is a metaphor for the mad woman. The third mask, *Fukai*, symbolizes the "deep woman,"—the "grief-laden," mature middle-aged mother. The highlight of the incredible tale told by Enchi Fumiko is the ritual of conception, followed by gestation, and birth. Because the author's very special use of the mask in her novel is archetypal in scope, it possesses a dynamism of its own and contains a numinosity and fascination which absorb the spirit and psyche of the protagonists as well as of the reader.

Ryo no onna

Mieko, the shamaness in Enchi Fumiko's novel, is identified with the *Ryo no onna* mask. Her outward expression—detached, meditative, and quietist—hides an inner world of torment and pain duplicated by the *Ryo no onna* mask. A dichotomy exists between the facade of complacency and Mieko's inner self, possessed by turbulent and repressed unconscious powers. The *Ryo no onna* mask alone knows the truth. As an archetypal power, it will dictate her pattern of behavior.

Mieko, a matriarchal force, has secreted everything personal in her life, rigidifying her ego in the process. Arrogating to herself the collective powers of the high priestess, she has successfully dominated both her own troublesome unconscious contents and the lives of those who are drawn into her orbit. Intellectually, she is a superior woman: the editor of a poetry magazine, a poet in her own right, well versed in matters of religion, and knowledgeable in matters of spirit possession.

Yasuko, her daughter-in-law, mourning the untimely death of her husband, Akio (meaning "Autumn's Growth" or "One born in Autumn"), who was killed by an avalanche when climbing Mount Fuji, has chosen to live with Mieko rather than return to her own family. Following Mieko's advice, she has decided to continue the research work begun by her husband on spirit possession during the Heian era, and auditing classes on Japanese literature at the University of Tokyo, given by Professor Ibuki, who had also been Akio's senior thesis director. That Ibuki is thirty-seven years old, married and a father, does not prevent him from feeling sensually attracted to Yasuko. His friend, Mikame, a medical doctor and also a student of spirit possession, likewise has his eye on the attractive widow.

The opening scene, which takes place in a cafe in Kyoto, sets the climate for the novel. Kyoto, the capital of Japan during the Heian era, was and still is the seat of temples, gardens, parks, and imperial palaces, known the world over for their beauty and mystery. That Enchi Fumiko chose this city as the locus of the early scenes of her novel underscores the importance not only of religious rituals but also of the aristocratic elements in *Masks*.

The introductory images are significant for their symbolic ramifications. On the table around which Ibuki and Mikame are seated there are "a single *white chrysanthemum* and an ashtray piled high with cigarette butts." Contemporary Japan is represented by the cafe, the ashtray, and the cigarette butts; its numinous and aesthetic past is identified with the white chrysanthemum, an image of crucial importance. Its petals, disposed in a circular pattern, represent the earthly counterpart of the sun's rays in all of their burgeoning purity, power, and eternality. Awesome, yet friendly, the sun in the guise of the chrysanthemum welcomes those who seek to be warmed by its glowing rays. The power of the flower's illumination—its numinosity—symbolizes cosmic intelligence. The chrysanthemum becomes a mediating force between the universal and the personal, the cyclical and the perennial, and between light and shadow (Michael Czaja, *Gods of Myth: Stone Phallicism in Japanese Folk Religion*, 187).

Ibuki and Mikame, friends since college days, believe themselves to be in full control of their lives, but by entering the world of spirit possession, which is traditionally a woman's area, they tread on dangerous ground. During their conversation, they mention a seance both had attended only a few weeks earlier. The medium, a woman who spoke in French in the voice of a male alpinist, told of his fatal fall into a crevasse while climbing the Matterhorn. Yasuko, who was present at the seance, was powerfully shaken by the experience, which recalled her husband's death on Mount Fuji. Ibuki and Mikame discuss the incident scientifically: did the medium have the power to "pick up the voices of real human beings from around the world, like a radio picking up air waves?" If so, the mind is comparable to a computer or word processor, possessing its own antennae, which are capable of tuning in and out of anything and everything, according to the length of the waves. An exciting and ambiguous world of imponderables emerges from this experience—a bit frightening even for these intellectually awakened men.

What also intrigues Ibuki and Mikame is the peculiar relationship between Mieko and Yasuko. The latter, they are convinced, is a medium figure, and the former a shaman spirit. Yasuko is psychologically fettered to her mother-in-law, her very vitality being fed and nurtured by the older woman; Mieko, an impassive and immutable force, by working her mysterious will is able to subdue the younger person.

Like the priestesses presiding at a Shinto shrine, there is something outerworldly about Mieko, as if she were inhabited by some transhuman power. Yasuko's unconscious identification with her mother-in-law prolongs the undeveloped nature of her childhood and her life as a young bride. To free herself from Mieko's influence would require a sacrifice of the *archetypal mother*, or the power represented by this force within her unconscious. Should such an amputation not take place, the younger woman would fall further under the domination of the older woman's personality and eventually become overpowered by it (C. G. Jung, *Collected Works*, 16, 179).

The ancient concept of possession by a spirit, demon, or ghost is today expressed in terms of an archetype—an alien energy or a mana figure which releases its *libido* (psychic energy) into an individual. Like a demon or djinn, the archetype represented by the *Ryo no onna* mask has invaded Mieko's unconscious, spreading its invisible poisons in the process. Mieko's other side—that of shamaness/priestess—remains exposed. She, like the sun, sees herself, unconsciously, as the Great Progenitrix, and, as such, an awe-inspiring force for Yasuko—a *tremendum*.

Yasuko, the medium, not only is caught up in and dominated by her mother-in-law's grieving archetype; she is also catalyzed by her energetic force. A woman medium, psychologically speaking, is one whose ego (center of consciousness) remains undeveloped and who is dominated by another's power, mood, or philosophy. So strong can this alien force (human or ideational) become that the medium woman unconsciously makes it her own. Yasuko, although somewhat aware of her identityless nature, does not realize to what extent she is being manipulated by her projection. She neither enjoys nor can she take advantage of her individuality or her life, her ego having yielded its authority to superior forces. That she may sometimes appear elusive, even secretive or subtle, simply indicates that she has no real identity, that she does not know who she is, and that she does not have any true understanding or recognition of her situation. Not necessarily negative, she will simply be unidentifiable—specterlike.

Yasuko feels confusion, annoyance, and a desire to free herself from what she senses to be her mother-in-law's domineering presence. She dreams of escaping into freedom, where she erroneously thinks she will gain independence and fulfillment.

Yasuko, a shadow figure, as we have already suggested, does not necessarily live out her mother-in-law's inferior traits. She lives out her weaknesses, or those characteristics which the ego has not yet recognized. Because she lacks lucidity, it may be said that Yasuko roams in dark realms in a state of psychological myopia. Her dependence upon Mieko will increase rather than decrease, transforming her eventually into her mother-in-law's spokeswoman and her tool.

Yasuko will remain a reflection throughout the novel; never will she come into her own. Her appearance at the cafe where Ibuki and Mikame are chatting is described as "a flame-red shadow [which] passed over the frosted glass window near their booth." In sharp contrast to her shadowy nature is the flame-red color of her coat, suggesting a fiery and passionate temperament as well as a highly charged and energetic personality. The incandescence she generates attracts men to her orbit. So, too, do the contrasting whiteness and iridescence of her skin tones, which glow with "the internal life-force of spring's earliest buds unfolding naturally in the sun." As a medium figure, Yasuko constellates Mieko's springlike enthusiasm and her own autumnal sadness. The younger woman is never separated from her entourage, and in that she blends into this entourage as well as reflecting it, she may be said to be all things to all men.

The reader's first direct contact with the matriarchal figure, Mieko, finds her seated in the back of a large car which is to take Yasuko, Ibuki, and Mikame to a Noh master's home. Her voice, which emerges "gay and youthful" as it comes "floating toward them from the interior of the car," offers auditive contact with the shamaness. Its reverberations from within the car, which may be considered a symbolic womb, are impressive in their power and transhuman dimension.

For the Japanese, sound, word, and non-sound are of supreme significance. They exist prior to manifestation and long after dissemination into the invisible domain. They both fill and absorb the universe. Like a magical filter, the tonalities and rhythms of Mieko's voice infiltrate the psyches of those present, effacing the barriers erected by consciousness, and immersing their egos into her protective yet constricting sphere. Lying back "languorously deep in the cushions, nodding slowly or smiling in agreement with everything Yasuko said," Mieko gives the impression of a remote background figure, never acting overtly, but merely directing the events through her radiant energies. Yasuko, by contrast, is "alert and vivid." The two women complement each other; they live in a world that no man can penetrate. Nevertheless, Ibuki and Mikame will attempt to lift the veil behind which the shamaness and her votary hide.

Having reached the Noh master's home, the visitors are shown a variety of female costumes. The beauty and artistry of these ancient garments, handed down from generation to generation, is breathtaking: "gray figured satin, stamped with a heavy gold-leaf pattern, embroidered with large, drooping white lilies." The range of brilliant and pastel colors may be looked upon as premonitory of the emotional patterns that will come into play during the course of the novel—a range of emotions stimulating and exciting, appeasing and serene, and destructive and cruel as well. Mieko and Yasuko realize that a whole *other* world exists in these costumes and that they contain life and breath.

Robes and weaving are significant for devotees of Noh, but even more importantly for shamanesses and priestesses of the Heian period. The gorgeous kimonos Mieko and Yasuko see in the Noh master's home are earthly counterparts of divine fabrics. As they cast their eyes upon them, they, too, begin spinning their webs—not concretely as yet, but figuratively. Caught up in the richness of the costumes' textures, designs, and colorations—manifold varieties of flowers, trees, and birds worked in brilliant and dark greens, blues, reds, and mauves—Mieko and Yasuko react affectively to this feast for the senses. Like the garments, which fuse disparate elements, they feel knit one to the other by unbreachable links, experiencing, in Ibuki's words, "a whole private worldless" domain.

The masks are brought out moments later. Yasuko is stunned most particularly by the expression worn by the *Zo no onna* mask: "the visage of a coldly beautiful woman, her cheeks tightly drawn. The sweep of the eyelids was long, and the red of the upper lip extended out to the corners of the mouth in an uneven and involved line, curving at the last into a smile of disdain. A haughty cruelty was frozen hard upon the face, encasing it like crystals of ice on a tree." Covering her eyes with her hands, Yasuko attempts to block out what she has just seen, thus rejecting the archetype imprinted in her mind's eye. Frozen cruelty, hardness, and iciness are the images she identifies with Akio's death. The shock of confrontation is so traumatic that she grows dizzy!

For Noh theatregoers (and Yasuko is conversant with Noh art) the mask not only severs the actor from the outer world, encouraging him to look inward, but it also takes on a numinosity of its own. For some, it embodies the spirit of an ancestor or the soul of a dead person paying a visit to the living. By implication, the mask is an entity capable of transcending barriers by destroying obstacles, and of renewing ties between the living and the dead. In that it is archetypal, it is a unifying, determinate form, which is capable of coalescing opposites. It thereby precedes creation and every manifestation of ordered form (Czaja, 8-10). The mask represents the primordial image of an aspect of the psyche that is nonperceptible but nevertheless filled with potential.

Why does the *Zo no onna* mask take Yasuko's breath away? The livingness and vibrancy of the unconscious content represented by the mask, so powerfully enchained within Yasuko's subliminal realm until now, breaks out of its closeted domain with such violence that it causes a momentary eclipse of the ego. The impact of the displacement of energies is such that it also smothers her spirit/soul or breath in the process, cutting off the oxygen feeding the brain. Whatever equilibrium, or semblance of equilibrium, she has possessed until now is destroyed, bringing on a state of confusion and dizziness. Yasuko fears the sensations represented by the cold, cruel, hard, and frigid ceremonial mask because they remind her of her dead husband, but also because of what these same sensations represent within her own psyche. Does she perhaps feel a certain frigidity on her part and has *feeling* been replaced in her world by icy impermeability? Can she still maintain a warm and deep relationship with a man?

If the *Zo no onna* mask takes its toll on Yasuko, the *Ryo no onna* mask, the next one brought to view, is even more frightening to her. Its "utter tranquility" of expression, and its "deeply inward" look remind her of Mieko. It is clear to Yasuko at this point that she must break away from Mieko's influence. She will, of course, continue working as her secretary, devoting her time to the poetry magazine, and will also pursue her research on spirit possession. But she must find her own niche in life lest Ibuki's appraisal of her become a reality: "like a woman wrapped in chains." She decides that she will marry Mikame, though she does not love him. It is the easiest way of escaping from her mother-in-law's dominion.

After leaving the Noh master's home, Yasuko and Ibuki take a train ride and observe Mount Fuji looming in the distance, "swathed in deep red clouds, as if it had risen that very moment from the earth." Mountains the world over and in all times have had special significance for humanity: Mount Meru for the Hindu, Mount Sinai for the Hebrew, the Mount of Olives for the Christian, Mount Kaf for the Muslim. Because of their verticality, they rise toward heaven, thus participating in transcendence. Volcanos—those energies necessary for hierophanies and theophanies—may be hidden in their bellies.

Mount Fuji plays a very special role, religiously and psychologically, for the Japanese. This sacred mountain, dotted with Shinto shrines, has always been looked upon by them as a spiritual ladder to be climbed. Each rung represents another stage in both a personal and collective evolution. Fuji's peak is usually hidden within a bed of white and greying clouds, which underscore its mystery, solitariness, and forlornness as well as its pristine purity. Unlike the spiritual images the Japanese most frequently evoke when in the presence of Mount Fuji, or the mountain's inspirational force for artists such as Hokusai and Hiroshigi or for poets like Saigyo and Jozan, the mountain image for Yasuko is one of death. This mountain had cost her the life of her husband four years prior to the opening of the story; in spite of the search party's efforts to unearth his body, it remained interred deep beneath glistening white mounds. Yasuko had walked up the mountain daily, meditating as she awaited its oracular pronouncements. As she stared at it from afar—and even at close range—it seemed to take on the contours of a "snow goddess, clutching Akio tightly to her, and refusing to give him up." The Goddess, a *vagina dentata*, froze her victims into paralysis, and then drained their blood.

The giant mountain force was feminine for Yasuko—perhaps a projection of Mieko. Powerful and rigid as her mother-in-law, her vise-like strength being lethal in both terrestrial and supraterrestrial ways, Mount Fuji had clutched and devoured Akio, and now was menacing her. She wondered whether her husband had been aware of his mother's constricting nature: perhaps this was the reason he had wanted to climb Mount Fuji in the first place—to get on top of things, reach great heights, prove his independence, his manliness, and his dominion over the mountain goddess. Had he wanted to stand *above* his mother?

Other reasons also suggested an identification between Mount Fuji and Mieko. Hadn't she spent her married years in the deep north—in the snowiest and coldest of areas? Mieko had spoken so frequently of the benumbing cold she had had to endure, as well as of the brilliant whiteness of the landscape, and the solitude and tranquility—perhaps the non-life—she had been forced to experience during those years. The whiteness, or counter-color, emphasized so continuously in Enchi's novel, reinforces the various motifs in *Masks*: death, absence, departure, and nocturnal-diurnal cyclical sequences. White absorbs everything around it—as does Mount Fuji, remote in its gleaming glaze and its frosted grandeur.

Akio's death should have encouraged Yasuko to go her own way. It had the opposite effect in that it reaffirmed her powerful bonds with Mieko. Was she in love with her mother-in-law? Ibuki wondered. Did they have lesbian relations? Not love, but admiration for Mieko's courage, assurance, vitality, strength, and calm are what attracted Yasuko to the older woman. Mieko had what Yasuko lacked. She was a woman in complete possession of herself. Still, there were aspects about her mother-in-law she did not understand: were she and Ibuki pawns in her game? extraneous pieces in a puzzle of her manufacture? Whenever Yasuko thought hard about these possibilities, she became almost paralyzed—as if she were choking.

In that Mieko's powers were archetypal—numinous—they were beyond her own comprehension. As the daughter of the head priest at a temple in Shinshu, she had certainly been indoctrinated into the world of spirits at an early age, and been taught to communicate with the *kami*. Upon her marriage, her husband, of the upper samurai class, took her to live in the far north, in the Hokkaido area, virtually buried the year round in snow and ice. Shut off from the outside world, deep in the heartland of the aboriginal people, the Ainus, Mieko learned about the culture of this indigenous race which had been influenced by the Ural-Altaic populations from Eastern Siberia and the Sino-Mongolians from China and Korea. She was taught firsthand the secrets of shamanism and ancestral totemism. The Ainus revered mountains and volcanos, considering them the central axis of the world, linking the three planes of the cosmos in a continuous process of regeneration.

Mieko had married at the age of nineteen. Unprepared for the harsh realities of life, for a time she bathed in the warm and serene seas of illusion. Her pregnancy gave her boundless joy but a strange accident ended her euphoria: the catching of her kimono on a protruding nail caused her to fall down a flight of stairs. Following a miscarriage, Mieko's trauma became particularly acute when she learned that the housemaid, who stood erect at the foot of the stairway during her fall, had "planted [the nail] strategically on the staircase." Only later did she understand the reasons and the power of the maid's hatred for her and for her unborn child: Mieko's husband had impregnated the maid prior to his marriage and again shortly afterward, so that she had been forced to undergo two abortions. The incident left Mieko with deep emotional scars, which neither vanished nor emerged into the light of day. They remained hermetically sealed within her depths. It was at this juncture that she created her *persona*. Her indomitable will and her rational principle now dictated her actions, and an ambiguous smile of seeming placidity was engraved upon her face. A moat existed henceforth between her inner impenetrable world and the outer accessible domain.

To the world outside, Mieko and her husband appeared to have resumed a normal relationship. Some years later she gave birth to twins: Akio, a boy, and Harume ("Spring Woman"), a retarded girl. Her husband's family, believing multiple births to be a sign of misfortune, forced her to give up one of the twins. Harume was registered as the daughter of a widowed aunt and sent to live far from home. No one saw the child again until after Akio's death.

Mieko's ordeals strengthened her ego and hardened her *persona*. As a result, she was highly organized, highly motivated, and always acted with a sense of equity and justice. Never, however, had anyone succeeded in peering beyond her *persona*. Yasuko, Mikame, and Ibuki have no inkling of her feeling toward them, but all three are fascinated, intrigued, and mesmerized by this incredible being.

In time, Yasuko and Ibuki enter into a liaison; he grows passionately fond of her even as Mikame desires to marry Yasuko. All seems to be functioning mechanically, according to some preconceived, mysterious plan.

Masugami

The second part of Enchi's novel opens as Yasuko awakens, terrified, from a nightmare. Stunned by the power of her dream and the unresolved unconscious energies which suddenly burst forth in a series of glazed images focusing on a mutilated Akio, Yasuko rushes into Mieko's room, then into her bed. Trembling she tells her mother-in-law in fits and starts that she actually saw Akio dug up from under the snow. Mieko holds her tightly in her arms, cradling her as a mother a child, soothing and comforting her as best she can.

Yasuko's dream is a reliving in part of a real incident. When she had joined the search party and climbed Mount Fuji, she had been given a long rod to poke about in the snow. She hesitated before using it, fearing she might stab Akio by mistake and hurt him in some way. Finally, she acquiesced, thrusting the rod into the snow, when she observed "a tiny deep hole of a blue that was so pure, so clear, so beautiful" it took her breath away.

Her dream was quite different. She actually *did* stab Akio with her rod: "I stabbed his dead face straight in the eye." In reality, when his body was recovered five months after his death, either because he had been dragged along by the avalanche or for some other unknown reason, one side of his face was intact, while the flesh on the other side had been torn away. "Beneath his left cheekbone his upper jaw had been fully exposed, revealing a line of white teeth" and on his forehead there was something "like a stab wound."

As Yasuko continues to relive her dream, Mieko continues reassuring her, telling her she was not at fault. As she speaks, her voice grows distant and her increasingly ambiguous expression "blurred into an even more indistinct white." Mieko's mental suffering, aroused by the vision of her son, is rapidly repressed. The indestructible and timeless *persona* once again takes over. In sharp contrast are Yasuko's "deep self-destructive urges" and her uncontrolled guilt and anguish. "I killed Akio again myself. I lost the power to keep him and him alone, alive inside me. That's the reason. That's what made me dream I stabbed him in the eye with that rod."

Focus on the *eye* yields some insights into Yasuko's projection. It was not Akio's eye she had stabbed, but her own—her spirit and intuitive powers or that sight which enables one to look deeply and openly within. By maiming his vision in her dream, she had, in effect, cut herself off from her real problem, blinding herself and her consciousness. Important, too, in the dream, are the feelings of guilt which emerge. Her affair with Ibuki is now experienced in a new light—as a violation of her husband's memory. Akio's real death by an avalanche had been viewed as a collective event; therefore, she assumed no responsibility for it. Her dream, however, pointed to her as the murderess and the blinder, guilty of having killed him a second time.

The entire stabbing incident may also be viewed as the maiming or destruction of Yasuko's *animus* (the masculine principle existing within her unconscious). Akio's death, then, is a premonitory image of the demise of her own subliminal maleness. Henceforth, Yasuko will yield completely to the woman's world—the matriarchate.

The dream marks a turning point in Yasuko's reactions. She no longer really *feels* anything for Ibuki; nor does she enjoy any kind of communication or relationship with him. Sex for her has become a completely impersonal act; it simply fulfills a need. Becoming more and more Mieko's "puppet," she lives out the *shadowy* destiny allotted to her by her archetypal mother. She even asks Mieko's advice as to whether she should marry or not. Yes, is the answer; she should not live on memories alone; and, by the same token, she should complete her work on spirit possession. Mieko also feels a change: "You are my real daughter," she tells Yasuko; "the woman in me that I tried, but failed to pass on to Harume, has found new life in you."

A daughter substitute, Yasuko continues to live out her shadow existence as the sensual aspect of Mieko, which has long since withered in the older woman. Mieko is the head; Yasuko, the body. The traditionally hereditary role of shamaness, passed on to Mieko by her father, is to be bequeathed to Yasuko, her substitute daughter. As Mieko's appendage—the bearer of the shadow—she is to become *actor* and carry out her will. Together they will work, as Amaterasu had with her weavers, transliterating their heavenly designs into earthly dimensions.

In time, Mieko reveals a confidence to Yasuko: only after the death of her son did she decide to bring Harume home to live with her. Since that time she has devoted most of her energies, emotions, and attention to this arrestingly beautiful but brain-damaged girl.

Harume is compared to "a large white flower bathed in light, magnificent in her isolation"—both physical and mental. As "she blinked slowly, moving her lashes like a dark butterfly beating its wings in time with its respirations, she resembled the Zo no onna mask," that of the "coldly beautiful woman" of exalted rank. Like her mother, she has an impassable and fixed expression, existing as she does in a different dimension—the transpersonal sphere. Unlike her mother, however, she is unable to return to the rational domain and communicate with others in a normal and logical way.

Mieko's plans for Harume are maturing. The *religious ritual* she has resolved to carry out, with the help of Yasuko, can now proceed as scheduled. Yasuko sets a rendez-vous with Ibuki, at his insistence. The locus of the meeting has been predetermined by her, as has been the time: nine o'clock in the evening, in what used to be her husband's study, where she now carries on her work on spirit possession. No one but she has been allowed in the room since Akio's death. A dark, cave-like area, enclosed and warm, like a mother's womb, it could be conceived now, symbolically speaking, as a receptacle for hidden energy. Alchemical mixtures could be cooked within this protected dwelling; magical forces could enact an initiation ritual.

Mieko has prepared Harume for the sacred phallic ritual. She has bathed, perfumed, and oiled her body most carefully, combined her long raven hair with loving tenderness, and colored her lips in bright camellia tones, so as to bring out her ripening sensuality. When all is in readiness and the purification procedure completed, Yasuko takes Harume by the hand and leads her to her study—the *temenos* for the enactment of the sacred mystery. The room glows pink from the lamp, as if it were the dawn of a new day and of a new life. Still, it is night, for in the garden the late moon sends "dark pine shadows across the frozen ground."

The emphasis is on darkness, blackness, night and the unconscious in this—Enchi's all-important transformation ritual. Darkness, illuminated by a glowing moon, provides for vegetation and fertility rituals to be enacted, thereby regulating the growing process—in realms deprived of light. An unconscious force, the moon represents passivity and receptivity—indirect rather than direct experience and knowledge. His power will make its way into Harume's unconscious, unnoticed. Like the moon, a reflection of the sun's rays, Harume is deprived of light, and a passive recipient in the sacrificial mystery about to take place.

The Japanese have always been moon lovers. The eerie and mysterious light which emanates from this body suggests a dim, insinuating, shaded world, never brilliant, and rather remote. Objects lit by moonlight are not individualized, but hazy and essentially obscure; they blend into the environment. The soft light of the moon's rays, moving about in complex designs and forms, times the modulations occurring in the secret world of gestation.

Night is sacred to the acolyte about to begin the phallic ritual. Ibuki steps into the dimly lit study where Yasuko has already placed wine and curacao. Like the mediums of old, and contemporary ones as well, she has provided her acolyte with spirits and drugs to increase his sensibility and diminish his level of consciousness, thus altering his body chemistry and affecting his nervous system. Ibuki imbibes magic brews.

The sacred space had now been sanctified. Ibuki holds Yasuko close and then feels himself dreaming, "transported into another realm"—spellbound.

> Giving himself over to her, he fell into the bed in the shadow of the curtain, his body enmeshed with hers . . . after closing his eyes in comfortable exhaustion, having been drawn again and again into dream after blinding dream, he started suddenly at the coldness of the hair on his arm in the dark. He pushed back the curtain by his pillow, and the fading light of the moon flowed in, illuminating in soft gray beams a woman's face of snowy whiteness, the heavy brows and thick downswept lashes alone black, as if drawn with a brush: Harume.

Stunned, Ibuki pulls away. Harume opens her eyes. She lies there exquisitely, in utter stillness, her face wearing the expression of the Masugami mask—the young madwoman. Ibuki wonders whether he has been drugged. Has he been dreaming? He drops off into another profound sleep, awakening later only to find Yasuko next to him in bed. Has she been with him all night? he asks. Yes, certainly. Or has it been Harume? No. She has her own room, Yasuko tells him emphatically. Ibuki is perplexed. "But in the night you changed into her, I'm sure of it. . . . Did you come I wonder, or was it I who went? . . . In the hands of someone like you, a man is destined to become a fool."

Ibuki, the male consort, has followed the dictates of the Great Mother with the help of Yasuko, her votary. His role in the grand scheme of things had been to fertilize the Mother through the maiden, to nourish and fructify her as well as the family, the race, and the nation. Subservient to the Great Mother, he becomes a follower, not an innovator. Under subdued lunar rays of the moon, that universal gauge whose function it is to govern the cycles of nature, Ibuki fertilizes the woman, in keeping with his *karma*. Acting in the world of shadows—in the subliminal sphere—he is no longer responsible for his actions. Confusion has set in. He is a being who has not come into his own; an unenlightened force; a funnel for transpersonal energies, and a vehicle of the shamaness's will.

The Maiden became Mother; death was transformed into life.

Fukai

Ibuki continues his trysts with Yasuko in Akio's study. Once more does the Noh Masugami mask appear to him in his dreams. Complications arise: Ibuki's wife, Sadako, who has hired a detective to follow her husband, learns that Ibuki is entering a "witches' den" in the evenings and that Harume is expecting a baby.

What is a *witch* that such power has been attributed to this kind of woman for so many centuries and in so many lands? Witches may be looked upon in part as materializations of the shadow. If what they represent is incompatible with ego, they may be incarnated as hideous and destructive forces. Such are Mieko and Yasuko for Sadako: evil and dangerous beings representing the basest of instinctual drives. Man-stealers, festering forces living in an airless and insalubrious terrain, they carry out their unregenerate practices at the most primitive of levels—by the light of the moon—like the Lamias, the Harpies, and the Hecates of the West.

Time passes. Mieko accompanies Harume for a medical visit: she is in her third month of pregnancy, but because of a retroflexed womb and her mental retardation, the doctor suggests an abortion. Should she go through with the pregnancy, he warns, she might die. But Mieko has no intention of allowing the pregnancy to be terminated.

When she had heard her daughter was expecting a baby, her "expression remained mistily vague and impalpable," but she had descended into another level of being where her joy could be experienced in the silence of solitude. Yasuko was entranced by the daring nature of Mieko's scheme, and joyful over the part she had played in its coming to fruition. The thought of a baby with Akio's blood flowing in its veins was tantalizing; Akio would be resurrected in the baby. The matriarchate was functioning to fulfill itself.

> You and I are accomplices, aren't we, in a dreadful crime—a crime that only women could commit. Having a part to play in this scheme of yours, Mother, means more to me than the love of any man.

Mieko had suddenly become more aware of the meaning of "the deep and turbid male strength within her"—the power that had guided her through her ordeals and her years of emotional wanderings. Like Amaterasu, she was her father's daughter; archetypal, she was mystery. Sleek, smooth, her mask tightly placed upon her face, she had become "gracious as a goddess"—an object of worship.

Mieko thought deeply of the infant gestating in Harume's belly, and she had a vision

> ... of an ancient goddess lying stretched out in the underworld, a prey of death. Her flesh was putrid and swarming with maggots, her decaying form covered with all manner of festering sores that smoldered and gave off black sparks. The luridness of the sight sent the goddess' lover fleeing in horror, and the moment that he turned and ran, she arose and swept after him in fury, all the love she had borne him transformed utterly into blinding hatred. A woman's love is quick to turn into a passion for revenge—an obsession that becomes an endless river of blood, flowing on from generation to generation.

Comparisons between Mieko and Izanami may be in order here. Had not Izanagi's heart been virtually broken, when his wife, Izanami, died in childbirth? Hadn't he followed her to the underworld kingdom of Yomi to bring her back? When he finally arrived there, he saw that her body had rotted away. "What a hideous and polluted land I have come to unaware," he thought as he fled in horror and haste, lest the Ugly Women of Yomi restrain him and prevent him from leaving (see Introduction).

As in the case of Izanami, aspects of Mieko died after she had given birth and after the discovery of her husband's betrayal with the maid. Her years of ordeal had strengthened her, but they had also rigidified her. Her obsessive hatred had led to a condition of stasis and virtual victimization by this irrational condition. What had died from disuse—her healthy outlook upon life—had become putrescent and transformed (as the dream indicated) into maggots. With the birth to be, however, a change was to take place within her psyche: the heretofore gangrenous elements were turning into living and healthy flesh. A symbol of futurity and continuity had awakened her creative and maternal urge and, with it, love was being resurrected. Ebullient, violent, and all-encompassing, love, which had withered so long ago, was emerging anew. She would be a woman fulfilled. Warmth and radiance glowed in her face; the persona was fluidifying, as communication between unconscious and conscious spheres resumed. The moat had been breached. Sensing the meaning of the change occurring within her, she allowed to trickle from her eye a "faint tear," which contained "all the anguish of which she never spoke." That violent and deprived side of her had been reabsorbed into the *whole*. No longer living in exile, she and her shadow were ready to join the real world.

The baby was born. Harume died of heart failure. She returned to her primordial condition in order to bring forth the new. Yu, the old nurse, holding the newborn in her arms, looked at it with the greatest love and tenderness: it was the image of Akio and Harume. No sooner had Yasuko taken the baby from Yu than she knew she loved it as her own. And when Mieko gazed upon its face, she felt herself peering into "the vast, mysterious depths" within her and suddenly realized she was eternal.

The child is the beginning and the end: the *renatus in novam infantiam*. Fruit of a shamaness' powerful will and longing, this child was Mieko's creation. Its gestation had taken place in the temple precinct where Harume had been brought up, and where she returned for her pregnancy. Hence it may be said that the infant had received the blessings of the *kami* and of Amaterasu, indicating the collective nature of this sacred creation born to a family—and to the World of the Mothers.

Some months later, the Fukai mask was brought to Mieko by the Noh master's daughter. Its numinosity and its sadness moved Mieko to her very depths. She gazed at

> the carved image [which] lay quietly with the yellowish hardness of a death mask. The long, conical slope of the eyelids, the melancholy, sunken cheeks, and the subdued red of the mouth with its blackened teeth—all conveyed the somber and grief-laden look of a woman long past the age of sensuality.

Bathed in the gentle light of moon-lit darkness, Mieko had become Universal Mother—the giver of life and the guardian of childbirth. Yasuko, the agent of her power, Ibuki, the inseminator, and Harume, the virgin, fulfilled their destinies in the enactment of a *Sacred Mystery*.

* * *

The circle has been completed. Women's creative force despoiled and desiccated throughout the centuries, has been returned to her in the twentieth century for good or for ill.

Conclusion

Is it not significant that the most archaic structure in existence in Japan is the Ise Shrine, erected in honor of the Sun Goddess Amaterasu? Although it has been reconstructed fifty-eight times since it was built in 260 C.E., hardly any change is evident from its original form.

Amaterasu is the Sun, the source of light and heat, and the engenderer of life. As the progenitrix of the Japanese nation, it is She who has bestowed divinity upon the Emperor. That he was obliged to renounce his holiness in 1946 indicates the power of this glowing and light-bringing force which is so deeply embedded in the Japanese psyche.

The Sun's power to illuminate identifies it, psychologically, with consciousness and knowledge—both speculative and intuitive—as well as with Cosmic Intelligence. The celestial glowing power also represents the *yang* principle: activity, energy, and fire. By way of contrast, the feminine *yin* is represented by the male Moon, Tsuki-yumi, associated with passivity, reflection, and water. Symbol for Japan's flag, the Rising Sun—Amaterasu/feminine power—is the nation's emblem.

The feminine principle held a significant place in Japan's culture and mythology since earliest times. In the *Nihongi*, mention is made of female chieftains (I, 194) who fought alongside the men. In historical times, shamanesses played important roles in religious services; and empresses reigned until the eighth century. Nor were women completely dependent upon men as was their destiny in later eras. In Heian times, women dominated the literary world. During the early centuries of feudalism women were not only allowed to inherit property, but also played a significant role in the feudal structure.

Was the male unconsciously fearful of feminine power? Was his need to feel superior to the woman a factor in his attempt to further his prowess? to lord it over her, relegating her to a restrictive and repressive world behind curtains? Did proving his worth at her expense yield him some semblance of security? Whatever the reasons—and these are complex and unfathomable—for his behavior over the centuries, the fact that Confucianism gained in prominence in Japan helped reinforce the male's fettering and shackling of women. Confucianism's strong puritanical bent, its view of women as simply procreative entities, with little or no love principle or conjugal intimacies to unite couples, served to diminish her place in aristocratic society. More and more prescribed and limited, she became wholly dependent upon the man. In the Tokugawa Period, her presence had become peripheral, subservient, a by-product of a man's life—a kind of entity necessary to his well-being. In the lower classes, particularly the peasantry, however, the situation was different. Women shared the burden of labor with the man, thereby maintaining some semblance of identity and self-sufficiency.

The Greater Learning for Women (*Dojikun*, III) by the Neo-Confucianist philosopher, Kaibara Ekken (1630-1714), sums up the moralistic views of his time. Women, he wrote, must be amiable, obedient, and virtuous.

1) A Womanly disposition, as shown in modesty and submissiveness.
2) Womanly language. She should be careful in the choice of words, and avoid lying and unseemly expressions. She should speak when necessary, and be silent at other times.
3) Womanly apparel. She should be cleanly, avoid undue ornament, and have a proper regard to taste and refinement.
4) Womanly arts. These include sewing, reeling silk, making clothes, and cooking.
4) Everything impure should be kept from a girl's ears. Popular songs and the popular drama are not for them. The *Ise Monogatari* and the *Genji Monogatari* are objectionable on account of their immoral tendency (W. G. Aston, *A History of Japanese Literature*, 239-40).

Kaibara Ekken's thirteen rules, which parents handed down to their daughters upon their marriage, include: respect and obedience for her parents-in-law; reverence and obedience to her husband; avoidance of jealousy; renunciation of the siesta; diligent housework; frugality in domestic matters; the keeping of young men at a distance; exclusion of a male domestic from the woman's apartments; avoidance of conspicuous colors and patterns in dress; compliance in all respects with her husband's wishes and those of his parents first, etc. (Aston, 240-41).

Because women had been taught to suppress their feelings and to hide behind a mask, their traditionally immobile features were interpreted as indications of a passive and weak nature. For many, however, their quiet dignity was, on the contrary, a sign of strength, of profound inner reserves, and extreme self-discipline. Woman was, indeed, Mystery—fearsome to some, alluring to others.

With the gradual elimination of the double moral standard in nineteenth- and twentieth-century Japan, increased opportunities for women's education became a reality—and incarceration gave way to freedom. There were, understandably, many examples of extremes in behavioral patterns, a case in point being the woman's need to prove her independence of the male by being as sexually active as he, with virtually no feeling attached to the act. Indeed, women were still cut off from their feeling world. Such comportment, however, rather than demonstrating a release from subjection suggested an *imitation* of male conduct—the reenactment of some unresolved psychological conflict.

Unconsciously, many women were imitating the man's ways, modeling their own activities and ideas upon those of the opposite sex rather than trying to probe their own inner world and discover their own groundbed. In this connection, Anais Nin wrote in *Notes on Feminism*:

> I see a great deal of negativity in the Women's Liberation Movement. It is less important to attack male writers than to discover and read women writers, to attack male-dominated films than to make films by women. If the passivity of women is going to erupt like a volcano or an earthquake, it will not accomplish anything but disaster. Their passivity can be converted to creative will. If it expresses itself in war, then it is an imitation of man's methods. To become a man, or like a man, is no solution (Anais Nin, *In Favor of the Sensitive Man*, 31).

Despite the extremes, woman in twentieth-century Japan generally came into her own. Not only had she discovered and developed her own remarkable creative faculties, as attested to by the plethora of women writers and artists, but in so doing she was also familiarizing herself with her own *nature*—her own needs and desires.

Woman had come the full circle. Having reintegrated her Amaterasu side into her *whole* psyche, she had once again become a sentient, spiritual, procreative, and earthly force. Like Amaterasu-o-hiru-me no Mikoto (Heaven-illumine-great-noon-female-of-augustness), her "resplendent luster . . . shone throughout all the six quarters" of the universe (*Nihongi*, 18).

Becoming *truly* woman, she had become *truly* her own person!

Bibliography

Ackroyd, Joyce, "Women in Feudal Japan," *Transactions of the Asiatic Society of Japan*, Third Series. 7, 1959.

Addis, Stephen, Ed., *Japanese Ghosts and Demons*. New York: George Braziller, Inc., 1986.

—, "The Three Women of Gion," pp. 241-264 in *Flowering in the Shadows*. Edited by Marsha Weidner. Honolulu: University of Hawaii Press, 1990.

Akiyama Terukazu, "Women Painters at the Heian Court," p. 159-184. Translated and Adapted by Maribeth Graybill in *Flowering in the Shadows*. Edited by Marsha Weidner. Honolulu: University of Hawaii Press, 1990.

Aston, W. G., *A History of Japanese Literature*. Tokyo: Charles E. Tuttle, 1977.

Behnke, Elizabeth A., "The Dimensions of Nothingness," *Main Currents in Modern Thought*. Jan.-Feb., 1974.

Bowring, Richard. *Murasaki Shikibu. The Tale of Genji*. Cambridge: Cambridge University Press, 1988.

Brock, Karen L. "Chinese Maiden, Silla Monk: Zenmyo and Her Thirteenth-Century Japanese Audience," pp. 185-218 in *Flowering in the Shadows*. Edited by Marsha Weidner. Honolulu: University of Hawaii Press, 1990.

Bunce, William K., *Religions in Japan*. Tokyo: Charles E. Tuttle, 1970.

Cahill, James, *Scholar Painters of Japan*. New York: Asia Society, 1972.

Campbell, Joseph, *The Mask of God. Oriental Mythology*. New York: The Viking Press, 1970.

Conze, Edward, *Buddhist Scriptures*. London: Penguin Books, 1959.

Czaja, Michael, *Gods of Myth: Stone Phallicism in Japanese Folk Religion*. Tokyo: Weatherhill, 1974.

Danly, Robert Lyons, *In the Shade of Spring Leaves*. New Haven: Yale University Press, 1984.

Davis, F. Hadland, *Myths and Legends of Japan*. Singapore: Graham Brash Ltd., 1989.

Dore, R. P., *Education in Tokugawa Japan*. Berkeley and Los Angeles: University of California Press, 1965.

Edinger, Edward, *Melville's Moby Dick. A Jungian Commentary*. New York: A New Directions Book, 1978.

Enchi, Fumiko, *Masks*. Translated by Juliet Winters Carpenter, New York: Random House, 1983.

Field, Norma, *The Splendor of Longing in the Tale of Genji*. Princeton: Princeton University Press, 1987.

Fister, Patricia, *Japanese Women Artists. 1600-1900*. Lawrence Spencer Museum of Art, University of Kansas. New York: Harper and Row, Pub., Inc., 1988.

—, "Women Artists in Traditional Japan," pp. 219-241; "The Life and Art of Cho Koran," pp. 265-294 in *Flowering in the Shadows*. Edited by Marsha Weidner. Honolulu: University of Hawaii Press, 1990.

Franz, Marie-Louise, von, *Projection and Re-collection in Jungian Psychology*. Translated by William H. Kennedy. London: Open Court, 1980.

Fukumoto, Hidéko and Catherine Pigeaire, *Femmes et Samourai*. Paris: Femmes, 1986.

Gossamer Years, The. Translated by Edward Seidensticker. Tokyo: Charles E. Tuttle, 1987.

Hall, John Whitney, *Japan From Prehistory to Modern Times.* New York: Delacorte Press, 1970.

Harding, Esther, *Psychic Energy.* Princeton: Princeton University Press, 1973.

Hawkridge, Emma, *The Wisdom Tree.* Boston: Houghton Mifflin Co., 1945.

Hendry, Joy, *Marriage in Changing Japan.* Tokyo: Charles E. Tuttle Co., 1981.

Jacobi, Jolande, *Complex Archetype Symbol in the Psychology of C. G. Jung.* Translated by Ralph Manheimn. Princeton: Princeton University Press, 1959.

Janeira, Armando Martins, *Japanese and Western Literature.* Tokyo: Charles E. Tuttle Co., 1970.

Jung, C. G., *Collected Works.* 3. Translated by R. F. C. Hull (New York: Pantheon Books, 1960). 12. Translated by R. F. C. Hull (London: Routledge and Kegan Paul, 1953). 16. Translated by R. F. C. Hull. New York: Pantheon Books, 1966.

Kawai, Hayao, *The Figures of the Sun Goddess in Japanese Mythology.* Unpublished Thesis presented at the C. G. Jung Institute, Zurich, December, 1964.

—, *The Japanese Psyche.* Translated by Hayao Kawai and Sachiko Reece. Dallas: Spring Publications, Inc., 1988.

Keene, Donald, ed., *Twenty Plays of the No Theatre.* New York: Columbia University Press, 1970.

—, *Dawn to the West. Japanese Literature of the Modern Era. Fiction.* New York: Holt, Rinehart and Winston, 1984.

Lippit, Noriko Mizuta and Kyoko Iriye Selden, Ed. and Trans., *Japanese Women Writers.* Armonk, New York: M. E. Sharpe, Inc., 1991.

Makoto, Ooka and Thomas Fitzimmons, Ed, *A Play of Mirrors*. Oakland University: Katydid Books, 1987.

Makoto, Ueda, *Modern Japanese Poets*. Stanford: Stanford University Press, 1971.

Malm, William P., *Japanese Music and Musical Instruments*. Rutland, Vermont: Charles E. Tuttle Company, 1990.

Maruoka, Daiji and Yoshikoshi Tatsuyo, *Noh*. Translated by Don Kenny. Osaka Joikusha Publishing Co., n.d.

Miner, Earl, *An Introduction to Japanese Court Poetry*. Stanford: Stanford University Press, 1968.

—, *Japanese Poetic Diaries*. Berkeley: University of California Press, 1969.

Miner, Earl, Hiroko Odagari, and Robert E. Morrell, *The Princeton Companion to Classical Japanese Literature*. Princeton: Princeton University Press, 1985.

Morris, Ivan, *The World of the Shining Prince. Court Life in Ancient Japan*. New York: Penguin Books, 1974.

—, *As I Crossed a Bridge of Dreams*. Translated by Ivan Morris. New York: The Dial Press, 1971.

Murasaki Shikibu, *The Tale of Genji*. Translated by Arthur Waley. Tokyo: Charles E. Tuttle and Co., 1970.

—, *Her Diary and Poetic Memoirs*. Translation and Study by Richard Bowring. Princeton: Princeton University Press, 1982.

Nakamura, Yasuo, *Noh*. Tokyo: Weatherhill-Tankosha, 1971.

Needham, Joseph, *Science and Civilisation in China*. 2. 5. Cambridge: Cambridge University Press, 1974. 1976.

Neumann, Erich, *The Origins and History of Consciousness*. New York: Pantheon, 1954.

New Larousse Encyclopedia of Mythology. New York: Hamlyn, 1959.

Nihongi. Translated by W. G. Aston. Tokyo: Charles E. Tuttle, 1984.

Nin, Anais, *In Favor of the Sensitive Man, and other Essays*. New York: Harcourt Brace Jovanovich, 1976.

Okamoto, Kanoko, *The Tale of an Old Geisha and Other Stories*. Translated by Kazuko Sugisaki. Santa Barbara, California: Capra Press, 1985.

—, "The River" (A Story). Translated by Kazuko Sugisaki. *Anais. An International Journal*. Vol. 1, 1983, pp. 69-80.

Parrender, Geoffrey, *Sex in the World's Religions*. London: Oxford University Press, 1980.

Paul, Diana Y., *Women in Buddhism*. Berkeley: University of California Press, 1985.

Pound, Ezra and Ernest Fenollosa, *The Classic Noh Theatre of Japan*. New York: New Directions, 1959.

Powell, Irene, *Writers and Society in Modern Japan*. Tokyo: Kodansha International Ltd., 1983.

Putzar, Edward, *Japanese Literature*. Tuscon: The University of Arizona Press, 1973.

Qamber, Akhtar, *Yeats and the Noh*. New York: Weatherhill, n.d.

Reischauer, Edwin O., *Japan Past and Present*. New York: Alfred A. Knopf, 1946.

—, *Japan the Story of a Nation*. Revised Edition. Tokyo: Charles E. Tuttle and Co., 1974.

—, *The Japanese*. Tokyo: Charles E. Tuttle and Co., 1979.

Rexroth, Kenneth and Ikuko Atsumi, Ed. and Trans., *The Burning Heart. Women Poets of Japan*. New York: A Continuum Book. The Seabury Press, 1977.

Robins-Mowry, Dorothy, *The Hidden Sun: Women of Modern Japan*. Boulder: Westview Press, 1983.

Rouselle, Erwin, "Spiritual Guidance in Contemporary Taoism,: *Eranos IV*. Edited by Joseph Campbell. Princeton: Princeton University Press, 1973.

Sansom, George, *A History of Japan, 1615-1867*. Stanford: Stanford University Press, 1981.

Shiffert, Marcombe Edith and Yuri Sawa, Ed. and Trans., *Anthology of Modern Japanese Poetry*. Rutland, Vermont: Charles E. Tuttle Co., 1972.

Shimizu, Yoshiaki, and Susan E. Nelson, *Genji: The World of a Prince*. Bloomington: Indiana University Art Museum, 1982.

Shiraishi, Kazuko, *Seasons of Sacred Lust*. Edited by Kenneth Rexroth and Ibuko Atsumi, John Salt, Carol Tinker, Yasuo Morita. 1978.

Shirane, Haruo, *The Bridge of Dreams*. Stanford: Stanford University Press, 1987.

Shuichi Kato, *A History of Japanese Literature*. Translated by David Chibbett. Tokyo: Kodansha International Ltd., 1979.

Sivin, Nathan, *Chinese Alchemy: Preliminary Studies*. Cambridge: Harvard University Press, 1968.

Sokyo Ono, *Shinto the Kami Way*. Tokyo: Charles E. Tuttle, 1969.

Sources of Japanese Tradition. I. II. Edited by Wm. Theodore de Bary. Compiled by Ryusaku Tsunoda, Theodore de Bary, Donald Keene. New York: Columbia University Press, 1964.

Stanley-Baker, Joan, *Japanese Art*. London: Thames and Hudson, 1984.

Stevenson, John, *Yoshitoshi's Thirty-Six Ghosts*. Hong Kong: Weatherhill/Blue Tiger, 1983.

Stone, Lee Alexander, *The Story of Phallicism*. Chicago: Pascal Covici, 1927.

Stone, Merlin, *Ancient Mirrors of Womanhood*. 2. New York: Sibylline Books, 1979.

Sugisaki, Kazuko, "Darkness of Passion: The Diary of Izumi Shikibu." *Anais. An International Journal.* Vol. 4, 1986, pp. 43-51.

—, "Staging the Dream—Japanese Noh Theater and the fiction of Anais Nin." *Anais. An International Journal.* Vol. 6, 1988, pp. 77-85.

—, "Ono-no-Komachi—The Legend and the Reality." *Anais. An International Journal.* Vol. 8, 1990, pp. 67-78.

Suzuki, Daisetz, T., *Zen and Japanese Culture*. Princeton: Princeton University Press, 1973.

Swann, Peter C., *A Concise History of Japanese Art*. Tokyo: Kodansha International Ltd., 1979.

Tanaka, Yukiko, Ed. and Trans., *To Live and to Write*. Seattle, Washington: The Seal Press, 1987.

Tanaka, Yukiko and Elizabeth Hanson, *This Kind of Woman*. Stanford: Stanford University Press, 1982.

Terry, Charles S., Ed. and Comp., *Masterworks of Japanese Art*. Tokyo: Charles E. Tuttle Company, 1959.

Thompson, Laurence C., *Chinese Religion: An Introduction*. Belmont, CA: Dickenson Publishing Co., 1969.

Tsuda, Noritake, *Handbook of Japanese Art*. Tokyo: Charles E. Tuttle, 1976.

Tsushima, Yuko, *The Shooting Gallery*. Translated by Geraldine Harcourt. New York: Pantheon Books, 1988.

Varley, H. Paul, *Japanese Culture*. Honolulu: University of Hawaii Press, 1984.

Ware, James R., *Alchemy, Medicine, Religion*. Cambridge: M. I. T. Press, 1966.

Week Ender, The, February 15, 1974.

We Japanese. Hakone: Fujiya Hotel, Ltd., 1950.

Weidner, Marsha, Editor, *Flowering in the Shadows. Women in the History of Chinese and Japanese Painting.* Honolulu: University of Hawaii Press, 1990.

Williams, C. A. S., *Outlines of Chinese Symbolism and Art Motives.* New York: Dover Publications, Inc., 1976.

Yosano Akiko, *Tangled Hair.* Translated by Sanford Goldstein and Seishi Shinoda. Lafayette: Purdue University Studies, 1971.

Index

Ainus 235
Akikonomu 58-9
Akoko *see*: Yosano Akiko
Akutagawa Ryunosuke 203, 223
Ama-tsu-hiko-no-ninigi no Mikoto 10
Amano-Uzume-no-Mikoto 9
Amaterasu (Sun Goddess) 3, 7-11, 31, 56, 81, 84-87, 93, 98, 110, 241, 243-44, 247
Amida Buddha 30, 52, 55, 77, 89
ancestral piety 16
anima 42, 44, 60, 61
animus 237
anti-Americanism 224
archetypal mother 229, 237
Ariwara no Yukihira 111, 119-20
Ariyoshi Sawako 225
Arsonist 200
Ashikaga Shogunate 102, 103, 110, 122, 123
Ashikaga Takauji 102
Ashikaga Yoshimitsu 102
Baba Akiko 182, 184-5
bamboo 18
Banshu Plain, The 222
Basho 134, 142, 145
"Battle Front" 224
"Beating" 224
birds 96
Bluestocking 194, 203
Bluestocking Society 194, 196, 200
bodhisattvas 83, 92
Book of Songs, The 141
"Boxcar of Chrysanthemums" 226
"Breast, The" 221
Buddha Breath 112, 116

Buddhism 3, 14-16, 21, 23-26, 28, 39-40, 54, 73, 84, 87, 92, 93, 101, 102, 110, 142, 203, 215
Buddhist nuns 37
Bungakkai (Literary World) 161-62
bunhinga 174
bunjin 173
bunjinga ("literary men's painting") 151-2, 153
bushido ("The Way of the Warrior") 105, 125
Byodoin temple 77
calligraphed poems 152
calligraphy 38
chanting (*joruri*) 137
Chine-jo 134
Chino Masako 172
Chronicles of Japan (Nihongi) 4, 5, 14
chrysanthemums 228
Chuang-tzu 147
Chuo Koron (Central Forum) 207
clothing 35-6
Collection of Ancient and Modern Times (Kokinshu) 17
Collection of New Style Poems 182
Collection of Nun Chiyo's Verses, A (Chiyo-ni kushu) 143
Collection of Ten Thousand Leaves (Manyoshu) 16
Columbine 185
Communist Party 179
Communist Writer's Federation 223
concubinage 27, 37, 93, 129
"Confessions of Love" 207
Confucianism 15, 16, 28, 31, 54, 93, 104, 151, 154, 180, 245

Index

Confucius 16
conjunctio oppositorum 84
Cosmic Intelligence 244
Courtesan Viewing Cherry Blossoms 150
"Crane Falls Sick, The" 203
Cranes 174
Creation 14
"Crested Ibis, The" 211
"Cry Baby" 210
Cuckoo, The 199
curtain of state (*kicho*) 73
daimyo 102, 105, 122-25, 151
Daini no Sammi 31
Daisetz Suzuki 140
dance 35
dance forms
    kagura 110
Daruma 138
Dazai Osamu 218
"Dead Sun" 190
Desert Flowers 225
dharmas 92
Diary of Izumi Shikibu, The 74, 90-101
Diary of Lady Murasaki, The 74
Diary of Sarashina, The 76-90, 101
divine ancestry of the Emperor 180, 181, 244
dreams 82-90
Drifting Clouds 211
Edo 154
Edo period 122, 123
Eisai 135
"Embrace, An" 219
Emperor Daigo 39
Emperor Daigo II 102
Emperor Fu Hsi 147
Emperor Gensho 14
Emperor Jimmu Tenno 10
Emperor Kami Yamato Ihare-biko 10
Emperor Meiji 154, 179
Emperor Mommu 138
Emperor Murakami 39
Emperor Reizei 91
Emperor Suinin 10
Emperor Taisho 180
Emperor Temmu 13, 17-19
Emperor Tenji 17, 18
Empress Akiko 91

Empress Eifuku 107, 108
Empress Gemmyo 13, 14
Empress Genmei 14
Empress Gensho 14
Empress Iwa-no-hime 17
Empress Jito 18, 19, 138
Empress Jito Tenno 14
Empress Kogyoku Tenno 14
Empress Koken 14
Empress Shoshi 31
Empress Suiko 14, 15, 147
emptiness 133
Enchi Fumiko 2, 195, 225-7
Enchi Yoshimatsu 226
Enomoto Seifu-jo 134
etiquette 28, 38, 94
face-saving devices 68-9
Farmer Labor Party 179
female/male relationship 5
feminine principle 244
fetish 70
feudalism 244
filial piety 16
Fire God (Ho-Masubi) 19
Fishing in the Moonlight 153
Five Amorous Women 131
"floating world, the" (*ukiyo*) 122, 127-30, 158, 162
Flock of Poor People, A 221
"Flowers at Dusk" 159, 160
Fox God 130
free verse poets 188-94
From the Caramel Factory 223
Fujimura Tadashi 207
Fujiwara clan 102
Fujiwara family 154
Fujiwara Michinaga 29
Fujiwara no Michinaga 39
Fujiwara Yasumasa 91
Fukai 227, 240-43
Fukuzawa Yukichi 177
"Full Moon" 200
Futabatei Shimei 161
games 37
gardens 52
Garment of Lovemaking, The 172
GE.GIMIGAM.PRRR.GIMGEM. 224
geishas (*gei*, performing arts) 122, 128, 129-30
General Oda Nobunaga 137
"Genius of Imitation, A" 208-9

Genji Monogatari 245
Genshin 55
gesaku ("literature of jestful writing") 156
gesaku bungaku ("jestful writing") 158
Girls Fording a Stream 149
Gold Pavilion 102
Gosenshu 22
Gossamer Years, The 32, 74
Great Learning for Women 123
Great Mirror of Manly Love, The 131
Great Mother 240
Greater Learning for Women, The 245
Grey Afternoon, A 223
"Growing Up" 163, 165
Hagino-ya (House of the Bush Clover) 156
Hagiwara Sakutaro 188
Haiku poets 141-7, 185-8
Hanagoromo (The Flowered Kimono) 186
Harada Yasuko 225
Harunobu 150, 163
Hashimoto Takako 185
Hayashi Fumiko 195, 210-14, 224
Hayashi Kyoko 225
Heian Aristocracy 34-9
Heian Art Diary, The 72
Heian dynasty 29, 32
Heian-kyo (Kyoto) 29, 76, 77
Heian Period 102
Hermitage by a Mountain Brook, The 103
hetaira 94
Hideyoshi Toyotomi 122-3
Hieda-no-Are 13, 14
Higuchi Ichiyo 155-65
Hirabayashi Taiko 195, 224-5
Hirahata Seito 187
Hiraiwa Yumie 225
Hiratsuka Raicho 194
Hirohito 179
Hiroshigi 233
Hishikawa Moronobu 131, 149
History of the Kingdom of Wei (Wei Chih) 12
Hoke Hakko 53
Hokusai 55, 233
Homa Matsuri 193

Honen 30
Horyuji temple 146
Hoshino Tatsuko 185, 187
Hotei 138
Hototogisu (The Cuckoo) 186
How to Compose Tanka 167
hyakki yako 55
"I Mean to Live" 225
"I" novel 208
I Saw a Blue Horse 210
"I" writers 204
Ichiyo see: Higuchi Ichiyo
Ihara Saikaku 131, 156, 162
Ike Gyokuran 137, 152, 153
Imperial Palace 34
Imperial Poetry Bureau 166
In and *Yo* 5
"In the Charity World" 224
"In Obscurity" 161
Inari 129, 130
incest 93
Ise Monogatari 245
Ishiyama Temple 98
Izanagi 5-7, 26
Izanami 5-7
Izumi Shikibu 32, 75, 91-2, 186
Izumi Shikibu Diary, The 32
Japan's first college for women 178
Japan's Imperial Line 3
Japanese Constitution of 1947 4, 181
Japanese Imperial dynasty 13
Japanese medical school for women 178, 195
Jigoku-e 55
jikkan ("actual feelings") 168, 169
Jocho 77
jogen 128
journey 78-82
Jozan 233
Kabuki 125, 196
Kaga no Chiyo 142-5
kagura 12, 57
Kaibara Ekken 123, 245
Kaji 135-6
kakemono 135
Kakinomoto Hitomaro 20, 138
Kamakura Period 102
kami 12, 14, 28, 54, 47, 112, 235, 243
Kamo no Mabuchi 125
Kamo Shrine 59
Kan'ami Kiyotsugu 111

Index

kanbuncho 155
Kano Masanobu 103, 148
Kano Motonobu 103, 148
Kano school of painting 70, 148
Kano Tan'yu 148
Kantan 200
karma 75, 96, 101, 240
Kasa no Iratsume 2, 21-2
Kataribe ("reciters") 14
Kawabata Yasunari 203, 219
Kitagawa Utamaro 131
Kitahara Takeo 207
Kitano Tenjin 139
Kitazono Katsue 192
Kiyohara Yukinobu 70, 148
Kiyoko Tsuda 185
Kiyonaga 150
Ko Raikin 152-53
Kobinshu 22
Kobori Jinji 224
Koda Rohan 155, 162, 195
Kojiki (Record of Ancient Things) 125
Kojiki (Records of Ancient Matters) 55, 56, 126
Kokinshu 27, 156
kokugaku 126
Komachi 186
Komachi at Sekidera 22
Kono Taeko 225
Kovalevskaya, Sonya 200
Kubokawa Tsurujiro 223
Kukai 30
Kuni-toko-tachi 5
Kunisada 55
Kuniyoshi 55
Kurahashi Yumiko 225
Kyonaga 163
Kyorai 134
Kyoritsu Women's College 185
Kyoto 102
Kyoto court 32
Lady Eifuku Mon'in 106, 107
Lady Ise 26-7
Lady Junii Tameko 107
Lady Jusammi Chikako 108, 109
Lady Kii 21
Lady Murasaki 72, 74, 76, 90, 105, 186
Lady Murasaki Shikibu 91
Lady Otomo no Yakamochi 21
Lady Rokujo 58-69

Land of Yomi (Hell) 7
Landscape 103, 153
Landscape with Fisherman 153
Landscape with Flowers and Birds 103
language
 Japanese 32
"Last Frost of Spring, The" 160
"Late Chrysanthemum" 211
libido (psychic energy) 66, 84, 229
"Lingering Affection" 214-18
Literary Style, The 207
Lotus Sutra 53, 82, 83, 93
love 92-101
"Love Promises Broken" 109
Machi 137
Machiko 200
Mahayana Buddhism 93
"Man Root, The" 192-4
Man who Spent His Life at Love-making, The 131
Manchuria 180
mandala 30
Manonobe 14
Manyoshu 27, 125
Masinobu 55
Masks 225, 226-43
masks
 Fukai 240
 Masugami 236
 Ryo no onna 227
Masugami 227, 236-40
Matriarchy 1, 3, 19, 226, 231
Matsukaze 111
Matsuya 135-37
maya 24, 25
Mayahanna Buddhists 82
"Me" 189
Meiji Civil Code 180
Meiji era 180
Meiji School for Girls 199
Mi Fu 174
miko 56, 126
militarism 222, 224
Minamoto-no-Yoritomo 102
Mincho 103
Ming dynasty 151
mirror 27
"Mirror of Velasquez, The" 189
Mishima Yukio 219
Mitsubishi 179

Mitsui 104, 179
Miyako no Hana (The Flowers of the Capital) 161
Miyamoto Yuriko 195, 221-2
moon 26, 27, 98, 239, 241
"Moor in Late Autumn, A" 108
Mori Arinori 177, 178
Mori Ogai 162
Mori Yoko 225
Moronobu 150, 163
Mother Mitchitsuna 32
Mother Syndrome 40-54
Mother, Universal 243
"Mother's Love" 204
Motoori Norinaga 125
Mount Fuji 81, 82, 228, 229, 233, 234, 236
Mountain Torrent 224
Mugaian Kihaku 143
Murasaki Shikibu 2, 28, 148
Musashino 159, 160
music 34
    sangaku 110
musical instruments
    ch'in 146
    koto 171, 175
Myamoto Kenji 222
Myojo (Morning Star) 167
Nakagawa Mikiko 182, 185
Nakajima Utako 156
Nakamoto Takako 225
Nakarai Tosui 156-62
Nakayama Miki 126
"Narcissus" 211-13
Native Land 225
Nembutsu 30
Neo-Confucianism 123, 158, 245
Neo-Shintoism 154
New Japanese Literature Association, The 222
New Life, A 200
"New Poetry Brotherhood of Tokyo, The" 167
"Nightingale in the Grove" 156
nihonga 174
Nihongi (Chronicles of Japan) 126, 244
nikki 72
Nin, Anais 246
nirvana 25, 92
Nishikawa Sukenobu 151

No-Hime 105
No Longer Human 218
Nobuko 221
Nobunaga 105, 106
Nogami Toyoichiro 199
Nogami Yaeko 195, 199-203
Noguchi Masaakira 176
Noguchi Shonin 155, 175-7
Noh masks 226, 227-43
Noh theatre 22, 106, 110-21, 125, 196, 199, 200, 226
Noh theatre characters
    kyogen 111
    shite 111, 114
    tsure 111, 114
    waki 111
Notes on Feminism 246
Oba Minako 225
Oda Nobunaga 122
Ofudesaki 126
Ohan 207
Ohashi 132
Oichi 106
Okamoto Kanoko 195, 203-6
Okuhara Seiko 155, 173-5
Okyo 55
Old School 166, 167
"On the Death of the Emperor Temmu" 19
"On the Full Moon of the Eighth Month" 109
"On the Last Day of the Year" 162
"On Preferring the Autumn Hills" 17
One Flower 221
"One Hundred Devils Out at Night" 55
Oneness 27, 140, 144
onnagata 151
Ono no Komachi 2, 22-6
Ono Ozu 137-9
Osaki Shiro 207
Otomo clan 19
Otomo no Sakanoe no Iratsume 19
Otomo no Yakamochi 19
Ozaki Koyo 160-62
Ozu ryu 139
Palace Scene in a Snowy Landscape, A 148
pantomime
    shushi 110
Paradise 89

Index

Patriarchy 1, 3
Peace Preservation Act 194
perfume 36
phallicism 192-4, 238-40
Phoenix bird 146
pictorial eroticism 132
Pillow Book 148
Pillow Book of Sei Shonagon, The 32, 75
"pillow-word" 26
Pimiko (Queen of Wa) 12-13
Po Chu-i 148
Poem-Pillow Picture Book, The 131
Poetic forms
    choka 17
    haiku 133, 134, 141, 168, 185, 186, 188, 202
    renga 106
    tanka 106, 156, 166-71, 182, 185, 188, 203
    waka 28, 126, 132, 140, 150, 175
"Poor, The" 210
"Powdered Face, The" 207
Primogeniture 181
Prince Atsumichi 91, 94
Prince Genji 34, 35, 39
Prince Kagami 17
Prince Konoye 154
Prince Saionji 154
Prince Shotoku 15, 147
Prince Tametaka 91, 94
Princess Nukada 17-19
Princess Yamatohime no Mikoto 56
Projection 84
prostitutes (*joro*) 127-9, 225
puer 61
puer aeternus 53, 69
Puppet-Maker, The 208
Pure Land 89
Pure Land Buddhism 31, 145
Pure Land Paradise Cult 77
Pure Land Paradise 52
Pure Land Sect 30
Record of Wandering 210
Records of Ancient Matters (Kojiki) 5, 14
Records of a Travel-Worn Satchel 134
Reizei Tamemura 137
renatus in novam infantiam 242
"Resignation" 196

Ryo no onna 227-36
Ryonen Genso 139-41
Sage Chou Mao-shu in a Lotus Pnd, The 103
Saicho 30
Saigyo 233
Saikai Toshihiko 224
Saito Fumi 182-4
salt 114
samisen 129
samsara 92
samurai 105, 124, 177, 180, 219
Sarashina Diary, The 32, 74
Sarashina Nikki 76
Sasaki Shogen 141
Sata Ineko 222-4
schizophrenia 62-68
screen of state 36
Scroll of Initiation 132
Seami Motokiyo 111
Sei Shonagon 32, 74-76, 90, 91, 148, 149
Seiko see: Okuhara Seiko
Sen no Rikyu 135
"Separate Ways" 163-5
seppuku 219
Series of Biographies of Women 123
Sesshu 103
Setouchi Harumi 195, 214-18
Setting Sun, The 218
sexual intercourse 92
sexual procreation 9
Shakyamuni 83
Shakyamuni Gautama 15
shamanesses 12, 17, 19, 57, 93, 226, 227, 231, 242, 244
Sharaku 163
"shasei" ("description of nature") 168
Shingon Buddhism 30
Shinto shamanesses 126
Shinto shrines 139, 229
Shinto temples 175
Shintoism 3, 5, 11, 16, 19, 23, 25, 28, 29, 31, 54, 47, 84, 87, 93, 110, 193
Shiraishi Kazuko 2, 188, 192-4
Shonin see: Noguchi Shonin
Shrines
    Hae 78
    Ise 10-11, 19, 31, 56, 244
    Ishiyama 78

Shrines (cont'd.)
  Kamo 31
  Kiyomizu 78
  Kurama 78
  Suma 31
  Sumiyoshi 31
  Tagata 193
  Toshogu 217
  Uzumasa 78
Shubun 103
Shuho 104
shunga 131
Signpost 222
Silver Pavilion 103
singing (*geiko*) 128
"Snowy Day, A" 161
Social Democratic Party 179
Soga rulers 14
"Song from the Depths of the Earth" 225
songs
  imayo 110
Soseki Natsume 195, 199, 204
spirit possession 54-8, 65-8
Spring Landscape 152
Stories of Wise and Strong Women 136
Style 207
Sugawara Michizane 139
Sugita Hisajo 185-7
Summer Mountains 174
Sun 26, 27
Susa-no-o (Storm God) 7-10
Sutra of the Perfection of Wisdom in Eight Thousand Verses, The 93
Suzuki 143
Suzuki Etsu 196
Suzuki Harunobu 131, 149
"Swirling Currents" 211
synchronistic event 51
Tada Chimako 188-91
Tagami Kikusha (nee Tagami Michi) 145-7
Tagami Shiko 142
Takahama Kyoshi 187
Takahashi Takako 225
Takizawa Bakin 158
"Tale of an Old Geisha, The" 204-6
Tale of Genji, The 2, 28, 29-71, 74, 104-5, 124, 148, 167, 186, 225
Talks on Tanka 167

Tamura Shogyo 196
Tamura Toshiko 195, 199
Tanabe Kaho 156
Tangled Hair 166
Tani Kankan 152-53
Tanizaki Junichiro 206
tanka poets 182-5
Taoism 55, 110, 133, 190
Tayama Katai 204
tea ceremony 216
teahouse poets 135-7
Tekkan Yosano 167, 169, 172
temenos 238
Tendai Buddhism 30
Tendai Sect 82, 84
Tenrikyo ("Teaching of the Heavenly Truth") 126
Thing Which Removes Red, The 226
"This Kind of Woman" 224
Three Imperial Regalia 10
"To Open a Grave" 207
"To Sting" 208
Togo Seiji 207
Tokugawa Hidetada 138
Tokugawa Ieyasu 137
Tokugawa Period 154, 245
Tokugawa Shogunate 122
Tokugawa society 129
Tokugawas 148
Tokyo Normal School for Women 178
Tomiko *see*: Yamakawa Tomiko
Tomiko Yamakawa 167
Tomioka Taeko 225
Torii Kiyonobu 132
Tosa Mitsuoki 70
Tosa Mitsuyoshi 70
Toshusai Sharaku 151
Town Where Eggs Fall, The 192
Toyo Muslin 194
True Pure Land Sect in Osaka 122
Tsuboi Sakae 225
Tsuki-yumi (God of the Moon) 7-8, 80, 98, 244
Tsukiji Little Theatre 225
tsukuri-e 70
Tsumura Setsuko 225
Tsushima Yuko 195, 218-21
Tu Fu 141
Two Bijin 177
Two Birds 152, 153
Two Gardens 222

Ukiyo Barbershop, The 130
Ukiyo Bathhouse, The 130
ukiyo-e wood-block prints 122, 127, 131, 132, 149, 163, 204
Uno Chiyo 195, 207-9
Utagawa Kuniyoshi 136
Utamaro 150, 163
utamonogatari 90
Vagabond's Song 210
vagina dentata 69, 206, 234
Viewing Maple Leaves by the Waterfall 149
"Vow" 196
Wa 12
Waiting Years, The 226
Waka Dedicated to Reizei Tamemura 136
Waka on Decorated Paper 133
Weathervane Plant, The 222
wen-jen-hua 151
Wholeness 242, 247
wind 116
Winter Landscape 103
witches 240
woman's hair 36
Women in the Arts 210
Women Practicing Arts in the Garden 177
"Women Writer, A" 197
Women's Democratic Club 222
women's equality 12
women's rights 31, 103-6
Women's Voice 197
woodblock prints *see: ukiyo-e*
Working Women 222-23
Yagi Mikajo 185, 187-8
Yamakawa Tomiko 155, 172-3
Yamamoto Michiko 225
Yamato clan 14, 19
Yamato court 15
Yamato rulers (*mononoke*) 56
yamato-e style 148, 149
Yamazaki Ryu-jo 149-51
Yasu Iwasaki 181
yin and *yang* 111, 113, 114, 118, 244
yoga 174
yokyoku 184
Yomiuri Shimbun 160
Yosami 20
Yosano Akiko 155, 166-72, 182
Yoshihito Taisho 179

Yoshimasa 102
Yoshioka Yayoi 178
Yoshitaki 55
Yoshiwara (moor of rushes) 127, 129
Young Actor Holding Narcissus 151
Yuasa Yoshiko 221
Yuri 136-7
Zen 103, 107, 109, 116, 121, 133, 135, 138, 139-41, 144, 145, 176, 190, 199, 215

NORMANDALE COMMUNITY COLLEGE
9700 FRANCE AVENUE SOUTH
BLOOMINGTON, MN 55431-4399